Columbia University

Contributions to Education

Teachers College Series

No. 746

AMS PRESS
NEW YORK

Cooperation between the Faculty of the Campus Elementary Training School and the Other Departments of Teachers Colleges and Normal Schools

By MARY I. COLE, Ph.D.

TEACHERS COLLEGE, COLUMBIA UNIVERSITY
CONTRIBUTIONS TO EDUCATION, NO. 746

Published with the Approval of
Professor Thomas Alexander, Sponsor

Bureau of Publications
Teachers College, Columbia University
New York City
1939

Library of Congress Cataloging in Publication Data

Cole, Mary Isabelle, 1904-
Cooperation between the faculty of the campus elementary training school and the other departments of teachers colleges and normal schools.

Reprint of the 1939 ed., issued in series: Teachers College, Columbia University. Contributions to education, no. 746.
Originally presented as the author's thesis, Columbia.
Bibliography: p.
1. Teachers colleges. 2. Laboratory schools.
3. Teachers, Training of. I. Title. II. Series: Columbia University. Teachers College. Contributions to education, no. 746.
LB2153.C57 1972 370'.733 76-176658
ISBN 0-404-55746-5

Reprinted by Special Arrangement with Teachers College Press, New York, New York

From the edition of 1939, New York
First AMS edition published in 1972
Manufactured in the United States

AMS PRESS, INC.
NEW YORK, N. Y. 10003

2.15

ACKNOWLEDGMENTS

THE AUTHOR wishes to express her sincere appreciation for the valuable guidance and counsel of her sponsor, Professor Thomas Alexander, and for the constructive criticisms and suggestions of her advisers, Professor Florence Stratemeyer and Professor J. R. McGaughy, of Teachers College, Columbia University.

She also desires to express her gratitude to Professor E. S. Evenden, Professor W. C. Bagley, and Professor Helen Walker, of Teachers College, for constructive criticism in assembling the data.

The author is especially indebted to the faculty members of the twenty-five teachers colleges and normal schools who furnished data for the study of present practice, and to the jury members who evaluated the score card.

M.I.C.

CONTENTS

Cooperation between the Faculty of the Campus Elementary Training School and the Other Departments of Teachers Colleges and Normal Schools

CHAPTER I

THE PURPOSE AND PLAN OF THE STUDY

Introduction

The problems involved in securing effective cooperative endeavor between the faculties of the laboratory school and the subject matter departments in normal schools and teachers colleges have constituted a recurring issue in the history of the teacher training movement.

According to Armentrout,[1] the laboratory or training school department was closely related to the theory department in the early normal schools. Both departments were housed in the same building, and each instructor who taught a course in educational theory supervised student teachers who were attempting to carry out the theory in practice in the laboratory school.

As teacher training institutions grew in enrollment, and the training school needed separate or larger quarters, the two parts of the school grew apart, each having a separate faculty. As the faculty personnel increased, the breach widened between the theory courses and the laboratory school until during the early part of this century, there was little or no correlation between the training school and the academic departments of the normal school. A few schools have felt no cleavage, notably the State Normal School at Oswego, New York,[2] which is still using President Sheldon's plan.

A documentary study of the proceedings of the National Education Association from 1874 to 1933 shows increasing effort in the solution of the problem. In 1874 a committee which included Dr. E. A. Sheldon, of Oswego, presented a picture of the ideal model school, embodying in the report the then current philosophy regarding

[1] Armentrout, W. D. *The Conduct of Student Teaching in State Teachers Colleges,* pp. 11–12. Colorado State Teachers College, 1928.

[2] Chittenden, M. D. "Oswego Normal and Training School Plan of Cooperation." *Educational Administration and Supervision,* May, 1925.

close relationship between theory and practice departments of normal schools.[3] At the 1888 meeting, C. H. Allen[4] questioned the practice of having adult students in a theory course teach fellow students as a class of children instead of using the model school for such experimental teaching. Again, at the 1896 meeting, Dr. Sheldon[5] recommended that the general principles which underlie the work of a teacher training institution should be arrived at through mutual agreement of the entire faculty, including training school critic teachers. Dr. L. W. Wilson[6] of the department of biology at the Philadelphia Normal School delivered an address at the 1899 meeting of the N. E. A. in which she attributed the cleavage between training school and college faculty to a need for specialists trained in teacher preparation. Her proposed plan of cooperative endeavor made no mention of professional training for critic teachers, recommending instead that the trained specialist from the academic departments outline the training school course of study, hold meetings with critic teachers, and supervise them.

Evidently the relation between theory and practice in the normal schools had reached a hiatus about 1903, for Part II of the *Second Yearbook*, and Part I of the *Third Yearbook* of the National Society for the Scientific Study of Education were devoted to suggested solutions. Seven studies of this problem, by such educators as John Dewey, Frank McMurry, David Felmly, and Sarah Brooks, were included in the two volumes. One of the seven, a report of an intensive survey of the relation of theory to practice made by the faculty of the State Normal University at Normal, Illinois, presented a plan of cooperative supervision of student teachers by critic teachers and normal school instructors.[7] In the *Third Yearbook*, Dr. Frank

[3] McVicar, M., Sheldon, E. A., and Greenough, J. C. "Training Schools in Connection with Normal Schools." *N.E.A. Proceedings,* 1874, pp. 230–233.

[4] Allen, C. H. "The Training School as an Adjunct of the Normal School." *N.E.A. Proceedings,* 1888, pp. 499–500.

[5] Sheldon, E. A. "The Practice School Versus a Public School." *N.E.A. Proceedings,* 1896, pp. 658–659.

[6] Wilson, L. W., "The Training School Should Be the Correlating Center of the Normal School." *N.E.A. Proceedings,* 1899, p. 899.

[7] Faculty of the State Normal University, Normal, Ill. "The Relation Between Theory and Practice in the Training of Teachers." *The Second Yearbook of the National Society for the Scientific Study of Education,* 1903, pp. 15–18.

McMurry[8] proposed a detailed plan for closer relationship between the Horace Mann Demonstration School and the academic departments of Teachers College, Columbia University. The advantages of housing the theory and practice departments in the same building to promote a more unified program of teacher training, were stressed by Miss Sarah Brooks.[9] Dr. John Dewey[10] urged that subject matter instructors professionalize their courses through closer contact with the work of the training school.

Apparently the plans incorporated in the *Yearbooks* of the National Society for the Scientific Study of Education were but a beginning in the solution of the problem, for a continuation of the documentary study of *N. E. A. Proceedings* reveals increasing space devoted to plans for coordinating training school and college departments. A pertinent article was presented in 1908 by J. A. H. Keith,[11] in which he proposed that the theory department should maintain an advisory rather than a supervisory relationship to the training school. C. B. Robertson[12] considered it the province of the educational theory department to lead in interdepartmental cooperation with the work of the training school. Dr. D. Finley[13] and J. W. Cooke[14] proposed that academic instructors be given time in their daily schedules for frequent visits to the training school, and for occasional experiments in teaching children for an entire term.

At the 1918 meeting of the N. E. A., Professor Harry A. Sprague[15] reported a composite picture of cooperative effort in thirty-seven

[8] McMurry, Frank M. "Theory and Practice at Teachers College, Columbia University." *Third Yearbook of the National Society for the Scientific Study of Education,* 1904, pp. 50–52.

[9] Brooks, Sarah C. "Relation of Theory to Practice." *Third Yearbook of the National Society for the Scientific Study of Education,* 1904, p. 42.

[10] Dewey, John. "The Relation of Theory to Practice in Education." *Third Yearbook of the National Society for the Scientific Study of Education,* Part I, 1904, pp. 21–30.

[11] Keith, J. A. H. "What Relation Should the Head of Theoretical and Scientific Education Sustain to the Practice School?" *N.E.A. Proceedings,* 1908, pp. 724–726.

[12] Robertson, C. B. "The Function of the Training School, Its Relation to the Department of Principles and Methods." *N.E.A. Proceedings,* 1908, pp. 561–566.

[13] Finley, D. "Normal School and the Training School." *N.E.A. Proceedings,* 1911, p. 700.

[14] Cooke, J. W. "The Practice School and the Work of the Heads of Departments in It." *N.E.A. Proceedings,* 1914, pp. 546–548.

[15] Sprague, H. A. "Coordination of Theory and Practice in Normal Schools." *N.E.A. Proceedings,* 1918, pp. 212–214.

state normal schools in twenty-two different states, basing it upon personal interviews with the individual faculty members in the thirty-seven schools. He found that these representatives reported little or no direct relationship between the departments of theory and practice.

The contributions which critic teachers might make in improving the academic and educational theory courses in the college departments were stressed by Dr. Lester Wilson in his dissertation, *Training Departments in the State Normal Schools of the United States*. He devoted his fourth chapter to the possibility of reciprocal cooperation between the normal and training departments and, in addition, reported questionnaire returns from forty-three normal schools. Examination of these data reveals but few contacts between the faculty of the training school and academic departments.

In the Louisiana[16] and Missouri[17] teacher training surveys, Professors Thomas Alexander and W. C. Bagley listed and applied definite principles for establishing desirable faculty cooperation. These suggested activities and administrative relationships were included in the questionnaire used to collect data for the 1933 picture of coordination which is discussed in Chapters III and IV of the present study.

The Department of Supervisors of Student Teaching of the N. E. A. in 1925 accorded major emphasis to the problem of faculty cooperation. Plans then in effect were presented at the conference, notably those at the teacher training institutions at Oswego, New York,[18] Frostburg, Maryland,[19] and Delaware, Ohio.[20] At this meeting, Professor E. S. Evenden[21] presented summarized data from his

[16] Bagley, W. C., Alexander, Thomas, Foote, J. *Report of a Commission on the Professional Education of White Public School Teachers in Louisiana*, 1924, pp. 177–203.

[17] The Carnegie Foundation for the Advancement of Teaching, *The Professional Preparation of Teachers for American Public Schools*. Bulletin No. 14, 1920, pp. 201–202.

[18] Chittenden, M. D. "The Oswego Normal and Training School Plan of Cooperation." *Supervisors of Student Teaching Yearbook*, 1925.

[19] Dunkle, J. L. "Plan of Cooperation at Frostburg State Normal School." *Supervisors of Student Teaching Yearbook*, 1925, pp. 16–20.

[20] Mead, A. R. "Cooperation of Academic and Professional Departments in Teacher Training Preparation at Ohio Wesleyan University." *Supervisors of Student Teaching Yearbook*, 1925, pp. 29–33.

[21] Evenden, E. S. "Cooperation of Teachers of Academic Subjects with the Training School." *Supervisors of Student Teaching Yearbook*, 1925, pp. 5–8.

questionnaire study and submitted definite proposals for effecting closer cooperation between the training school and normal school instructors. Again in 1929 he challenged the critic teachers to be the aggressors in promoting reciprocal relations[22] with the subject matter instructors.

Several recent studies in professional education of teachers have included findings and recommendations regarding reciprocal cooperation between training school and college faculty. Notable among these are Dr. Noble L. Garrison's[23] study of the status and work of the training supervisor,[24] and his analysis of current practice in coordination of college and training school work.[25] Dr. L. A. Eubank[26] devoted one chapter of his dissertation to articulation of the laboratory school with the college. In the 1931 proceedings[27] of the Texas Teacher Training Conference, Dr. Thomas Alexander made specific recommendations for coordinating the laboratory schools with the subject matter departments. A major part of the 1932 meeting of the American Association of Teachers Colleges was devoted to addresses recommending ways for securing closer correlation between the theory departments of the institution and the training school. A plan of reciprocal relations between college and training school faculty which is being used experimentally at the State Teachers College, Milwaukee, Wisconsin, was reported by President Frank E. Baker[28] at the 1933 meeting of the American Association of Teachers Colleges. Another published account of the work of one school in effecting cooperative activities between normal school and college faculty

[22] Evenden, E. S. "The Critic Teacher and the Professional Treatment of Subject Matter: A Challenge." *Supervisors of Student Teaching Yearbook,* 1929, pp. 39–48.

[23] Garrison, Noble L. *Status and Work of the Training Supervisor.* Teachers College Contributions to Education, No. 280, Bureau of Publications, Teachers College, Columbia University, 1927, pp. 10, 76–98.

[24] Referred to as critic teacher throughout the present study.

[25] Garrison, Noble L. *Current Practice in Coordination of College and Training School Work.* Michigan State Normal College, 1929.

[26] Eubank, Louis A. "The Organization and Administration of Laboratory Schools in the State Teachers Colleges," pp. 34–60. Northeast Missouri State Teachers College, Maryville, Mo., 1931.

[27] Alexander, Thomas. "Cooperative Planning for Teacher Training Standards in Texas." North Texas State Teachers College, *1931 Conference Proceedings,* pp. 138–143.

[28] Baker, Frank E. "Integrated Professional Experiences as the Basis for Learning and as a Substitute for Formal Courses in Education." *Twelfth Yearbook, American Association of Teachers Colleges,* 1933, pp. 70–85.

was presented by the faculty of the State Normal School at Towson, Maryland.[29]

Recently, many other plans for coordinating the training school and college departments have been published. Notable among them are those by Professor A. R. Mead,[30] Miss Lenora Johnson,[31] and Miss Edna Neal.[32]

Periodical literature concerning this problem in teacher training institutions has appeared in increasing amount since 1925; hence the writer saw a need for more complete study of one specific phase of the problem, that of cooperation between the faculties of the campus elementary training school and the academic department of state teachers colleges and normal schools.

Statement of Problem

The type and extent of cooperation between the faculty of the training school and the other departments of teachers colleges and normal schools varies with on-campus and off-campus laboratory schools. It also differs at the various levels—elementary, junior high, and senior high school. Because this is generally accepted as true, this study will consider such cooperation between the academic departments and the campus elementary laboratory school[33] only.

The purpose of the study may be specifically stated as follows:

1. To present a picture of present practice regarding such cooperation gained through personal visitation of a representative sampling of state teachers colleges and normal schools throughout the United States.
2. To present a score card, which was evaluated by a carefully selected jury of educators who are authorities in this field, to be used for self-surveys by teacher training institutions.

[29] Towson, Maryland (faculty study). "A Plan for the Closer Coordination of Professionalized Subject Matter and Student Teaching in a Normal School." *Educational Administration and Supervision,* April, 1930, pp. 257–286.

[30] Mead, A. R. *Supervised Student Teaching,* pp. 615–627, Johnson Publishing Co., 1930.

[31] Johnson, Lenora. "Cooperation Between Training School and Subject Matter Instructors." *The Virginia Teacher,* February, 1931, pp. 29–36.

[32] Neal, Edna. "Closer Co-ordination Between Professionalized Subject-Matter Instructors and the Training School." *Kentucky School Journal,* May, 1933, pp. 39-41.

[33] An elementary school including only the first six grades.

Sources of Data

Present Practice Study. The material for this section of the study was collected in the following manner.

A representative sampling of schools was visited and the information obtained through personal interview with critic teachers, college course instructors, and administrators.

Similar questionnaires were presented to each of these groups. The content of each questionnaire was identical, the variation in form being explained by the use of the personal pronoun.

In the teacher training institutions visited, one member of each academic department was interviewed regarding his cooperation with members of the training school faculty. Differences in enrollment and number of college departments caused this number to vary from ten to twenty-five people in a school. In addition, three or more critic teachers for each grade from kindergarten to sixth grade in the campus training school, were interviewed regarding their cooperation with members of the academic departments.

In addition to these individuals, the administrative officers who were most cognizant of this phase of work gave information and the picture of their plan of cooperation. In every school the director of training or principal of the training school was interviewed, and in many schools, both the president of the teacher training institution and the dean of the college assisted in explaining their plan.

Manner of Selecting Schools Visited. The writer toured the United States by automobile and railroad, making visits to a representative sampling of state teacher training institutions which had campus elementary training schools, or which used city schools within a ten-minute walk of the college buildings. An automobile route was laid out along main federal highways which would cover desired territory east of the Rocky Mountains. The nearest schools which fulfilled the needs of this study were noted.[34]

A letter was sent to one teachers college or normal school located on or near this route in each state, explaining the nature of the study and requesting permission to visit at a stated date during the spring

[34] Institutions were selected on the basis of information given in the *Educational Directory,* 1931, Bulletin No. 1, 1931, U. S. Office of Education; and from the 1930–1931 catalogues of these institutions.

or summer of 1931. The majority of the schools granted this permission, but in cases where it was not granted, another school near the planned route was substituted. Visits to schools in each of the forty-eight states were not possible because of such factors as spring or summer vacations.

The investigator covered 6,500 miles by automobile on this part of the tour, visiting eighteen schools in as many states.

After this information had been obtained, a railroad route to include states not covered by the automobile tour was arranged, and letters were written to the schools in these states.[35] As it was nearing the end of the summer, it was possible to visit only seven institutions on this part of the tour, which brought the total number visited to twenty-five, representing Far-Western, Mid-Western, Southern, and Eastern sections of the United States.

A composite picture of the findings in each school was drawn up from the questionnaire data gained through the interview method. This picture of 1931 practice was submitted during the summer of 1933 to the director of training at each school visited. He was requested to approve the report as it stood or to indicate changes which had occurred during the two-year period.

The changes reported, which were few in number except for two schools (where the entire organization had been revised), have been incorporated in the body of the study.

Formulation of the Questionnaire

Suggested Cooperative Activities. The topics originally included in the questionnaire were derived from various plans of cooperation as suggested in the current professional literature on this subject and from term papers on file in Teachers College, Columbia University. Tentative forms of the questionnaires were presented to three groups of major students in the Professional Education of Teachers department at Teachers College, Columbia University, for suggestions and additions. Some items were added, others clarified and expanded. The revised list of topics was presented to the seminar group in the above named department for further revision.

[35] For the names and locations of these schools, see Appendix A.

The suggestions were incorporated in two questionnaires, one for college instructors, the other for critic teachers, and were again presented to the same three major groups and seminar for final criticism before being used in the personal interviews in schools visited.

Data Regarding the Directions Given for Filling in the Questionnaire. Each questionnaire asked that the instructor answering give the frequency with which he participated in any named activity. The following terms were suggested:

Y Not oftener than once a year[36]
T Not oftener than once a term (quarter or semester)
M Not oftener than once a month
W Not oftener than once a week
O Oftener than once a week, but not daily
D Daily[37]

The greatest source of uncertainty in meaning which the investigator encountered in securing and interpreting frequencies was how much time was spent per day when an activity was recorded. For instance, in several cases, college department instructors who were training school supervisors recorded daily participation. Clearly, a person who spent half a day in any cooperative activity and one who spent one class period a day in the same activity would not be recording comparable data. The majority of the individuals interviewed stated that they were unable to give accurate account of the number of hours or periods spent each time they participated in a cooperative activity. Therefore, such fine distinctions as "weekly, one hour each time" are not used in the tabulation of data. However, whenever an instructor spent more than one class hour (usually 50 minutes) on the particular item, mention is made of it in the discussion of the table covering the data.

The frequency notation "once a term" was used to indicate that the instructor participated in any given type of cooperative work once each term, though in some cases that means once per semester

[36] Academic year of nine months; summer sessions not considered in this study.

[37] Other frequencies, such as "twice a month," "four times per quarter," and "twice a term," were used by the persons interviewed, which have been included in the tables and in discussion of each activity.

and in others each quarter. It seemed inadvisable to separate these recordings in the tabulations since the implication is that the instructor participated once in each division of the academic school year. Had an instructor given the frequency of three times a year when the semester plan was used in his school, this would have been recorded. This did not occur in any case.

The questionnaire for the academic instructors asked for rather specific data in many cases. For instance, in item I A 1 of the questionnaire, instructors were asked to list the number of students they observed each term, the number of times each student was observed, and on what subject matter. These questions were found impractical, and the replies thereto inaccurate since a large majority of the instructors believed they could not reliably answer in such detail. Their reasons were: (1) that the number of students observed varied from term to term and from day to day; (2) that they observed whatever happened to be in process of teaching at the time they were able to observe. Because of such criticism of the questionnaire, details on these items have been omitted from the tables and the discussion in the following pages. Frequency of observation is recorded with the instructor's title, which usually indicates in which subject the instructor is interested. For instance, an instructor in the Teaching of Arithmetic would naturally observe student teachers who were teaching arithmetic to training school children. An exception to this rule would be the case of training school supervisors who also teach elementary education courses in the college. Clearly, these supervisors would observe the teaching of students in all elementary school subjects.

In tabulating many of the items included in this study, it was found that instructors participated in the activity in more than one way, and therefore listed such participation under two or more of the categories on the questionnaire. For example, the Later Elementary Education instructor might, in company with the critic teacher, observe teaching by student teachers once a week. She might also, in company with the critic teacher and other interested faculty members, observe once a month; and once a semester might observe the teaching of students unaccompanied. To say that this instructor observed the teaching of student teachers not oftener than once a week is not giving a true picture, since these monthly and once-a-term observations are additional and bring the total observations to 47 or 48 per academic year of thirty-six weeks. No method of summing up these activities for individuals has been used in the following tables except in cases where few frequencies occur for any given type of college instructor or when a note is used to show that frequencies under more than one category were reported by the same individual.

The original data contributed by a critic teacher, in any given school, listed the college instructors who cooperated with her and what cooperation she in turn gave to college instructors. It was necessary to check this information against that furnished by college instructors and administrative officers to show the total time individual faculty members from the college departments spent in a given activity in the training school rather than to show such time spent in specific grades or classes in the school. For instance, the tables may show that an academic instructor observes the teaching of student teachers with a frequency of once a month, when in fact he has observed the teaching of nine critic teachers once a year each. This standard has been used throughout the study: that time refers to total time spent in an activity rather than time with an individual.

In case a college instructor cooperates with only one or two critic teachers instead of all, such fact is mentioned in discussion of a table. With few exceptions, the Early Elementary Education instructor tends to cooperate with critic teachers in the primary grades in the training school, and similarly, the Later Elementary Education instructor with critic teachers in the intermediate grades.

Classification Assigned to Faculty Members

Because instructors in different schools may teach courses with similar content but varying titles, arbitrary groupings of data have been set up and used in the tables. They are as follows:

1. *Academic departments*, *college department*, *subject matter departments*, or *theory departments* refers to the teacher training institution exclusive of the training or laboratory school. The term *college instructor* is used to designate those members of the faculty who teach courses other than student teaching to college students.

2a. *College department instructors who supervise students in the training school* includes those people who are regularly scheduled not only to teach college courses in elementary education but to aid in the supervision of student teachers. To these persons the official titles for the position found in the schools visited were:

Assistant Director of Training
Supervisor of Elementary Training
Supervisor of Practice Teaching
Supervisor of Student Teaching

Seven of the twenty-five schools visited have supervisors of this type. Their relationship to the critic teachers is coordinate rather than supervisory in five of the seven. The other two use city public schools for practice purposes, the state assuming no part in payment of salaries to the grade teachers.

2b. *Special subject instructors who supervise their own subject in the training school* includes those instructors who teach college courses in the following departments: Fine Arts, Home Economics, Industrial Arts, Music, Penmanship, Physical Education, and in addition to this college teaching, supervise student teachers or teach children in the training school in these respective fields. For brevity in this study such instructors are often referred to as special supervisors.

3. *Critic teacher* is used to include the term training school supervisor because the former is in use in the majority of the schools visited. The terms *grade teacher* or *room teacher* refer to the critic teachers who are not paid by the state but are public school teachers in the city.

4. *Director of training* is used in referring to the coordinating officer in each institution who directs and unifies the work of the training school and represents the student teaching department in the college faculty council or other group meetings which only one person from the school is expected to attend. The varying titles for the position found in the schools visited were:

Director of Demonstration School
Director of Teacher Training
Director of Practice Teaching
Director of the Training School
Head of the Department of Teaching
Superintendent of the Training School
Supervisor of Practice Teaching

In sixteen of the twenty-five schools visited, this officer teaches one or more courses in the education department.

5a. *Early elementary education* is used to include such courses as Primary Technique, Primary Methods, Teaching in the Primary Grades, being the title that is most commonly used for such courses.

5b. *Later elementary education* is used to include such courses as Intermediate Grade Technique, Intermediate Grade Methods, Upper Grade Methods, and Teaching the Fundamental Subjects in the Intermediate Grades.

6. *General education course instructor* refers to those instructors who offer types

of education courses and so cannot be described as instructor in any one type. Such instructors often teach a combination, as Educational Psychology, Tests and Measurements, History of Education, Classroom Management, and Educational Administration. Such an individual is referred to as General Education course instructor throughout the study.

7. *Student teaching* is used to include the terms *directed teaching*, and *practice teaching*.

8a. *The teaching of arithmetic* was selected to include such courses as Arithmetic for the Grades, Arithmetic Methods, Teaching of Arithmetic in the Elementary School, and Professionalized Subject Matter in Arithmetic. The same criterion was applied to all the courses of this nature, so that they are called Teaching of Geography, Teaching of History, Teaching of Reading, Teaching of Physical Education, Teaching of Public School Art, Teaching of Public School Music, etc. For variety in terminology, *professionalized subject matter courses* is used as an alternate term in the discussion of the tables.

8b. *Head of department* is used to designate the departmental head or chairman when this official cooperates with the training school faculty, unless he is the instructor in the professionalized subject matter courses. If the latter is true, he is listed as an instructor in the specific courses.

CHAPTER II

A WEIGHTED EVALUATION OF A LIST OF COOPERATIVE ACTIVITIES AS REVEALED BY A SCORE CARD

It was indicated in Chapter I that one of the major purposes of this study was to evaluate the cooperative activities which were gathered from the literature of the teacher training field and from faculty members of teacher training institutions. It is the purpose of this chapter to describe the technique used for such evaluation and to present the results of this effort. The score card was selected as the appraisal instrument for evaluating the many ways suggested for bringing about cooperation between the faculty of the campus elementary school and the other departments of teachers colleges and normal schools.

The Score Card as a Rating Instrument for Utilizing Judgments

Evaluation by jury rating has been employed in educational research by many investigators. An exhaustive discussion of the various survey-appraisal procedures with a description of the research studies which illustrate each is given by Good, Barr, and Scates in their recent volume on the methodology of educational research.[1] They list and discuss the types of rating and the various applications that have been made of them in order of their increasing complexity or refinement of technique. According to these experts, score cards[2] represent the most elaborate form of rating instrument for utilizing judgments directly when compared with the other techniques—direct comparison,[3] check-lists,[4] and rating scales.[5] The score card

[1] Good, Carter V., Barr, A. S., and Scates, D. E. *The Methodology of Educational Research,* pp. 409–439. D. Appleton-Century, New York, 1936.

[2] *Ibid,* p. 429.

[3] *Ibid,* p. 412.

[4] *Ibid,* p. 418.

[5] *Ibid,* p. 424.

is said to differ from the check-list primarily in calling for an evaluation of each aspect of the object to be rated, rather than merely rating its presence or absence.

The most common application of the score card has been in the field of rating school buildings. Dr. George Strayer and Dr. Nicholaus Engelhardt have published an impressive number of score cards for school buildings[6] of various types which are used in their surveys of school systems. The score card technique has had a number of additional applications to subjects closely related to buildings such as selection of building sites, architectural service and building plans, school building utilization, school housing program, structural and housekeeping sanitation, and janitorial services. Score cards have also been used for school seating, school budget, school record and reports, guidance, organization of junior high schools, publicity material and parent-teacher association, elementary school practices, appraising of colleges, and accrediting of high schools. They have been used for rating the homes of pupils, appraising other institutions and community conditions, selection of textbooks, grading student teachers, and evaluating silent reading lessons.[7]

Underlying Assumptions and Limitations of Jury Appraisal

One of the assumptions underlying the score card as an appraisal technique is: "It is assumed that better judgment can be secured on the significant aspects of an object (or situation) by centering attention on one aspect at a time." [8]

Good, Barr, and Scates question this principle by stating that, though it is not difficult to select certain aspects of a situation, perhaps certain intangible elements which are crucial are omitted. An illustration of this danger which may be cited from the present study is the factor of personality adjustments among faculty members. The reason for lack of cooperation in many instances may not be

[6] References to seventeen such score cards may be found in "School Buildings, Grounds, Equipment, Apparatus and Supplies," *Review of Educational Research,* II, December, 1932, No. 5.

[7] Good, C. V., Barr, A. S., and Scates, D. E. *The Methodology of Educational Research,* pp. 432–437. D. Appleton-Century, New York, 1936.

[8] *Ibid,* p. 437.

one of educational philosophy but of personal antipathy, or professional jealousy. The same writers say:

A second fundamental assumption involved in all of the instruments which yield a general total or composite rating is that general value can be approximated by a summation of the values of parts. Even granting that the first question has been satisfactorily answered, and that all of the really significant aspects have been included in the rating, there is still room for question that any mathematical functions (such as a weighted sum) of these separate ratings will yield a relative value that corresponds well with one's reaction to the object or situation as a whole. . . . This second question also forces a new interpretation of the first one, for the aspects (or elements) must be significant not only when viewed independently but when viewed in the light of their contribution to the picture as a whole.[9]

An example of this limitation of the jury technique of appraisal may be discovered in the present study. In the survey of present practice, certain of the institutions visited seemed to have almost ideal coordination of college and training school staff. Yet, when the author (for experimental purposes) attempted to apply the final form of the score card to such schools, they failed to attain a significantly higher total than some of the others. The explanation probably lies in the fact that certain activities are not needed in an institution when a high degree of coordination exists between some of the other elements. To be specific, in one teachers college no definite distinction was made between critic teachers and college staff, each assuming the work and title of the other at given intervals.[10] In that school it would not be essential that the college staff should 'aid' the training school staff in supervising student teachers, for they would have complete supervision at regular intervals. Since this section of the score card was allotted fifty-eight points by the juries, the score for that school would be reduced considerably if many such lacks occurred.

Good, Barr, and Scates[11] state that from the practical standpoint these problems are not so acute for the following reasons:

1. Improvements in practice or in objects (such as school buildings) are for the most part made in terms of details.

2. The instruments are not likely to be applied at any one time to

[9] *Op. cit.*, p. 438.
[10] See page 235 of this study.
[11] *Op. cit.*, p. 438.

the appraisal of objects or practices which vary fundamentally. That is, a score card for buildings would not be applied to some experimental building that was constructed to suit an entirely special philosophy of education, or that was built on some new theory of building construction which sought to make an epochal advance.

3. It is possible to include in any schedule elements of varying generality, some very detailed, some rather broad, so that a hierarchy of levels is represented. The problem of losing elements of organization or pattern through dividing things is thus met, at least in part.

4. It is probable that administrative action will always be tempered by general opinion and common sense—sometimes to the exasperation of the technical research worker, but not always to the detriment of education.

The underlying assumptions concerning the practical versus the ideal situation in the use of appraisal instruments is best summarized by Good, Barr, and Scates:

> The foregoing remarks concerning the practical situation have no implications of the ideal situation. But we must always temporize ideals with practical considerations. Perhaps an ideal instrument would be so cumbersome and expensive of effort and time that its use would not be warranted. Possibly a combination of ratings and general judgment will ultimately be found to be more desirable than the scientist's dream of a perfect instrument. After all, appraisal schedules are normative instruments; they reflect general tendencies, tempered by the superior and by the inferior, but they represent in the main the things we are most used to. Differences in objects or practices which involve questions of changing philosophies and points of view must be evaluated by other means—principally by human beings giving their best attention directly to the consideration of requirements and consequences. The problems of human values may be studied scientifically, but they can never be supplanted by science without our having surrendered our prerogatives as human beings.[12]

Development of the Score Card and Selection of the Jury Members

The technique used in collecting and organizing the items of cooperative activity which made up the questionnaire has been described in Chapter I.[13] A score card containing the items used in the questionnaire was designed for evaluating present practice in co-

[12] *Ibid*, p. 439.
[13] See page 8.

operation between college and training school faculty. This score card, containing opportunities for evaluating the major items from the questionnaire, was submitted to three juries for relative evaluation of items in terms of teacher training institutions of varying enrollments. A jury selected because of special ability in the particular field concerned is often used to judge validity of principles and practices. Charters and Waples,[14] after making an exhaustive analysis of the duties of teachers, used a jury to validate the relative importance and difficulty of the various activities involved. Rutledge[15] stated ninety-six principles for administration of teachers colleges and normal schools and submitted these principles for validation to a jury of outstanding men in the field of educational administration. Morrison[16] set up twenty criteria for evaluating administrative organization in teachers colleges and submitted them to a jury of thirty teachers college presidents for evaluation.

For the purpose of securing a valid evaluation of the many suggested cooperative activities, it seemed that the highest degree of validity would be assured by the combined judgment of a jury made up of a small number of the most outstanding men in two fields of teacher training: professors of education and directors of training. For this study it was believed that a jury of twenty-five was sufficiently reliable. Charters and Waples[17] found that the predicted coefficient of correlation between the judgment scores of one group of twenty-five persons and an infinite number was $.949 \pm .015$. This correlation indicates that the judgment scores of twenty-five[18] jurors as used in this study would be changed but little by increasing the size of the jury.

The members of each of the three juries were selected from the following two groups of educators who were adjudged to be cogni-

[14] Charters, W. W. and Waples, D. Douglas. *The Commonwealth Teachers Training Study,* pp. 24–30, 493–535. The University of Chicago Press, 1929.

[15] Rutledge, Samuel A. *The Development of Guiding Principles for the Administration of Teachers Colleges and Normal Schools,* Chapters II and III, pp. 5–54. Bureau of Publications, Teachers College, Columbia University, 1930.

[16] Morrison, Robert H. *Internal Administrative Organization in Teachers Colleges,* Chapter II, pp. 8–26. Bureau of Publications, Teachers College, Columbia University, 1933.

[17] *Ibid,* p. 70.

[18] Thirty were selected to provide for the possibility of incomplete returns.

zant of the underlying principles of teacher training in theory and in practice:

I. Forty-five authorities in the field of the professional education of teachers, as evidenced by published writings since 1925; in *Educational Administration and Supervision* (a periodical journal); *Yearbooks of the American Association of Teachers Colleges; Yearbooks of Supervisors of Student Teaching.*

II. Directors of training in forty-five teachers colleges located in each geographical area of the United States.

Directors of training were excluded from Group I above, so that with three exceptions[19] each individual was a dean of a school of education or a professor of education in a college or university in the United States. For the purpose of brevity, members of this group will be referred to throughout the study as professors of education.

Thirty members, fifteen from each of Groups I and II above, composed a jury. Each jury was requested to distribute the points on the score card in terms of a teacher training institution with a different student enrollment, assuming that student teaching facilities were adequate. Jury I distributed points for schools having more than 1,000 students enrolled, July II for schools having 500 to 1,000 students enrolled, and Jury III for schools having fewer than 500 students enrolled.

When the juries had been chosen, the score cards were mailed to each juror with the request that he distribute 1,000 points among the various items listed so that each should carry a number that indicated his estimate of its importance in relation to each and all of the other items in the score card.

Returns were not complete so that the averages in Table I represented:

Jury I	Weighted evaluation in terms of schools with 1000 or more students enrolled.	
	Professors of education..........	11 cases
	Directors of training............	11 cases

[19] The presidents of two teachers colleges and one normal school sent in the evaluated score card.

Jury II In terms of schools with 500 and 1000 students enrolled.
Professors of education.......... 11 cases
Directors of training............ 12 cases

Jury III In terms of schools with fewer than 500 students enrolled.
Professors of education.......... 14 cases
Directors of training............ 11 cases

In Table I, the average number of points given by the two groups in each jury are tabulated for each item in the score card. In addition the average number of points assigned by each jury and the average number of points assigned by the three juries combined, are recorded for each item.

Reliability of Average Weights Assigned to Score Cards

Eleven different correlations were computed to determine the reliability of the evaluations made on the score card. First, the correlations between the weights assigned by professors of education and by directors of training within a given jury were computed by using the averages of the 57 Arabic-numbered subdivisions only. The following correlations were found:

Jury I,[20] for schools with over 1,000 students enrolled....... .81 ± .03
Jury II,[21] for schools with 500 to 1,000 students enrolled.... .67 ± .05
Jury III,[22] for schools with fewer than 500 students enrolled. .82 ± .03

A relatively high degree of correlation is shown within each jury. Since it is lower in Jury II than in the others, we may assume that there is less agreement between professors of education and directors of training as to the relative value of cooperative activities in average-sized [23] schools than in large or small ones. This may be due to the fact that it is more difficult to assign weights for an average-sized[23] school.[24]

[20] Average of weights assigned by 11 professors of education and 11 directors of training.

[21] Average of weights assigned by 11 professors of education and 12 directors of training.

[22] Average of weights assigned by 14 professors of education and 11 directors of training.

[23] Size as evidenced by student enrollment. The jury members were not informed that there were other juries or that other enrollment numbers had been suggested.

[24] This difference, however, is not very reliable and might be attributed to chance.

TABLE I

Allotment of 1,000 Points to a List of Cooperative Activities*

	Jury I More than 1,000			Jury II 500 to 1,000			Jury III Fewer than 500			All Juries
	P	D	Both	P	D	Both	P	D	Both	
I. *Participation of Members of the College Departments in the Functions of the Training School*	336	306	321	341	314	327	264	260	262	303
A. By aiding the training school staff in supervising student teachers	58	62	60	61	65	63	44	60	52	58
1. By observing the teaching of student teachers in the training school	11	20	15	15	17	16	10	12	11	14
2. By holding conferences with student teachers to evaluate and analyze the teaching they have observed the students do	14	13	14	15	18	17	10	13	12	14
3. By helping student teachers plan work they are teaching in the training school	17	11	14	13	15	14	11	21	16	15
4. By giving student teachers a rating or grade	6	6	6	6	9	7	7	5	5	6
5. By working out and revising manuals or handbooks to be used by student teachers in the training school	10	12	11	12	6	9	6	9	8	9
B. By aiding in carrying on the training school curriculum	74	75	75	100	81	90	60	62	61	75
1. By constructing and revising courses of study for the training school	11	12	12	18	11	14	9	9	9	12
2. By assisting in the application of details and the enrichment of state or city prescribed courses of study which are used by the training school	8	9	8	14	10	12	8	8	8	9

* Allotments made by three juries, each composed of professors of education (P) and directors of training (D). Consult page 30 for a statement concerning interpretation of the data in this table.

TABLE I (*Continued*)

	Jury I More than 1,000			Jury II 500 to 1,000			Jury III Fewer than 500			All Juries
	P	D	Both	P	D	Both	P	D	Both	
3. By aiding in the selection of such materials of instruction and equipment as textbooks, supplementary books, physical education equipment, art materials, slides, maps, moving pictures, science laboratory equipment, etc.	8	9	8	13	10	11	8	9	8	9
4. By participating in the testing of training school children	8	10	9	9	10	10	7	5	6	8
5. By participating in analyzing the results of tests administered to training school children, and planning remedial measures	9	10	10	11	9	10	7	8	8	8
6. By participating in such training school activities as assembly programs, school publications, parent-teacher association programs, field trips, etc.	6	6	6	7	8	8	4	4	4	6
7. By participating in the community activities of the training school (e.g., civic projects—community chest, clean-up campaign, safety projects, historical and patriotic pageants, health clinics; recreational activities: story telling at the library, community entertainments, boy or girl scout hikes, etc.)	7	7	7	7	7	7	7	6	6	7
8. By aiding in planning and conducting experiments and new techniques in the training school (e.g., experiments regarding student teachers, children in the training school, types of teaching, new material)	17	12	15	21	16	18	10	13	12	15

TABLE I (*Continued*)

	Jury I More than 1,000			Jury II 500 to 1,000			Jury III Fewer than 500			All Juries
	P	D	Both	P	D	Both	P	D	Both	
C. By having college classes observe teaching done by critic teachers in the training school	74	75	74	47	62	55	58	55	57	62
1. By preparing for observation in the training school	28	21	24	15	19	17	20	18	19	20
2. By visiting in the training school to observe	23	31	27	16	19	18	18	18	18	21
3. By following up observation in the training school	23	23	23	16	24	20	20	19	20	21
D. By personally teaching children in the training school	50	38	44	55	44	49	29	27	28	40
1. By teaching for college classes to observe	12	11	12	15	16	16	9	8	8	12
2. By teaching without observers to try out an experimental unit	23	15	19	24	13	18	8	11	10	15
3. By teaching occasional units in fields where more of an authority than the critic teacher	15	12	13	16	15	15	12	8	10	13
E. By assisting in adjusting personality problems in the training school	34	26	30	37	28	32	29	25	27	30
1. By aiding in adjusting personality problems of training school children (e.g., stealing, lying, non-cooperative behavior)	12	10	11	14	7	10	12	7	9	10
2. By aiding in adjusting personality problems of student teachers (e.g., non-cooperative behavior, inferiority feelings)	22	16	19	23	21	22	17	18	18	20

TABLE I (*Continued*)

	Jury I More than 1,000			Jury II 500 to 1,000			Jury III Fewer than 500			All Juries
	P	D	Both	P	D	Both	P	D	Both	
F. By aiding in determining policies of the training school	46	30	38	41	34	38	44	31	37	38
1. By deciding which students are prepared to begin student teaching, using previously set-up standards as to who shall be admitted to student teaching	16	13	15	16	14	15	20	13	16	15
2. By determining the length and content of student teaching (e.g., time and content of observation, participation, responsible teaching, conferences, lesson planning, etc.)	14	7	10	12	10	11	11	8	9	10
3. By determining the kind and amount of contacts the students should have with the training school throughout their training courses prior to student teaching	16	10	13	13	10	12	13	10	12	13
II. *Participation of Members of the Training School Staff in the Functions of the Other College Departments*	*185*	*213*	*199*	*223*	*184*	*203*	*249*	*198*	*224*	*209*
A. By aiding in formulating the college curriculum	56	73	64	94	47	69	110	69	89	74
1. By participating in determining the content of college courses	21	34	27	40	22	31	43	25	34	31
2. By participating in the selection of such college materials as textbooks, supplementary books, laboratory equipment, etc.	12	19	15	16	10	13	24	20	22	16
3. By participating in planning new experiments and techniques in the college departments (e.g., size of college classes, having consultant advisors for students, etc.)	23	20	22	38	15	25	43	24	33	27

TABLE I (*Continued*)

	Jury I More than 1,000			Jury II 500 to 1,000			Jury III Fewer than 500			All Juries
	P	D	Both	P	D	Both	P	D	Both	
B. By participating in the teaching of college courses	72	68	71	73	69	71	85	72	79	74
1. Through offering occasional units in college courses where the training school faculty member is more of an authority on that unit than is the regular college instructor (e.g., lesson planning, units of work)	28	24	26	36	23	29	33	27	30	29
2. By aiding students who are preparing work for their college classes (e.g., obtaining data for case studies, conferences regarding routine details of classroom management, etc.)	30	24	27	20	21	21	24	23	24	24
3. Through teaching entire college courses	14	20	18	17	25	21	28	22	25	21
C. By being cognizant of the content of college courses	57	72	64	56	68	63	54	57	56	61
1. By visiting college courses	27	36	31	32	31	32	27	27	27	30
2. By having recent outlines of the college courses	30	36	33	24	37	31	27	30	29	31
III. *Participation of the Entire Faculty in Activities Which Concern the Teacher Training Institution as a Unit*	*254*	*255*	*254*	*232*	*273*	*253*	*218*	*274*	*246*	*251*
A. By determining the policies of the institution relative to such matters as entrance requirements, attendance regulations, school athletics, graduation requirements, scholarships, loan fund, etc.	31	45	38	34	25	30	36	27	32	33
B. By agreeing upon the methods by which common equipment may be made accessible to faculty members, students, and training school children	22	32	27	15	33	24	30	29	30	27
C. By participating in planning such college activities as college assembly, social programs, departmental clubs, school publications, special day programs, commencement, etc.	24	26	25	18	24	21	21	24	23	23

TABLE I (*Continued*)

	Jury I More than 1,000			Jury II 500 to 1,000			Jury III Fewer than 500			All Juries
	P	D	Both	P	D	Both	P	D	Both	
D. By cooperating on the placement of graduates..	46	33	40	33	31	32	27	29	28	33
E. By follow-up work with graduates............	68	53	60	64	65	65	47	90	67	64
1. By visiting graduates in the field to supervise their first year of teaching experience and to gain material for revising and improving the training curricula........................	29	16	22	23	20	22	14	32	22	22
2. By presenting to the resident faculty the findings of field workers who visit students in service	13	13	13	11	17	14	12	22	17	15
3. By considering the written appeals for teaching helps from graduates.................	12	12	12	11	14	12	10	17	13	12
4. By holding conferences with graduates who return to the institution to visit.............	14	12	13	19	14	17	11	19	15	15
F. By publishing as a joint enterprise such professional literature as:.......................	63	65	64	68	95	81	57	75	66	71
1. Student teaching manuals................	6	7	6	6	12	9	8	9	9	8
2. Courses of study for the training school.....	7	11	9	9	16	12	9	11	10	11
3. Courses of study for the college courses.....	5	7	6	7	11	9	6	9	7	7
4. Rating scales for student teachers..........	7	7	7	4	6	5	6	6	6	6
5. Reports of experiments in college departments	8	6	7	8	8	8	5	7	6	7
6. Reports of experiments in the training school	10	7	9	10	12	11	7	8	8	10
7. Children's textbooks.....................	6	6	6	8	8	8	5	6	5	6
8. College textbooks........................	5	4	4	7	7	7	3	5	4	5
9. School news bulletins....................	4	4	4	3	5	4	3	7	5	4
10. Reports of cooperative activities within the college................................	5	6	6	6	10	8	5	7	6	7

TABLE I (*Continued*)

	Jury I More than 1,000			Jury II 500 to 1,000			Jury III Fewer than 500			All Juries
	P	D	Both	P	D	Both	P	D	Both	
IV. *Certain Administrative Devices Which May Facilitate Cooperation*	*225*	*226*	*225*	*204*	*229*	*217*	*269*	*268*	*268*	*237*
A. Through faculty personnel	119	130	124	123	141	132	146	141	143	133
1. By having an administrative officer whose work is to direct the coordination of the training school and the other departments of teacher training institutions	29	27	28	27	34	30	36	40	38	32
2. By having a consultant advisor for each student who advises him throughout his pre-service training and who decides when the student is ready to do student teaching and when ready to graduate	14	10	12	13	12	13	18	15	16	14
3. By having supervisors of each grade level in the training school (e.g., primary, intermediate, upper)	9	20	14	12	12	12	19	13	16	14
4. By requiring that every member of the faculty shall have had some experience in teaching in the types of school for which he is preparing teachers	20	11	16	18	18	18	14	15	14	16
5. By paying equal salary for equal training and experience to every member of the faculty, including the training school staff	18	27	22	15	23	19	25	19	22	21
6. By adjusting the service load of each member of the college faculty to provide for regular contacts with the training school	15	18	16	18	21	19	17	22	20	18

TABLE I (*Continued*)

	Jury I More than 1,000			Jury II 500 to 1,000			Jury III Fewer than 500			All Juries
	P	D	Both	P	D	Both	P	D	Both	
7. By adjusting the service load of each member of the training school staff to provide for regular contacts with the college departments....	14	17	16	20	21	21	17	17	17	18
B. Through the status of the training school......	106	96	101	81	88	85	123	127	125	104
1. By having a training school building which is accessible to the college faculty............	32	30	31	25	20	23	36	27	32	29
2. By interlocking the training school and the college departments......................	25	22	23	19	26	23	33	31	32	26
3. By basing each professional course of the college upon constant observation in the training school from the freshman year to graduation..	26	25	26	21	23	22	30	40	35	28
4. By requiring participation teaching in the training school in each year of the student's study, leading to responsible room teaching in the last year...........................	23	19	21	16	19	17	24	29	26	21

This table should be read as follows:

(1) The total number of points given 1, 2, 3, 4, and 5 should equal the number of points allotted to A; those given to 1, 2, 3, 4, 5, 6, 7, and 8 should equal that allotted to B; those given to 1, 2, and 3 should equal that allotted to C; and so on through the list.

(2) The total number of points given A, B, C, D, E, and F should equal the number of points allotted I; those given A, B, and C should equal the amount allotted to II; those given to A, B, C, D, E, and F should equal the amount allotted to III; and those given to A and B should equal the amount allotted to IV.

(3) The total number of points given Parts I, II, III, and IV should equal 1,000.

The fourth computation was a determination of the correlation between weights assigned by professors of education in the three juries combined, and those assigned by the directors of training in the juries combined. Using the 57 Arabic-numbered subdivisions only, the resulting coefficient of correlation was .77 ± .02. The fifth computation was made between the same two groups, using the 17 lettered subdivisions only, which gave a correlation of .87 ± .02. It is evident from this difference that the judges were more reliable in distributing 1,000 points among 17 items than among 57.[25] The above high correlations lead to the conclusion that the reliability of the evaluations within a jury is substantial, and that it was a valid technique to include in each jury both professors of education and directors of training. Since the former group represents the theory in education, and the latter the practice, we may conclude that there is a comparatively high degree of correlation between theory and practice relative to desirable cooperative activities for teacher training institutions.

The next set of correlations was computed for the weights assigned by the three juries, in terms of schools with three different enrollment ranges, using the 57 Arabic-numbered subdivisions only. Correlating the weights assigned by Jury I (for schools with over 1,000 students enrolled) with those assigned by Jury II (500 to 1,000 students enrolled) gave a result of .92 ± .02. In like manner correlating Jury I (over 1,000) and Jury III (fewer than 500) gave a result of .895 ± .02. The result of correlating Jury II with Jury III gave .88 ± .02. Similar computations were made, using the 17 lettered subdivisions only. Correlating the weights assigned by Jury I with those assigned by Jury II gave a result of .95 ± .02; Jury I with Jury III, .94 ± .02; and Jury II with Jury III, .89 ± .03.

These high correlations lead to the conclusion that size of school as evidenced by differences in student enrollment makes little difference in the relative weight assigned to a list of cooperative activities by juries composed of professors of education and directors of training.

[25] It is not so much the difference in the number of categories which matters as it is the familiar fact that there is usually better agreement on the broader categories than on their subdivisions.

The validity of these data is claimed on the following grounds: first, those educational experts selected for the juries represent two groups of specialists who, because of superior training and intimate contact with the problems in teacher training, are in a position to give sound opinions; and second, the judgments are consistent and reasonable.

Analysis of the Four Major Sections of Score Card

Following is a tabulation of the relative weight assigned to the four major sections of the score card:

	Jury I Over 1,000			Jury II 500 to 1,000			Jury III Less than 500			All Juries
	P[1]	D[2]	B[3]	P	D	B	P	D	B	
I. Participation of members of the college departments in the functions of the training school	336	306	321	341	314	327	264	260	262	303
II. Participation of members of the training school staff in the functions of the other college departments	185	213	199	223	184	203	249	198	224	209
III. Participation of the entire faculty in activities which concern the teacher training institutions as a unit	254	255	254	232	273	253	218	274	246	251
IV. Certain administrative devices which may facilitate cooperation	225	226	225	204	229	217	269	268	268	237

[1] Professors of Education. [2] Directors of Training. [3] Both Groups within a Jury.

The combined judgment of the juries places the greatest emphasis on Part I, Participation of members of the college departments in the functions of the training school, and the least emphasis on Part II, Participation of members of the training school staff in the functions of the other college departments. This difference is misleading unless the subdivisions are read through as the jurors were instructed to do before making any division of the 1,000 points. The appraisal instrument would have been simpler to weight if an equal number of activities had been listed under each division and subdivision, but such a procedure would have padded the score card with unimportant activities. Only those items were included [26] which were discussed in the literature of the field, or were suggested by students in graduate classes at Teachers College, Columbia University.[27]

Part I of the score card includes 24 cooperative activities; Part II has only 8.[28] An examination of the individual weighted activities indicates that even greater importance is assigned to the items in Part II than is assigned to those in Part I. Matching similar activities from each part will show this to be true.

Part I A 3	By helping students plan work they are teaching in the training school..........................	15 points
Part II B 2	By aiding students who are preparing work for their college classes..........................	24 points
Part I D 3	By teaching occasional units in fields where more of an authority than the critic teacher.......	13 points
Part II B 1	Through offering occasional units in college courses where the training school faculty member is more of an authority on that unit than is the regular instructor.......................	29 points
Part I B 3	By aiding in the selection of materials of instruction for the training schools................	9 points
Part II A 2	By participating in the selection of materials of instruction for the college.................	16 points
Part I F 2	By aiding in determining the length and content of student teaching..........................	10 points
Part II A 1	By participating in determining the content of college courses...............................	31 points

Doubtless the difference in weight assigned to the two parts would have been much greater had the jurors considered Part I of more importance than Part II, in view of the fact that there are three times as many items in the former as in the latter. It is the author's conclusion that the high values placed upon all of the items in Part II are due to each juror's attempt to indicate that Part II is highly important in comparison with Part I. This difference would not be apparent if one studied only the totals for the four major sections.

[26] Good, Barr, and Scates, *op. cit.*, p. 439.
[27] See Chapter I, page 8.
[28] Part III has 18 divisions; Part IV has 11 divisions.

At this point the author should state that in her judgment the assigned weights are highly significant, for they are the product of much time and thought on the part of the jury members. Several of the jurors attached notes to the score card lamenting the amount of time they had been required to spend in giving accurate and careful consideration to the weighting. The rather high correlations attest to the reliability of their judgments.[29]

There are several differences apparent in the weight assigned to the four sections in terms of schools of different enrollments, and in terms of the two groups within a jury.

1. Jury III, which evaluated the activities in terms of an institution with fewer than 500 students enrolled, indicates that certain administrative devices which may facilitate cooperation are as important as the informal participation of the college staff in the work of the training school.[30] This correlates well with present practice, for the investigator found that the smaller teacher training institutions usually had rather definite administrative programs for achieving coordination.

2. Size of the college apparently has no influence upon the importance of Part III, Participation of the entire faculty in activities which concern the teacher training institution as a unit. This section has been assigned at least one-fourth of the 1,000 points by each jury, which would indicate that those activities represent significant types of faculty coordination. Within the jury for schools with fewer than 500 students enrolled, there is a rather large difference in the weight assigned—218 points by the professors of education and 274 points by the directors of training. An examination of the activities which comprise this section shows the difference to be chiefly in the relative importance assigned to Part III E, By follow-up work with graduates (47 and 90 points). The professors of education may have based their judgment upon the assumption that in small schools, with fewer faculty members, it is more difficult to arrange for a member of the college faculty and a member of the training school staff to be away from the campus at the same time. In the study of present practice several directors of training in the smaller schools

[29] See pages 20, 29.
[30] See page 30.

mentioned follow-up work with graduates as one of their activities. In each case this director also taught college courses. Perhaps the directors of training, considering themselves members of both college and training school faculty, find this to be a highly satisfactory way of coordinating theory and practice.

3. The activities listed in Part I, Participation of members of the college departments in the functions of the training school, are those which are more definitely the work of the training school staff. The weights assigned show that the professors of education are consistent in placing a slightly higher value on Part I than the directors of training place on it. Such a difference might have been predicted because, though in theory this function seems highly desirable, the latter group may see a need for solving many practical problems which influence the efficient administration of the plan.

For similar reasons one might expect the directors of training to weight Part II, Participation of members of the training school staff in the functions of the other college departments, more heavily than would the professors of education. This conclusion is true for Jury I (large schools), but in Juries II and III the professors assign much more importance to the activities than do the directors.

Summary of Four Major Sections of the Score Card

1. The weights assigned show that the professors of education are consistent in placing a slightly higher value on Part I than do the directors of training. Also, one may assume from a comparison of the means for each jury that to these educational experts Part I is relatively more important in schools of over 500 than in small schools with fewer than 500 students enrolled. The investigator found that in practice no one size of school seemed to predominate in the emphasis given to participation of the college departments in the work of the campus training school.

2. In Jury II the professors of education assign more weight to Part II of the score card than do the directors of training. The reverse is true of Jury I. The mean judgment of the three juries shows a slight tendency to attach more weight to Part II as the size of the school decreases.

3. There is a slight tendency for the directors of training to assign

more importance to Part III than do the professors of education. This difference increases as the size of school decreases. The mean weights given Part III by the juries are so similar that one might assume that size of school had little influence on the importance of having the entire faculty participate in activities which concern the school as a unit.

4. The two groups of officials on a given jury are in closer agreement regarding the importance of Part II than upon the other three parts.

4a. Jury III shows a tendency to place more value on administrative devices which facilitate cooperation than do Juries I and II.

5. In comparing the relative weight which a given jury assigns to the four parts, we find that the two groups in Jury I are more consistent with each other than are similar groups in Juries II and III.

6. A study of the weights assigned by the three juries to each major part shows that there is little real difference between such means for schools of 500 to 1,000, and over 1,000 enrollment. It may be said that the mean weights assigned to the four major parts of the score card by Juries I and II are in closer agreement with each other than with those assigned by Jury III.

7. These data suggest that the judgment of two juries instead of three would have been sufficient to show where differences in emphasis on cooperative activities should appear.

Influence of Size of School or of Jury Membership upon Score Card Appraisal

1. Having college classes observe the teaching of critic teachers in the campus training school (I C 2)[31] received heavy weighting. Both groups in Jury I (large schools) accorded importance to this activity. They felt that it was more important for college instructors to observe the teaching of critic teachers than to do the teaching themselves (I D 1), unless such teaching was done without observers (I D 2).

Jury II (schools of average size) indicated that it is almost as important for college instructors to teach for observers as to

[31] See Table I.

observe the teaching of critic teachers. The professors of education in Jury II indicated that it is even more important that college instructors teach without observers in trying out experimental units than to teach for observers.

Jury III (small schools) felt that it was much more important for college instructors to observe the teaching of critic teachers than that they, themselves, teach for observers. This jury accorded much less importance to teaching without observers than did the other two juries. This judgment is probably based upon the assumption that not all college instructors are successful teachers of children and that in schools with a small enrollment the number of faculty members who could teach children successfully would be negligible. This weighting is not in keeping with present practice, for the investigator found that college instructors in the smaller institutions taught children for observers more frequently than in the larger ones.

2. The directors of training in Juries II and III accorded much less prominence to having college faculty aid in adjusting personality problems of training school children than did the professors of education. Perhaps the former group has found that this type of adjustment does not lend itself well to cooperative effort.

3. Educational literature suggests that members of the college faculty may aid in determining the length and content of student teaching (I F 2).[32] This item received rather low weighting by the juries, but in each case the professors of education assigned more points to it than did the directors of training. The latter group may have felt that this task is more definitely the work of the training school and therefore does not lend itself well to cooperative enterprise.

4. The professors of education assign even greater importance than the directors of training to the following ways in which the training school staff may participate in the work of the college departments:

a. By participating in planning new experiments and techniques in the college departments (II A 3).[32]

b. Through offering occasional units in college courses where the training school faculty member is more of an authority on that unit than is the regular college instructor (II B 1).[32]

[32] *Ibid.*

5. The three juries agree upon the importance of having the critic teachers participate in determining the content of college courses. This would indicate that size of school has little or no influence upon the value of the activity, but there is no consistency of agreement between the two groups within a jury. Directors of training accord greater importance than the professors of education in Jury I (large schools), but the latter group assigns it more weight within the two juries for smaller schools.

6. Except in small teacher training institutions, directors of training think it more important that the training school staff should offer courses in the college than do the professors of education. The present practice survey found that directors of training, usually, and critic teachers, frequently, are assigned to this work. Size of school, however, had no relation to the existence of the plan.

7. The publication of professional literature as a joint enterprise is suggested as an important cooperative activity in teachers colleges regardless of size. The directors of training weight this activity more heavily than do the professors of education but the latter are more consistent among themselves in their evaluation.

8. Each jury assigns importance to having an administrative officer whose work is to direct the coordination of the training school and the other departments of teacher training institutions. It is difficult to explain why the need for such an official is weighted as more important as the size of the school decreases. Perhaps this difference is due to chance, for such an officer would seem more essential to the organization as the size of the school increases, with its many accompanying problems of coordinating all the representative interests of the college.

9. Size of school has little influence upon the relative importance of the following items, nor is there great disagreement within the juries as to their importance:

Part IV A 6—By adjusting the service load of each member of the college faculty to provide for regular contacts with the training school.

Part IV A 7—By adjusting the service load of each member of the training school staff to provide for regular contacts with the college departments.

It is surprising that these items[33] did not receive the highest

[33] See Table I.

weighting on the score card, since the existence of all the other activities seems dependent upon these two.

The fact that they do not achieve the expected ranking is a criticism of the technique used in formulating the score card rather than an inconsistency in the jury appraisals. The investigator feels that these two should be considered as one item since their final identical weights imply that each is as important as the other. The statement on the score card should read: By adjusting the service load of each member of the training school and college faculty to provide for regular reciprocal contacts. If one reads the two items just preceding the ones under discussion on the score card,[33] it becomes evident that items IV A 6 and IV A 7 should have been stated as one in order to be comparable with the others in that subdivision.

10. Professors of education assign slightly greater value than do the directors of training to having a training school building which is accessible to the college faculty. Perhaps this is a chance difference, for there seems to be no valid explanation for this inconsistency.

11. Item IV B 3, by basing each professional course of the college upon constant observation in the training school from the freshman year to graduation,[33] received heavy weighting by all the juries but was considered most important for schools with enrollments of less than 500 students. Perhaps this difference is based upon the assumption that such a program is more easily administered in schools with small enrollments.

Ranking of Cooperative Activities According to Mean Weight Assigned by the Combined Juries

Since the allotment of points to a lettered subdivision is somewhat dependent upon its number of Arabic-numbered subdivisions, it seems more valid to compare the latter groups. Table II contains the 57 Arabic-numbered subdivisions listed in rank order according to the mean weight assigned by the combined juries.

The investigator is aware that to list the cooperative activities in rank order as in Table II is not an entirely reliable technique since the jury members were not directed to assign weights to each Arabic-numbered subdivision so that these items might eventually be listed in rank order. However, since correlations are high between

[33] See Table I.

TABLE II

Ranking of 57 Cooperative Activities According to Mean Weight Assigned by the Combined Juries*

Cooperative Activity	Mean Weight out of 1,000 Points	Location on Score Card
1. College maintains an administrative officer whose work is to direct the coordination of the training school and the other departments of teacher training institutions.......	32	IV A 1
2. Critic teachers participate in determining the content of college courses..................................	31	II A 1
3. Critic teachers have recent outlines of the college courses	31	II C 2
4. Critic teachers visit college courses to observe..........	30	II C 1
5. Critic teachers offer occasional units in college courses where the training school faculty member is more of an authority on that unit than is the regular college instructor (e.g., lesson planning, units of work)................	29	II B 1
6. Training school building which is accessible to the college faculty....................................	29	IV B 1
7. Each professional course of the college is based upon constant observation in the training school from the freshman year to graduation..............................	28	IV B 3
8. Critic teachers participate in planning new experiment and techniques in the college departments (e.g., size of college classes, having consultant advisors for students, etc.)....	27	II A 3
9. Training school and college departments are interlocked in relationship..................................	26	IV B 2
10. Critic teachers aid students who are preparing work for their college classes (e.g., obtaining data for case studies, conferences regarding routine details of classroom management, etc.)..................................	24	II B 2
11. Training school and college faculty visit graduates in the field to supervise their first year of teaching experience and to gain material for revising and improving the training curricula....................................	22	III E 1
12. College instructor has college classes visit in the training school to observe...............................	21	I C 2
13. College instructor has college classes cooperatively following up observation in the training school............	21	I C 3
14. Critic teachers teach entire college courses............	21	II B 3
15. Equal salary for equal training and experience is paid to every member of the faculty, including the training school staff....................................	21	IV A 5
16. Participation teaching is required in the training school in each year of the student's study, leading to responsible room teaching in the last year.......................	21	IV B 4

* Items III A, B, C, and D might have been included because they have no subdivisions and have been considered as Arabic-numbered subdivisions by the juries. See pages 25, 26.

TABLE II (*Continued*)

Cooperative Activity	Mean Weight out of 1,000 Points	Location on Score Card
17. College instructors have college classes prepare cooperatively for observation in the training school	20	I C 1
18. College instructors aid in adjusting personality problems of student teachers (e.g., non-cooperative behavior, inferiority feelings)	20	I E 2
19. The service load of each member of the college faculty is adjusted to provide for regular contacts with the training school	18	IV A 6
20. The service load of each member of the training school staff is adjusted to provide for regular contacts with the college departments	18	IV A 7
21. Critic teachers participate in the selection of such college materials as textbooks, supplementary books, laboratory equipment, etc.	16	II A 2
22. College requires that every member of the faculty shall have had some experience in teaching in the types of school for which he is preparing teachers	16	IV A 4
23. College instructors help student teachers plan work they are teaching in the training school	15	I A 3
24. College instructors aid in planning and conducting experiments and new techniques in the training school (e.g., experiments regarding student teachers, children in the training school, types of teaching, new material)	15	I B 8
25. College instructors teach in training school without observers to try out experimental units	15	I D 2
26. College instructors cooperate in deciding which students are prepared to begin student teaching, using standards previously set up as to who shall be admitted to student teaching	15	I F 1
27. Training school and college faculty who visit students in service present the findings to the resident faculty	15	III E 2
28. Training school and college faculty hold conferences with graduates who return to the institution to visit	15	III E 4
29. College instructors observe the teaching of student teachers in the training school	14	I A 1
30. College instructors hold conferences with student teachers to evaluate and analyze the teaching they have observed the students do	14	I A 2
31. Each college instructor is a consultant advisor to individual students, advising them throughout their pre-service training and deciding when the student is ready to do student teaching and when ready to graduate	14	IV A 2
32. College maintains supervisors of each grade level in the training school (e.g., primary, intermediate, upper) who are also college instructors	14	IV A 3

TABLE II (*Continued*)

Cooperative Activity	Mean Weight out of 1,000 Points	Location on Score Card
33. College instructors teach occasional units in training school, in fields where more of an authority than the critic teacher	13	I D 3
34. College instructors cooperate in determining the kind and amount of contacts the students should have with the training school throughout their training courses prior to student teaching	13	I F 3
35. College instructors teach in training school for college classes to observe	12	I D 1
36. College instructors aid in constructing and revising courses of study for the training school	12	I B 1
37. Training school and college faculty consider the written appeals for teaching helps from graduates	12	III E 3
38. Members of training school and college faculties publish as a joint enterprise courses of study for the training school	11	III F 2
39. College instructors aid in adjusting personality problems of training school children (e.g., stealing, lying, non-cooperative behavior)	10	I E 1
40. College instructors cooperate in determining the length and content of student teaching (e.g., time and content of observation, participation, responsible teaching, conferences, lesson planning, etc.)	10	I F 2
41. Members of training schools and college faculties publish as a joint enterprise reports of experiments in the training school	10	III F 6
42. College instructors cooperatively work out and revise manuals or handbooks to be used by student teachers in the training school	9	I A 5
43. College instructors assist in the application of details and the enrichment of state or city prescribed courses of study which are used by the training school	9	I B 2
44. College instructors aid in the selection of such materials of instruction and equipment as textbooks, supplementary books, physical education equipment, art materials, slides, maps, moving pictures, science laboratory equipment, etc.	9	I B 3
45. College instructors participate in analyzing the results of tests administered to training school children, and in planning remedial measures	9	I B 5
46. College instructors participate in the testing of training school children	8	I B 4
47. Members of training school and college faculties publish, as a joint enterprise, student teaching manuals	8	III F 1

TABLE II (*Continued*)

Cooperative Activity	Mean Weight out of 1,000 Points	Location on Score Card
48. College instructors participate in the community activities of the training school	7	I B 7
49. Members of training school and college faculties publish courses of study for the college courses as a joint enterprise	7	III F 3
50. Members of training school and college faculties publish reports of experiments in college departments as a joint enterprise	7	III F 5
51. Members of training school and college faculties publish reports of cooperative activities within the college, as a joint enterprise	7	III F 10
52. College instructors cooperate in giving student teachers a rating or grade	6	I A 4
53. College instructors participate in such training school activities as assembly programs, school publications, parent-teacher association programs, field trips, etc.	6	I B 6
54. Members of training school and college faculties publish rating scales for student teachers as a joint enterprise	6	III F 4
55. Members of training school and college faculties publish children's textbooks as a joint enterprise	6	III F 7
56. Members of training school and college faculties publish college textbooks as a joint enterprise	5	III F 8
57. Members of training school and college faculties publish school news bulletins as a joint enterprise	4	III F 9

the groups within a jury and between juries, such a table seems justified as an aid to the reader in comparing the picture of present practice discussed in Chapters III to VI with the relative importance of the cooperative activities found in the twenty-five schools visited.

An examination of the upper third of the ranked cooperative activities in Table II reveals that only three are from Part I, the others being equally divided among Parts II, III, and IV. Though ranking twelfth, thirteenth, and seventeenth in the list, these activities represent the most generally accepted way in which college instructors participate in the functions of the training school.

Limitations of the Score Card

Reasons for declaring the ranked list in Table II to lack complete statistical reliability are based upon the following possible limitations of the score card:

1. More weight may be assigned to one or more of the four major headings than the number and importance of the subdivisions would warrant. Although the directions for distributing the 1,000 points recommended that the entire score card be read through twice before allotting weight to such headings, it is an accepted fact [34] that to retain as many as 17 lettered subdivisions and 57 Arabic-numbered subdivisions in mind in relation to each other would decrease reliability. Therefore, to rank the subdivisions from the four large groups in one list is less valid than to rank the subdivisions within each of the four major parts of the score card. These latter ranks may be easily read from Table II, since the column at the extreme right gives the exact number and location of each item in the score card. For example, the three items ranking highest in Part I are C 2, C 3, and C 1.

2. It is possible that Part IV, Certain administrative devices which may facilitate cooperation, was weighted heavily because of its title rather than because of the number and importance of the subdivisions. Many authorities in the field of teacher training feel that one of the most effective ways to promote cooperative endeavor is through administrative devices. Such a viewpoint is quite valid since many

[34] Conclusive evidence through experiments has shown that reliability in evaluations decreases as the number of items increase.

of the suggested activities in Parts I, II, and III could not be carried out unless items A 6 and A 7 in Part IV, relating to adjustment of service loads, were in force. It is possible that there are more subdivisions which should have been included, but the present list represents the best judgment of the groups mentioned in Chapter XII to whom the score card was submitted for additions and different groupings.

3. The lettered subdivision titles are not equally inclusive. For instance, Part I B includes eight Arabic-numbered subdivisions, Part I C includes three. Table II shows that, where there are many subdivisions to a given item on the score card, those subdivisions rank lower in the number of points out of 1,000 allotted. In like manner, where there are few subdivisions to a given item, they tend to rank high on the score card. The writer feels that subdivisions in Parts III F, I B, and I A may not be of less importance than others on the score card, and probably would have received more weight if all other sections had the same number of subdivisions.

4. The items in Part I, Participation of members of the college departments in the functions of the training school, have not been paired with Part II, Participation of members of the training school staff in the functions of the other college departments. For example, Part I E suggests that college faculty members may assist in adjusting personality problems in the training schools, but it is not balanced in Part II by an item suggesting that the training school faculty assist in adjusting personality problems of students in college courses. The reason for this difference is that only those subdivisions were included which were suggested by educational experts in theory or in practice.[35]

5. Administrative devices for facilitating cooperation, other than those included in Part IV, may be found in Parts I, II, and III. To illustrate, Part I F, By aiding in determining the policies of the training school, might be called an administrative device if such cooperation were effected by the "training school cabinet," suggested by Professor Bagley.[36] The devices grouped in Part IV are those which

[35] Chapter I, page 8.

[36] Learned and Bagley. *The Professional Preparation of Teachers for American Public Schools.* The Carnegie Foundation for the Advancement of Teaching, *Bulletin 14*, 1920, pp. 201–202.

were not covered by the titles applied to the other three major sections of the score card.

6. The score card gave no opportunity for negative weighting, but several judges assigned a weight of zero to certain items. No subdivision was considered sufficiently undesirable to receive a weight of zero in the average weights assigned by any jury or any group within a jury.

Suggested Use of the Score Card for Self-Survey of a Teacher Training Institution

Need for Validated Standards

Printed score cards used in surveying elementary school organization[37] or college buildings[38] show the maximum weight for each subdivision in either five or a multiple of five, permitting the use of a five-point scale of evaluation in scoring that item in a given school. If the weights assigned by Jury I are used in scoring the degree of cooperation between the faculty of the campus elementary training schools and of the other departments in a teachers college with over 1,000 students enrolled, the weights tabulated in Table I should be rounded off in numbers of 5 or a multiple of 5. The same would be true in using the average weights assigned by Juries II and III.

Before the score card can be used as a basis for surveying a teacher training institution, certain standards must be validated upon which to base the evaluation of a given subdivision. This has been partially done by the juries who weighted the cooperation activities. In Part II of the booklet containing the score card items each jury member was asked to rank various methods[39] for carrying out the cooperation activities in the order of their usefulness in the size of school for which he had weighted Part I.

These methods were to be ranked in order of preference, using 1 to indicate first preference; 2, second preference; and 3, third preference; etc. The means of the ranks assigned were computed for

[37] Mort, P. R. and Hilleboe, G. L. "A Rating Scale for Elementary School Organization." Bureau of Publications, Teachers College, Columbia University, 1930.

[38] Evenden, E. S., Strayer, G. D. and Engelhardt, N. L. "Score Card for College Buildings." Bureau of Publications, Teachers College, Columbia University, 1929.

[39] These methods were those suggested by the groups to which the questionnaires were submitted for revision, clarification, and additions. See Chap. I, page 8.

the two groups within a jury, and for the three juries; then averaged into a single mean, representing the combined judgment of three juries. These data are not collected into one table but may be found in Chapters III to VII, accompanying the discussion of the extent to which cooperative activities are in progress in the twenty-five state teachers colleges and normal schools visited. The ways in which the cooperative activities might be performed were used in the questionnaires and therefore appear across the top of each table in the succeeding chapters. Jury ranking of the items is included in the discussion of each cooperative item to aid the reader in comparing present practice with the judgment of experts. In many instances the suggested methods for a given activity received similar or identical mean ranks, showing that there is probably more than one acceptable way of effecting a given type of cooperation. It might also reveal that two or three methods are equally undesirable, for the ranking technique shows relative preference rather than importance of each item.

The juries of experts were not asked to indicate the most desirable frequency of performance for each item on the score cards, though the personally presented questionnaires collected such information, which is presented in Tables III through XXXIV.

Though these additional data would have added to the values of the present study, it is doubtful whether the judges would have been willing to give further consideration to the score card, since the first two types of information required more time than one can reasonably ask of such authorities.

Differences in Organization in the 25 Institutions Visited

The investigator found that administrative organization, faculty personnel, and facilities for student teaching influenced the reciprocal relations between training school and college faculty in the report of present practice given in the succeeding chapters of this study. Certain of the following types of organization made comparisons complicated:

1. One campus and one off-campus elementary training school (5 cases).
2. One campus and several off-campus elementary training schools (9 cases).
3. Only a campus elementary training school (8 cases).
4. Only city elementary schools used for laboratory purposes, one[40] of these being nearer the college buildings than the others (3 cases).

5. Student teaching conducted in both secondary and elementary education: campus school only (8 cases); elementary on campus, secondary off campus (3 cases); both on campus and off campus (7 cases).
6. Critic teachers teaching college courses in addition to supervising student teaching (7 cases).
7. Training school supervisors employed in addition to critic teachers, each carrying a part-time teaching load in the college (7 cases).
8. Special critic teachers in fine arts (8 cases), music (6 cases), and physical education (6 cases), who taught no college courses.
9. Special supervisors in music (17 cases), fine arts (15 cases), physical education (16 cases), home economics (1 case), industrial arts (1 case), penmanship (2 cases), who carried a teaching load in the college and supervised their field in the training school.
10. Directors of training who gave full time to one elementary training school; who divided time among several training schools—campus and off-campus; who taught college courses in addition to directing the laboratory school work; no director of training employed, and campus training school principal also a critic teacher (1 case).
11. A principal of the campus elementary training school employed in addition to the director of training, who also taught college courses (7 cases); who gave full time to directing the campus training school (6 cases).
12. Each member of the academic faculty supervising student teachers one term out of every four (1 case), city schools used for student teaching but state assuming no responsibility in paying the city teachers.
13. City schools used for student teaching purposes, but the city teachers not paid by the state and therefore all supervision of student teachers done by the education department in the college (1 case).
14. Professionalized subject matter (methods) courses taught in: education department only; in each subject matter department concerned (4 cases); and in both education and subject matter departments.[41]
15. Head of an academic department offering courses in professionalized subject matter in certain schools; in others these courses taught by another member of the department concerned.

Proposed Plan for Scoring the Degree of Cooperation Between Campus Elementary Training School and College Faculties in an Individual School

Since the above differences within teacher training institutions would influence the relative feasibility of carrying out certain of the cooperative activities, it is suggested that the entire faculty within

[40] A school within a ten-minute walk of the college buildings was considered a campus school if only city schools were used.

[41] No frequency is given here because the frequencies of departments within a school varied.

a given school cooperate in making a self-survey. Let us assume that the three sets of score card evaluations in Table II apply to all state teachers colleges and normal schools which train elementary school teachers, but that the way of effecting these activities varies within each school.

The relative value of a given method of carrying out any one of the cooperative activities included in Parts I and II of the score card would no doubt vary among departments. To illustrate, it may be of value for the members of the education department to observe the teaching of student teachers *with the critic teacher,* at least once a week, though it may be advisable for the children's librarian to so engage but once a term and *in company with the critic teacher and members of other college departments.* Again, perhaps the members of the music department should participate *weekly* in planning training school assembly programs, *in company with student teachers and critic teacher,* though the members of the French department[43] should so participate but once a year, and then only with the critic teacher.

Assuming that there is a difference in the frequency and manner in which individual college departments should conduct the reciprocal relations in Parts I[44] and II[45] of the score card, the following plan is suggested for scoring an individual department.

1. Four juries selected from faculty members of the institution should be asked to set up standards for carrying out the cooperative activities for a given department of the school, e.g., the history department. These juries should be composed as follows:

Jury I. All instructors within the department being considered.

Jury II. All instructors from the other academic departments of the college (excluding those who are also administrative officers, training school supervisors, and critic teachers who may teach college courses).

[43] Referring to the campus elementary training school.

[44] Part I. Participation of members of the college departments in the functions of the training school.

[45] Part II. Participation of members of the training school staff in the functions of the other college departments.

Jury III. Administrative officers of the school: president, dean of instruction, dean of the college, director of training, principal of campus training school, etc.

Jury IV. All critic teachers and training school supervisors, whether or not they may also teach college courses.

2. Using the items in the second section of the score card booklet as possible standards, the four juries should rank each method for carrying out an activity on a scale of 1 to 5, score 1 representing the degree of greatest importance, score 5 representing the degree of least importance. In addition these juries should rank suggested frequencies[46] with which the activity should be done by the department being studied.

Setting up the standards as to method and frequency for effecting the activities in Part III should be done by three juries—Jury I, administrative officers; Jury II, each member of all academic departments combined; Jury III, all training school critic teachers and supervisors. Compute mean rankings for each jury, then combine them into one mean for each item. At a meeting attended by all members of the faculty, score the school on the items in Part III, basing the judgments upon the evaluated standards shown by the mean of the combined judgments of the three juries.

Since most of the items in Part IV, Administrative devices which may facilitate cooperation, are matters of record or policy, the school may be scored without previous jury rankings of standards. The scoring of the institution in terms of these administrative devices for facilitating cooperation may be done at the same faculty meeting at which Part III is applied. After this meeting, write in the scores for Part IV on the score card and add the total number of points, out of a possible 1,000, earned by the school on Parts I, II, III, and IV. A discussion and comparison of the points earned on all parts of the score card by the school should be made the center of several faculty meetings.

[46] Suggest those frequencies which appear in Tables III to XXXIV, based on the survey of present practice.

CHAPTER III

THE PARTICIPATION OF MEMBERS OF THE COLLEGE DEPARTMENTS IN THE FUNCTIONS OF THE TRAINING SCHOOL

A COMPOSITE picture of the extent to which members of the college departments participate in the functions of the campus elementary training school in twenty-five state teachers colleges and normal schools in the United States, will be shown in this chapter through a discussion of the data presented in Tables III through VI.

I. PARTICIPATION OF MEMBERS OF THE COLLEGE DEPARTMENTS IN THE FUNCTIONS OF THE TRAINING SCHOOL

A. BY AIDING THE TRAINING SCHOOL STAFF IN SUPERVISING STUDENT TEACHERS

A majority of the leaders in the field of teacher training who have written on the problem of coordination of training school and college faculty recommend that college faculty members aid the critic teachers in the supervision of student teachers in the training school. In an address before the Department of Supervisors of Student Teaching of the N.E.A. in 1925, Dr. E. S. Evenden made this proposal:

> Increase the responsibility of the subject-matter teachers for the supervision of practice teaching in their fields. This should include approval of lesson plans, some regular observations of teaching, and attendance at conferences between practice teachers and critics or supervisors.[1]

In 1929, in an address to the same group, Dr. Evenden recommended that the critic teachers

> . . . issue special invitations to individual staff members to visit the training-school rooms during designated periods to observe students at work in their fields.[2]

[1] Evenden, E. S. "Cooperation of Teachers of Academic Subjects with the Training School." *Supervisors of Student Teaching Yearbook*, 1925, pp. 5–8.

[2] Evenden, E. S. "The Critic Teacher and the Professional Treatment of Subject Matter: A Challenge." *Supervisors of Student Teaching Yearbook*, 1929, pp. 39–48.

Dr. Thomas Alexander, in an address delivered at a conference for the study and discussion of teacher training in Texas, stressed twelve major types of cooperative activities. Notable among these was the following, which is quoted to explain further the scope of Tables III, IV, and V in this chapter.

> The next factor which should be mentioned is what might be called cooperative supervision of the student teacher's work. This should begin long before the student teacher actually goes into the training school to do class-room teaching. It has to do with teaching the student to plan and organize the units of work which he will later use in his practice activity. The administrative set-up should be such that each student in practice will receive the combined attention of the subject-matter and theory teachers, class-room supervisor, and the director of training. . . . Systematic lesson planning under a cooperative scheme of supervision will do more than anything else to tie up the work of the various departments.[3]

To the above quotations regarding this phase of cooperation might be added many others, but their inclusion here would be repetitious.

The first five tables in this phase of the study show the extent to which members of the college departments aid the training school staff in the supervision of student teachers as found in the twenty-five schools visited.

1. *Aiding the Training School Staff by Observing the Teaching of Student Teachers in the Training School*

When the subject of observing student teaching was treated in the questionnaire, four categories were suggested, giving faculty members opportunity to state the manner in which they observed the teaching of student teachers in the training school.

The rank importance of each category, as determined by the three juries,[4] is given on page 51. Jury I refers to teacher training institutions with over 1,000 students enrolled, Jury II to institutions with 500 to 1,000 enrolled, and Jury III to institutions with fewer

[3] Alexander, Thomas. "Coordination of the Laboratory Schools with the Subject-Matter Departments in the College." *Cooperative Planning for Teacher Training Standards in Texas.* Bulletin, North Texas State Teachers College, Denton, Texas, May, 1931, p. 141.

[4] Chapter II, pp. 47-48.

than 500 enrolled. For brevity the letter P is used for professors of education, D for directors of training, and M for mean of each jury.

Since Table III gives a summary picture of findings in the schools visited, disregarding differences in enrollment, only the mean ranking of the juries would apply in ascertaining the extent to which the twenty-five teacher training institutions are in accord with expert judgment.

	Jury I			Jury II			Jury III			Mean of Juries
	P	D	M	P	D	M	P	D	M	
1. That they observed in company with the critic teacher	1.6	1.1	1.3	1.2	1.4	1.3	1.1	1.3	1.2	1.3
2. That members of the academic departments observed the teaching of student teachers alone, no other faculty member being present	2.6	3.2	2.9	1.9	2.1	2.0	2.9	2.6	2.8	2.6
3. That they observed in company with the critic teacher and members of other college departments	2.5	2.3	2.4	3.1	3.0	3.0	2.7	2.9	2.8	2.7
4. That they observed in company with members of other college departments	3.4	3.5	3.4	3.8	3.5	3.7	3.2	3.3	3.2	3.4

Analysis of Table III in Terms of Instructors Listed

In considering the extent to which members of college departments cooperated with members of the training school staff, the writer found it difficult to assign to each person a definite title which could be used throughout the study, since in the majority of the schools visited each instructor taught a combination of courses. For example, a member of the English department may have offered Children's Literature, The Teaching of English, and three courses in English subject matter. If this instructor participated in the functions of the training school, he is referred to as the "Teaching of English instructor" since it is primarily because of this professional course that he has an interest in the work of the laboratory school.

TABLE III

Frequency with Which College Instructors Observe the Teaching of Students in Campus Elementary Training School*

Faculty Members	Frequency: Alone, No Other Faculty Member Present					In Company with Critic Teacher						In Company with Members of Other College Departments			In Company with Critic Teacher and Members of Other College Departments		Activity Initiated by				Total Number Who Observed	Number of Such Instructors in 25 Schools
	Daily	Twice Weekly	Weekly	Monthly	Once a Term	Daily	Twice Weekly	Weekly	Monthly	Once a Term	Yearly	Monthly	Once a Term	Yearly	Weekly	Once a Term	Administration	College Instructor	Critic Teacher	Mutual		
Children's Literature Instructor	1									1							2				2	9
College Department Instructors (Supervisors)																						
Educational Psychology[ba]		2														1[b]	2				2	2
Teaching of Elementary School Science[b]		1					1									1	1				1	1
Teaching of Elementary School Subjects[o]	2[i]	4[n]	2[i]	2[i]			6[j]	2[i]		2[i]							10[o]				10[o]	10
Teaching of Reading[b]				1			1										1				1	1
Tests and Measurements[a]	1																1				1	1
Dean of College					1		1[k]						1[k]			1[k]	1[k]		1		2	20
Director of Training (Teaches Education Courses)																						
Directed Observation			1		1		1			1							3				3	3
General Education courses[h]	1	1	2		1				1	1				1		1	5	1			6	9
Introduction to Teaching	1			1		1	1		1							1	3				3	3
Later Elementary Education	1						1										1				1	1
Director of Training (no courses)[g]	1		2	1	1	2	1	3	2			2	1	1	1	2	7			1	8	8
Early Elementary Education Instructor			1						1	1							2			1	3	8
Educational Psychology Instructor				2	1				3	2	1						2	5	2		9	19[c]
Fine Arts Department Head	1								3								1			2	3	18[c]
General Education Instructor[h]									1	1							1		1		2	21

TABLE III (*Continued*)

Faculty Members	Frequency: Alone, No Other Faculty Member Present					Frequency: In Company with Critic Teacher						Frequency: In Company with Members of Other College Departments			Frequency: In Company with Critic Teacher and Members of Other College Departments		Activity Initiated by				Total Number Who Observed	Number of Such Instructors in 25 Schools
	Daily	Twice Weekly	Weekly	Monthly	Once a Term	Daily	Twice Weekly	Weekly	Monthly	Once a Term	Yearly	Monthly	Once a Term	Yearly	Weekly	Once a Term	Administration	College Instructor	Critic Teacher	Mutual		
Kindergarten Department Head										1									1		1	2
Later Elementary Education Instructor			1							1							2				2	4
Music Department Head			2	1													1	2			3	20[3]
Nursery School Director				1					1											1	1	1
Physical Education Department Head									1		1						1			1	2	18[a]
President of College	1				1				2[1]	1								3[1]	1	1	5	25
Principal of Training School (Teaches)																						
Directed Observation		1						1		1							2		1		3	4
Teaching of Reading	1																1				1	1
Sociology Instructor										1								1			1	25
Special Subject Instructors (Supervisors)																						
Teaching of Home Economics	1																1				1	1
Teaching of Industrial Arts	1																1				1	1
Teaching of Penmanship		2					2										2				2	2
Teaching of Physical Education	7[m]	3[m]				1	2	1	1								12[m]			1	13	16
Teaching of Public School Art	5	2				1	1	1	1								7	1		1	9	15
Teaching of Public School Music	7	5	1				3	2	1							1	12	2		1	15	17
Teaching of Arithmetic Instructor	1			1	1		1			2						1	3	1	1		5	13
Teaching of Elementary School Science Instructor									1								1				1	8
Teaching of Elementary School Subjects Instructor			1[e]		1			1[e]		1							1[e]	1			2	4
Teaching of English Instructor	1			1	1			2	2	1						1	2	1	1	1	5	15
Teaching of Geography Instructor	1	2	1		2		1			3							3	1	3	1	8	17

TABLE III (*Continued*)

Faculty Members	Frequency: Alone, No Other Faculty Member Present					In Company with Critic Teacher						In Company with Members of Other College Departments			In Company with Critic Teacher and Members of Other College Departments		Activity Initiated by				Total Number Who Observed	Number of Such Instructors in 25 Schools
	Daily	Twice Weekly	Weekly	Monthly	Once a Term	Daily	Twice Weekly	Weekly	Monthly	Once a Term	Yearly	Monthly	Once a Term	Yearly	Weekly	Once a Term	Administration	College Instructor	Critic Teacher	Mutual		
Teaching of History Instructor	1	1			1[e]			1		1[e]						1[e]	2	1		1	4	13
Teaching of Nature Study Instructor		1					1										1	1			2	5
Teaching of Penmanship Instructor					1												1				1	8
Teaching of Reading Instructor		1					1	1									1	2			3	3
Visual Education Instructor										1									1		1	1
Total	35	26	14	11	13	5	25	15	22	23	2	2	2	2	1	11	100	23	13	13	149	373

* This table should be read as follows: Read from left to right to determine: (1) the frequency with which college instructors of a given title observe students teach in the campus training school, under one or more of the four suggested categories; (2) who initiated the activity; (3) total number of such instructors who observed in comparison with (4) total number of instructors, so entitled, who might have observed in the twenty-five schools.

[a] Educational Psychology and Tests and Measurements instructors are from same school.

[b] Educational Psychology, Teaching of Elementary School Science, and Teaching of Reading instructors are from the same school.

[c] In remaining schools head of department is training school supervisor—considered under that title.

[d] Last two columns show number who observed; number bearing that title who might have observed.

[e] Same instructor appears under more than one category.

[f] See page 55 for explanation of total.

[g] Director of training teaches no college courses.

[h] Instructors who teach several different courses in education department.

[i] These two persons are in same school.

[j] These six persons are in three schools.

[k] No director of training in this school. This work is in charge of dean of women.

[l] One official teaches Professional Ethics.

[m] One training school supervisor is physical education department head.

[n] These four persons represent two schools.

[o] These ten persons represent five schools.

Column (a) of the section marked total, at the extreme right of Table III, indicates the number of instructors of a given title, for example, Teaching of Arithmetic instructor, who reported observation of student teachers. Column (b) gives the number of such instructors in the 25 schools who would be listed under that title if there had been one hundred per cent participation. For example, nine of the institutions have an instructor who teaches Children's Literature courses only and therefore would appear under the title "Instructor of Children's Literature." Of the nine, only two were reported as participating in the observation of student teachers.

The majority of the faculty members who signified observation of the teaching of student teachers in the training school are from the following groups: (1) the education department, (2) training school supervisors, (3) administrative officers. The writer has questioned the validity of including in Table III instructors in subjects[5] such as music, art, physical education, penmanship, industrial arts, and home economics, who supervise these fields in the training school. Obviously, this is not cooperation between members of the college department and the training school faculty, since in these subjects one person is responsible for both the training school and the college work. The decision to include them was based upon the fact that 50 per cent of them observe in company with critic teachers.

To be entirely consistent, the critic teachers who teach college courses should also be included in this table. Such critic teachers, however, make supervision of student teachers their major work and teaching of college courses only a small part of their service load. One school in the 25 uses a modified Oswego[6] or Frostburg[7] plan whereby the college instructors in Early and Later Elementary Education are the training school critic teachers. Since these members spend a part of every day observing the teaching of student teachers, unaccompanied by any other faculty member, it seemed best to consider them as critic teachers throughout this study. In three ad-

[5] See definition of terms, p. 12, item 2b.

[6] Chittenden, M. D. "The Oswego Normal and Training School Plan of Cooperation." *Educational Administration and Supervision*, Vol. X, May, 1925, pp. 325–332.

[7] Dunkle, J. L. "Plan of Cooperation at Frostburg State Normal School." *Supervisors of Student Teaching Yearbook*, 1925, pp. 16–20.

ditional schools critic teachers offer one college course each term in Early or Later Elementary Education. Three of the 25 schools have a kindergarten critic teacher who carries a half-time teaching load in Kindergarten-Primary Education, but they conduct a forenoon kindergarten only in the training school. Again, three of the schools visited delegate the course in Directed Observation to the critic teachers so that it is not a college course but a training school course, offered in addition to Directed Teaching. The special subject instructors who supervise their subject in the training school differ from the critic teachers who teach college courses in that their major duty is teaching of college courses rather than supervision of student teachers in the training school. This criterion excluded all critic teachers from being considered college department instructors in Table III.

In Table III, in considering the administrative officers who observed the teaching of student teachers, we find two college deans listing this as a part of their work. In one of the institutions, this officer participated in the activity because no director of training was employed, this work being included as part of his regular duties.

Five of the directors of training who teach no college courses but aid the critic teachers in the supervision of student teachers have one or more off-campus training schools under their supervision and therefore give little time to observing the teaching of individual students.

Directors of Training Who Teach Courses in the Education Department

In sixteen schools, the director of training also teaches college courses in the education department. Thirteen of these officers report participation in the observation of student teachers. Three others supervise both campus and off-campus training schools, which means their time devoted to observing is divided between two or more schools. One of these officers, who teaches Introduction to Teaching and Later Elementary Education, observes in the campus training school only once a month since the major part of his observation time is spent in the off-campus schools. This teachers college employs a non-teaching principal for the campus training school. Another of these thirteen directors of training, who teaches several education courses, observes daily. He represents a teacher training institution in which the room teachers are not paid by the state and therefore have little part in the supervision of student teaching. A similar statement may be made regarding the director listed as teaching Introduction to Teaching and observing twice weekly, but in company with the room teacher.

In two others of the thirteen schools the directors of training carried such a heavy teaching program of General Education courses that they were able to observe not oftener than once a month, and once a term respectively. One of these thirteen officials, who teaches Introduction to Teaching, spends a part of every day observing students in a campus training school. This is due to the administrative setup of the institution, which expects that every faculty member will spend considerable time in such activity.

The fourteenth school employs a director of training who teaches courses in the department of education and is administrative supervisor of three off-campus schools which are a part of the city school system, no campus school being used. This school maintains two supervisors of student teaching so that this duty is not considered a part of the director's work. As has been previously cited, one institution employs no director of training but this work is incorporated in the office of the dean of the college. Both of the teaching directors of training not yet accounted for offer courses in the education department and are administrative supervisors of both campus and off-campus schools. In one of these schools, the principal of the campus school supervises the student teaching in the elementary field while the director of training supervises the students in the secondary field; and in the other one, supervisors of Early and Later Elementary Education are responsible for this type of supervision.

Campus Training School Principals Who Teach Courses in the Education Department

Five of the 25 schools in this study have a principal of the campus training school who teaches courses in the department of education. In each case, this officer is employed in addition to the director of training. Four of these teaching principals observe students during their student teaching period. The fifth principal gave as a reason for not participating in this activity the fact that this institution employs Early and Later Elementary Education supervisors who are responsible for this work.

Presidents of the Teacher Training Institutions Who Observe Teaching

Five of the 25 teachers college presidents observe the teaching of student teachers. The frequency of observation varies from daily to once a term. There is no trend to show whether presidents from schools with large or small enrollments report this activity since this was recorded for schools with enrollments (according to the last biennial survey report[8]) ranging from 609 to 2,739.

College Department Instructors Who Supervise the Teaching of Student Teachers

Seven of the schools visited in this survey of cooperation between the faculties of the college and the training school departments maintain college instructors who supervise the teaching of student teachers as a part of their scheduled service load. In one school, two people, in addition to the director of training, supervise student teachers in the elementary education field. These are the instructors in Educational Psychology and in Tests and Measurements. This institution, which was cited before in the discussion of the director of training, uses a city school for laboratory purposes but the state does not remunerate the room teachers. Therefore, the supervision of student teachers is carried on entirely by these education department instructors who record daily or twice weekly participation in this work.

Another of these schools, which also uses city schools for laboratory purposes, rotates supervision of this type among the entire normal school faculty. The college instructors in Educational Psychology, Teaching of Elementary School Science, and the Teaching of Reading were spending at least two days a week as training school supervisors at the time this survey was made.

[8] United States Office of Education. *Biennial Survey of Education in the United States, 1928–1930*. Washington, D. C.

The remaining five schools maintain two[9] supervisors each; one for Early Elementary grades and one for Later Elementary grades. These instructors teach the college courses in their respective fields. Since the frequency of observation is the same for both supervisors in a given school, this work has been combined under the heading "Teaching the Elementary School Subjects" in Table III, two frequencies being given for each school.

In one of the five institutions, three city schools are used for observation, participation (preliminary teaching), and student teaching. The city teachers are paid by both city and state and therefore carry a larger part in the supervision of students than in the other two situations mentioned above where city schools are used for laboratory work. However, the work of these critic teachers is supplemented by two people from the normal school who teach the courses in Early and Later Elementary Education. These supervisors observe the teaching of students at least once a week in company with the critic teacher, and at least once a month unaccompanied by the critic teacher or any other member of the faculty.

The second of the five institutions is conducting an experiment whereby students enter student teaching before completing college courses in Early and Later Elementary Education. As questions arise during their teaching, these students go to the college instructors in these fields for individual conference. These instructors spend at least two days a week in the training school observing the teaching of such students.

The supervisors in another of the five institutions mentioned above aid the critic teacher in both campus and off-campus training schools in the supervision of student teachers. These officials spend a half day once a week on this work in the campus training school.

Another of the five which sponsor this type of organization uses only a campus training school but maintains two supervisors in Early and Later Elementary Education who teach college courses and spend at least two days a week in the training school observing the teaching of student teachers.

[9] Two of these institutions mention three such supervisors for primary, intermediate, and upper grades. Only the first two are included in this study since the third supervisor works in the junior high school field.

In the fifth institution, these supervisors teach the theory courses in Early and Later Elementary Education and spend a part of every day in the supervision of student teachers in both campus and off-campus training schools.

Instructors in the Special Subject Departments Who Are Also Training School Supervisors

Physical Education. Of the 16 institutions in which a college instructor is also a training school supervisor in the physical education field, 13 report that they observe the teaching of student teachers with varying frequency. Six of the 25 institutions maintain a physical education critic who teaches no college courses. In two of these six schools, the head of the physical education department reports joint observation of student teachers with this critic teacher.

An explanation for the absence of cooperation of this type in five of the schools was given as follows:

1. One institution has no physical education department and the responsibility for this work is taken by the individual critic teacher of each grade.

2. Two other schools have no major department in this field but the college instructor in physical education teaches the training school children. The supervisors in these two institutions take no part in the observation of student teachers in the elementary school subjects.

3. Two of the teacher training institutions which use city training schools have no major students in physical education and do not observe the teaching of student teachers in the elementary school subjects.

Public School Art. Nine of the 15 schools which maintain fine arts supervisors in the training school, who also teach college courses in this field, report that these supervisors observe the teaching of student teachers. In two of the schools visited, the head of the fine arts department reports that he, in company with the art supervisor, observes the teaching of students majoring in this field. One of the eight institutions has a fine arts critic teacher in the training school who is aided once a month by the head of the fine arts department in the observation of student teachers.

The absence of such cooperation in six of the schools is explained as follows:

1. For financial reasons, one institution uses the city art supervisor in the campus training school, since it is a part of the city public school system. The college department of fine arts does not observe the teaching of student teachers in this training school, although the institution grants a degree to students who have fulfilled the requirements in this major subject field.

2. Two schools maintain no major department in fine arts but the college instructor teaches this subject in the training school.

3. Four others of the 25 schools visited have no major students who would do student teaching in this field, and the college instructors in fine arts show no apparent cooperation with the training school critic teacher of each grade who is responsible for the teaching of art as well as other elementary school subjects.

Public School Music. Of the 17 teacher training institutions which have a training school supervisor in public school music who is also a member of the college department, 15 report participation in the activity being discussed. In no one of these institutions did another member of the academic department observe the teaching of student teachers. Six of the schools have a special music critic teacher in the training school and in three cases, the head of the music department observes the teaching of major students in this field in company with this critic teacher.

We may find in the following an explanation for the absence of cooperation of this type in four of the schools:

1. Two institutions use city training schools and have no students majoring in the field of music.

2. As cited above in the case of fine arts, one institution uses the city supervisor of music, for financial reasons. The college department of music, which has major students, does not observe the teaching of student teachers in the training school.

3. In one other institution which does not grant a degree or diploma in music, the college instructor teaches music to the training school children. This instructor takes no part in the observation of student teachers.

To summarize regarding the fine arts, music, and physical education departments in their relation to the training school, we may say that the fact that the same instructor is both college instructor and supervisor in many of the schools would be an evidence of coordination between theory and practice. However, few members of the college departments who are not supervisors cooperate with their special supervisors or critic teachers in the observation of the teaching of major students.

Penmanship. In two of the 25 schools, the college instructor in penmanship is also a special supervisor in the training school. Both report that this official observes the teaching of student teachers. The college instructor in the Teaching of Penmanship is a member of the commercial department in another institution. Though this official is not the training school supervisor, he reports observation of student teachers once a term.

In accounting for the remaining schools with respect to this subject, we may say that in seven schools where penmanship is taught in the college department, no apparent cooperation in the supervision of student teachers is noted; the eighth institution uses city schools and therefore has no jurisdiction over this work; and fourteen schools list no course in the Teaching of Penmanship in the college course offerings.

Industrial Arts. Of the 12 schools which report courses in the Teaching of Industrial Arts in the academic department, only one instructor observes the teaching of student teachers and this because it is a part of his scheduled work. This lack may be accounted for because in the majority of cases this work seems to be for secondary rather than for elementary education majors. In each case where such a course is taught in elementary schools only, the instructor also offers courses in fine arts or in other elementary education subjects and his work is therefore discussed under another heading.

Specialized Courses in Elementary Education (i.e., Early Elementary Education, Later Elementary Education, Teaching of the Elementary School Subjects, and Technique of Teaching). Fifteen of the 25 schools which were visited have one instructor who teaches Early Elementary Education courses only. In three of these 15 schools, such courses are taught by a critic teacher; and in three others, the Early Elementary Education instructor is also a training school supervisor.[11] In the seventh, the director of training teaches such courses. Since the above-mentioned seven staff members are considered under the headings which are represented by their official titles, they will not be included in this discussion. Four of the instructors from the eight remaining schools, which offer such work, report that they observe the teaching of student teachers. There is no uniformity about this observation as is shown in Table III. Such observation ranges from twice a week to only once a term.

Ten of the 25 schools maintain an instructor who teaches only Later Elementary Education courses. In each of these ten schools, there is also an instructor in Early Elementary Education. Similar conditions operate here as in Early Elementary Education regarding instructors in this work, namely, Later Elementary Education courses are taught by critic teachers in three schools, and the college instructor in this field is also a training school supervisor in three schools. Of the four remaining Later Elementary Education instructors, two report that they observe the teaching of student teachers. Here again, the frequency ranges from weekly to once a term, showing no uniformity.

In four of the schools not mentioned in the above two paragraphs, the courses in Early and Later Elementary Education are taught by the same instructor and therefore this instructor is referred to as Teaching of the Elementary School Subjects instructor throughout the study. Two of these four indicated that they observe the teaching of student teachers, one with a frequency of once a week, the other once a term.

In three institutions where no courses in Elementary Education *in toto* or Early or Later subdivisions are offered, this work is called Technique of Teaching. In two of these schools, such instructors are training school supervisors and therefore are tabulated under that heading. In the third institution, no participation in this phase of the study was recorded by the Technique of Teaching instructors.

A record of the manner in which teaching method is cared for in

[11] See definition of terms, p. 12, item 2a.

the schools which do not offer specialized courses in Elementary Education follows:

1. Three institutions offer professionalized subject matter courses in each academic department. Discussion of the cooperation of instructors in such courses appears with the course title, i.e., Teaching of Arithmetic, Teaching of Geography, etc.

2. Fifteen of the schools included in this study offer "teaching" courses in both the education and subject matter departments.

(*a*) One institution included courses with similar titles in both departments, i.e., Teaching of History in both education and history departments.

(*b*) Eleven institutions offer Early and Later Elementary Education courses in the education department in addition to the professionalized subject matter courses in the academic departments.

(*c*) In the other three schools of the above-named fifteen, the "teaching" courses in the education department are called Technique of Teaching.

General Education Course and Educational Psychology Instructors

Each of the 25 schools visited has one or more instructors who teach a variety of education department courses not closely related to the work of the training school, such as History of Education, Educational Supervision, Principles of Education, etc. Only two such instructors from the entire group record observation of student teachers and this not because of any particular course which they teach but because of a general interest in the training school. The same reason for such observation was given by nine Educational Psychology instructors with whom observation of this type varies from once a month to once a year.

Instructors from the Subject Matter Departments Who Observe the Teaching of Student Teachers

Teaching of Elementary School Science—Teaching of Nature Study. The science department in nine of the schools visited offers a course in the teaching of Elementary School Science. Two of these instructors, one of whom is designated as a training school supervisor, indicate observation of student teachers. The science department in five other schools offers a course in teaching nature study, as elementary science. Two of these instructors observe student teachers. Since no one of the 25 schools offers both the Teaching of Science and the Teaching of Nature Study, we may summarize by saying that 14 out of the 25 schools offer some course in teaching in the science department, three of whose instructors observe the teaching of student teachers.

The Teaching of English. The English department in 13 of the schools considered offers a course in teaching English in the elementary grades. Of these instructors, three observe the teaching of student teachers. One institution offers such a course in the education department, taught by a member of the English department. This instructor observes the teaching of student teachers with a frequency of once a month. One of the schools, with an enrollment during the academic year of over 2,500 students in the teacher training courses, maintains an instructor in the education department who offers professionalized subject matter courses only in English, literature, and related fields. This instructor reports that he observes the teaching of student teachers at least once a term. To summarize, of the 15 faculty members who are called Teaching of English instructors throughout this study, five observe the teaching of student teachers.

The Teaching of History. The data show that the history department in 13 of the 25 schools offers a course in the Teaching of History. Of this number, only four signify that they participate in observing the teaching of student teachers, this varying from once a day to once a term. One of these instructors explained that he observed daily because he wished to determine whether or not his teaching course was functioning in practice. The instructor who recorded twice weekly participation in this activity is a member of the institution which requires that every instructor offering teaching courses spend considerable time observing in the training school. The same is true of the instructor who said he observed at least once a week in company with the critic teacher. One instructor indicated that he observed once a term in each of the following ways: alone, with the critic teacher, and in company with the critic teacher and other college instructors. This staff member was from the institution where supervision is rotated among the various academic faculty members and had himself been such a supervisor the preceding year.

Teaching of Reading. According to the analysis of the courses offered, only two of the schools have an instructor who offers the Teaching of Reading as distinct from the Teaching of English. Both of these instructors record participation in the observation of student teaching. In one of these schools, the work in reading holds so important a place in the college curriculum that students do remedial teaching with training school children under the guidance of this instructor. He observes these student teachers at least twice a week, since this phase of the reading work is largely under his supervision. The third Teaching of Reading instructor who recorded participation in this activity is a member of the English department but offers this course in the education department. He observes the teaching of reading in the training school twice weekly in company with the critic teacher since he is studying the extent to which his teaching course is functioning in student teaching.

Analysis of Frequencies in Table III in Terms of Various Ways in Which Faculty Members Observe the Teaching of Student Teachers

The majority of the college faculty members who gave some positive answer to this section of the study, as shown in Table III, reported that they observed student teachers in more than one of the four categories listed at the top of the table with varying frequency. For instance, one Teaching of History instructor said that he observed students teach, unaccompanied by any other faculty member, once a term, but that he also observed their teaching in company with the critic teachers with the same frequency and, in addition, in company with members of other college departments together with the critic teacher. No method of recording the fact that the same instructor observed in several ways is shown in the table since the frequency for a given instructor is recorded under its appropriate heading. For example, in Table III, it is shown that 149 different faculty members recorded some degree of participation in the observation of student teachers, but due to the fact that such observation might be done in more than one way, summation of the frequency of observation in the three possible categories totals 210 instead of 149.

To determine the total number of instructors of each subject, e.g., Teaching of Reading, who participate in the activity considered in Table III, the column headed "Activity initiated by" should be used, since only one mark is given for each instructor, regardless of the number of categories under which he recorded participation, or in the total column.

Alone, No Other Faculty Member Present. According to Table III, 100 of the 149 observers, or 67 per cent, report that they observe the teaching of students unaccompanied by any other faculty member. However, 34 of these 100 persons, or 34 per cent, are special subject instructors whose regular duties include supervising in the training school, i.e., physical education, public school art, public school music, etc. This group would observe the teaching of their student teachers unaccompanied by critic teachers since the latter are not usually considered specialists in these fields. During the teaching of these special subject student teachers, the critic teachers are in conference with other student teachers. Of the 34 special subject instructors who are training school supervisors, 21 record observation activity daily, 12 twice weekly, and 1 weekly. No case of less frequent observation is recorded under this heading. Of the remaining 66 who record observation of the teaching of students unaccompanied by the critic teacher, 15 observe daily, 14 twice weekly, 13 weekly, 11 monthly, and 13 once a term, there being no marked preference for any plan.

In Company with the Critic Teacher. Ninety-two of the 149 observers, or 62 per cent, report observation of the teaching of student teachers in company with the critic teacher. Of this number, 17 are the special subject instructors who are also training school supervisors, all of whom record such observation within a range of daily to monthly. The remaining 75 who observe with the critic teachers show a range of frequency of visit from daily to yearly. However, 19 of this number record monthly and 23 once-a-term observation, implying that this group of instructors observe seldom.

In Company with Members of Other College Departments. Table III shows that only six of the 149 instructors observe the teaching of students in company with other college instructors, the critic teacher not present. Individual examination of their papers shows them to be administrative officers only: One dean of college; four directors of training who teach no college courses; and one director of training who teaches General Education courses. Since the critic teachers in only one of these six schools teach college courses and consequently would have occasion to be away from the practice school during visitation by these college administrators, there seems no logical reason for such non-co-attendance.

In Company with the Critic Teacher and Members of Other College Departments. Twelve of 149, or 8 per cent, of the college instructors record the observation of student teachers in company with the critic teacher and other college instructors. Only one person, a director of training who teaches no college courses, says that he does so frequently—that is, once a week. The other eleven say they do so not oftener than once a term. In the one case, where the director of training observes weekly, the reason for the frequency is the conduct of an experiment in student teaching in which members of the education department are equally interested and responsible for the success of these students.

Seven of the 11 remaining observers are from one institution with a small enrollment, which utilizes city schools for laboratory purposes. Every instructor in this teacher training institution is required to keep in close touch with what is being done in the training schools.

The group of college department instructors who are training school supervisors in the general fields should receive separate consideration since this is an important feature of their labor load. Of the 15 such supervisors, each reports that he observes with varying frequency unaccompanied by the critic teacher; 10 of them that they observe with the critic teacher weekly or oftener and two that they do so once a term. Two of these supervisors report that they also observe with the critic teacher and another college instructor once a term. These two officials represent the institution which has been mentioned previously, in which it is the policy for the training school supervisors to observe jointly the teaching of student teachers at least once a term.

Activity Initiated by. In the majority of instances where college instructors observe the teaching of student teachers, it appears to be due to the consideration that the administration has designated this as part of their regular work. Of the 149 instructors who observed students teach, 100, or 67 per cent, reported that they did so because it was one of their duties as suggested by the administration of the school. Twenty-three individual college instructors, or 15 per cent, initiated the activity for themselves. In 13, or 9 per cent of the cases, the critic teacher requested the college instructor to observe the teaching of students. It is apparent from the list of persons who did so for this reason that the majority are members of the administrative staff or represent departments which usually are not as closely in touch with the training school as the education department is.

Thirteen, or 9 per cent, of the individuals stated that they observed the teaching of students through a *mutual* agreement with the individual critic teachers. Three of these are instructors in Teaching of Physical Education, Teaching of Public School Art, and Teaching of Public School Music, who observe only once a month because the supervision of these students rests in the hands of the critic teachers, such students not majoring in these special fields.

2. *Aiding the Training School Staff by Holding Conferences with Student Teachers to Evaluate and Analyze the Teaching They Have Observed the Student Do*[12]

The findings in Table IV are closely linked with the findings in Table III since evidently only those persons listed in Table III as observing the teaching of student teachers could hold conferences with student teachers to evaluate and analyze the teaching they had observed. A comparison of the two shows that with few exceptions members of the administrative staff of the training school, the education department, and the Special Subject instructors, who are training school supervisors who observe, also have conferences with the student teachers following the observation of their teaching.

[12] For uniformity and clarity, the topics from the questionnaire will be used as headings for discussion of present practice.

TABLE IV

Frequency with Which College Instructors Hold Conferences with Student Teachers to Evaluate and Analyze the Teaching They Have Observed the Student Do in the Campus Elementary Training School*

Faculty Members	Frequency: Alone with Student Teacher						In Joint Conference with Student Teacher and Critic Teacher			In Joint Conference with Student Teacher, Critic Teacher, and Members of Other College Departments		Activity Initiated by					Total Number Who Conferred	Number of Such Instructors in 25 Schools
	Daily	Twice Weekly	Weekly	Twice Monthly	Monthly	Once a Term	Weekly	Monthly	Once a Term	Monthly	Once a Term	Administration	College Instructor	Critic Teacher	Mutual	Student		
Children's Literature Instructor		1					1					2					2	9
College Department Instructors (Supervisors)																		
Educational Psychology[eb]	1[b]	1							1			2					2	2
Teaching of Elementary School Science[e]			1									1					1	1
Teaching of Elementary School Subjects[h]	2[f]		6[g]				2	4				10					10[h]	10
Teaching of Reading[e]		1										1					1	1
Tests and Measurements[b]	1											1					1	1
Director of Training (No Courses)[c]				2	1	1	3					5					5	8
Director of Training (Teaches Education Courses)																		
Directed Observation		1							1				1		1		2	3
General Education Courses[d]	1				2	1						4					4	9
Introduction to Teaching	1	1	1						1			2				1	3	3
Early Elementary Education Instructor					1	1						1				1	2	8
Educational Psychology Instructor						1						1					1	19
Fine Arts Department Head					1								1				1	18*
General Education Course Instructor[d]		1					1						1				1	21
Kindergarten Department Head						1								1			1	2
Later Elementary Education Instructor						1										1	1	4
Music Department Head			2										1			1	2	20*
Principal of Training School (Teaches Directed Observation)		1			1	1		1	1			1	1	1			3	4

TABLE IV (*Continued*)

Faculty Members	Frequency: Alone with Student Teacher						In Joint Conference with Student Teacher and Critic Teacher			In Joint Conference with Student Teacher, Critic Teacher, and Members of Other College Departments		Activity Initiated by					Total Number Who Conferred	Number of Such Instructors in 25 Schools
	Daily	Twice Weekly	Weekly	Twice Monthly	Monthly	Once a Term	Weekly	Monthly	Once a Term	Monthly	Once a Term	Administration	College Instructor	Critic Teacher	Mutual	Student		
Special Subject Instructors (Supervisors).																		
Teaching of Home Economics		1										1					1	1
Teaching of Industrial Arts		1											1				1	1
Teaching of Penmanship			1									1					1	2
Teaching of Physical Education	3	3	6				2	1				8	4				12	16
Teaching of Public School Art	2	2	4			1	2			1		5	4				9	15
Teaching of Public School Music	3	3	5	1	1		4	2				10	4				14	17
Teaching of Arithmetic Instructor	1		1			1			1			2	2				4	13
Teaching of Elementary School Science								1				1					1	8
Teaching of Elementary School Subjects			1											1			1	4
Teaching of English Instructor	1		1	1			1	1				2		2			4	15
Teaching of Geography Instructor	2		1	1		1			1		1	1	1	1	1	1	5	17
Teaching of History Instructor			2			1	1		1		1	3			1		4	13
Teaching of Nature Study Instructor			1					1					1				1	5
Teaching of Penmanship Instructor						1						1					1	8
Teaching of Reading Instructor		2					2					1	2				3	3
Total	18	19	33	5	7	12	19	11	7	1	2	67	24	6	3	5	106	281

* No answer from one school (4 per cent).

[a] One additional category, In joint conference with student teacher and members of other college departments, was included on the questionnaire but received no frequencies.

[b] Educational Psychology and Tests and Measurements instructors are from same school.

[c] Director of training teaches no college courses.

[d] Instructors who teach several different courses in education department.

[e] Educational Psychology, Teaching of Elementary School Science, and Teaching of Reading instructors are in same school.

[f] These two persons are in same school. [g] These six persons are in three schools. [h] These ten persons represent five schools.

[i] See page 55 for explanation of total.

None of the college presidents or the college deans who observed the teaching of student teachers conferred with these students about the teaching they observed. This is not surprising since the supervision of student teaching is not generally considered a part of the work of these administrative officers, but is delegated instead to other members of the faculty. Of the directors of training who teach no college courses, five of the eight also confer with the students. It was explained in two of the three instances where no conference is recorded that these officers supervise both campus and off-campus schools and have no time for such activity.

Nine Educational Psychology instructors observe the teaching of students but only one follows up this activity. That the other eight carry a heavy teaching schedule is the reason given for failure to follow up the observation by suggestion and criticism.

Every education department instructor who is a training school supervisor reports that he not only observes the teaching of students but confers with the student to evaluate and analyze this teaching. An attempt was made to estimate the amount of time spent in each conference but the instructors were reluctant to give more precise answers than are recorded in Table IV.

As in Table III, the closest cooperation between college departments and their students, as to conferences regarding teaching observed, is shown under the heading "Special subject instructors who are training school supervisors." In the case of the instructors in physical education and public school art, each who observed, as is shown in Table III, also conferred with the student regarding such observations. All but one of the Public School Music instructors who observed conferred later with the student. Fewer departmental heads in the special subject departments conferred with the students whose teaching they had observed. Three heads of the fine arts department were recorded in Table III, and but one in Table IV; three music department heads observed while two conferred; of the two physical education department heads who observed, neither conferred. Such reduction in frequency between Table III and Table IV was explained in the following manner. The special subject supervisor discusses the observation with the head of the department and then carries the suggestions made by the latter to the student teacher.

The majority of the instructors from the academic departments, who are not designated as supervisors but who observe students teach, also confer with them afterward.

Initiation of the Conference with Student Teachers. The majority of observers if they conferred with student teachers stated that they did so because this duty was assigned to them by the administrative organization of the school. Sixty-eight of the 106 conferees, or 64 per cent, gave this reason for participating in the activity. Twenty-four of the remaining 42, or 23 per cent, stated that they engaged in this activity on their own initiative. Seven, or nearly 7 per cent, said they did so at the request of the critic teachers. Only three members gave *mutual* agreement with the critic teacher as their reason for participating. A new reason for participation is included in Table IV which did not occur in Table III, namely, five instructors reported that the student teacher requested a conference regarding the work observed.

Frequency Analysis as to Various Ways in Which Faculty Members Hold Conferences with Student Teachers to Evaluate and Analyze the Teaching Observed. Expert opinion, as indicated by the mean judgment of the three juries regarding rank value of the four ways in which faculty members may confer with student teachers, is not in perfect accord with the findings presented in Table IV.

	Jury I Over 1,000			Jury II 500 to 1,000			Jury III Less than 500			Mean of Juries
	P	D	M	P	D	M	P	D	M	
1. In a joint conference with the student teacher and critic teacher......	1.9	1.1	1.4	1.5	1.4	1.4	1.2	1.4	1.3	1.4
2. With the student teacher alone................	2.0	2.9	2.4	2.0	2.1	2.0	2.3	2.5	2.4	2.3
3. In a joint conference with the student teacher, critic teacher, and members of other college departments............	2.6	2.7	2.6	3.0	2.9	2.9	2.9	3.2	3.0	2.9
4. In a joint conference with the student teacher, critic teacher, and members of other college departments............	3.6	3.4	2.5	3.5	3.6	3.6	3.6	2.9	3.3	3.1

The juries' judgment indicated that preferably such conferences should be conducted with the critic teacher present, but Table IV shows that this is seldom done in the 25 schools. Instead, present practice selects the method placed second in importance by the juries for, in the 106 instances where college instructors observe and follow up their observation with conferences with the student teacher, ninety-four, or 89 per cent, report that they hold such conferences *alone* with the student teacher. As in Table III, the college instructors from the special departments, i.e., music and art, who are training school supervisors, should be considered separately. Thirty-seven, or 39 per cent of these 94 persons, are included in this group. The majority of them hold such conferences frequently; eight, daily; ten, twice weekly; sixteen, weekly; one, twice monthly; one, monthly; and one, once a term. Of the remaining 57 who confer with the students *alone,* ten do so daily; nine, twice weekly; seventeen, weekly; four, twice monthly; six, monthly; and eleven, once a term.

Thirty-seven persons of the total 106, or 35 per cent, say they confer with students in joint conference with student teacher and critic teacher. Eleven of the 37 are from the group of special supervisors. A possible trend is evident as to frequency in this category since 19 confer weekly, eleven monthly, and seven once a term.

The personnel of conference groups ranked third and fourth by the juries receive similar weight in practice.

Only three out of 106 instructors, or 2.8 per cent, say that they confer with students in company with the critic teacher and other college instructors. Two of these who do so once a term are from the same small institution which recorded in Table III that they visited in company with these same mentioned people. Another person, a Teaching of Public School Art instructor who supervises in the training school, said that she held these conferences monthly with the critic teacher and the principal of the training school who teaches Elementary Education courses.

Although the questionnaire included a heading asking if members conferred with students in joint conference with this student teacher and members of other college departments, no instances were reported which show that the critic teacher is present if such conferences are attended by other faculty members.

To complete the discussion of Table IV, it should be mentioned that one school recorded no answer to this part of the questionnaire.

An examination of the tabulation for this school in Table III showed that most of the observation by members of the college faculty was done infrequently. In five of seven cases the instructors observed once a term. The director of training, who does not teach college classes, recorded more frequent observation, and that weekly. The one remaining person giving more frequent observation was the nursery school director who observes monthly. Since both of these are considered as members of the training school staff, we may say that in this one school no one from a college department observes the teaching of student teachers oftener than once a month.

3. Aiding the Training School Staff by Helping Student Teachers Plan Work They Are Teaching in the Training School

According to Table V, giving aid to students in planning the work which they teach in the training school is reported by 124 instructors. With the exception of one instructor in sociology, each of the 124 who report this work is an instructor in a course which is closely related to the preparation for student teaching, such as the Teaching of Geography. In no case did an instructor in an academic department who taught no professionalized subject matter courses record participation in aiding student teachers with lesson planning.

Forty-seven of the 124, or 38 per cent, report that they aid in planning because the administration of the school has designated it as a part of their service load. Twenty-one of the 47 are special subject instructors who supervise in the training school. Eight others who report it to be part of their service load, are from the group of education department instructors who are also training school supervisors.

Twenty of the 124 cases, or 16 per cent, report that they confer with students from personal volition. Twelve special subject instructors who supervise check this reason but the general college department instructor who is a training school supervisor also does so.

Eleven of the 124, or 9 per cent, report that they confer at the request of the critic teacher who has the student teacher under supervision; ten others indicate that they do so by mutual agreement with the critic teacher. A large number, 36 out of 124, or 29 per cent, give such aid at the request of the student teacher himself.

TABLE V[a]

Frequency with Which College Instructors Help Student Teachers Plan Work They Teach in Campus Elementary Training School

Faculty Members	Frequency: Alone with Student Teacher						In Joint Conference with Student Teacher and Critic Teacher			In Joint Conference with Student Teacher, Critic Teacher, and Members of Other College Departments		Activity Initiated by					Total Number Who Helped Plan	Number of Such Instructors in 25 Schools
	Daily	Twice Weekly	Weekly	Twice Monthly	Monthly	Once a Term	Weekly	Monthly	Once a Term	Monthly	Once a Term	Administration	College Instructor	Critic Teacher	Mutual	Student		
Children's Librarian			1	1												2	2	5
Children's Literature Instructor		1	1[b]				1[b]				1[b]	1[b]				1	2	9
College Department Instructors (Supervisors)																		
Educational Psychology[ed]	1[d]				1							1		1			2	2
Teaching of Elementary School Science					1									1			1	1
Teaching of Elementary School Subjects	2[f]		2[f]		2[f]			4[i]				6[g]					6	10
Tests and Measurements[d]	1											1					1	1
Director of Training (Teaches Education Courses)																		
Directed Observation			1				1					1					1	3
General Education Courses[c]	1							1				2					2	9
Introduction to Teaching	1															1	1	3
Early Elementary Education Instructor		1	1											1		1	2	8
Educational Psychology		1	1									1					1	19
Fine Arts Department Head					2			1								2	2	18
General Education Course Instructor[c]		1[b]				1	1[b]						1[b]			1	2	21
Later Elementary Education Instructor		1	1											1		1	2	4
Music Department Head			1				1								1		1	20

TABLE V (*Continued*)

Faculty Members	Frequency: Alone with Student Teacher						In Joint Conference with Student Teacher and Critic Teacher			In Joint Conference with Student Teacher, Critic Teacher, and Members of Other College Departments		Activity Initiated by					Total Number Who Helped Plan	Number of Such Instructors in 25 Schools
	Daily	Twice Weekly	Weekly	Twice Monthly	Monthly	Once a Term	Weekly	Monthly	Once a Term	Monthly	Once a Term	Administration	College Instructor	Critic Teacher	Mutual	Student		
Principal of Training School (Teaches Education Courses)																		
Directed Observation		1											1				1	4
Teaching of Reading							1					1					1	1
Teaching of Elementary School Subjects		1	1[b]						1[b]			1[b]	1				2	2
Sociology Instructor					1								1				1	25
Special Subject Instructors (Who Supervise)																		
Teaching of Home Economics		1										1					1	1
Teaching of Industrial Arts			1									1					1	1
Teaching of Penmanship		1														1	1	2
Teaching of Physical Education	1	3	6		1	2						4	6		1	3	14	16
Teaching of Public School Art	1	4[b]	7[b]		1		1[b]	1[h]		1[b]		7	3[b]		2[h]	1	13	15
Teaching of Public School Music		7	7[b]		1				1[b]			8[b]	3	2	1	1	15	17
Teaching of Arithmetic Instructor		2	2	1	3	1						2		1	1	5	9	13
Teaching of English																		
English Department Head		1										1					1[k]	7
Teaching of English Instructor		1	2	2	1							2	2	1	1		6	15
Teaching of Elementary School Science	1[h]				1[b]	1	1	1[h]	1[b]			1				3[h]	4	4
Teaching of Geography																		
Geography Department Head			2													2	2[l]	6
Teaching of Geography Instructor		5[bh]	1	1	4	1	1[h]		1[b]			2[b]		2		8[h]	12	17

TABLE V (*Continued*)

Faculty Members	Frequency: Alone with Student Teacher						In Joint Conference with Student Teacher and Critic Teacher			In Joint Conference with Student Teacher, Critic Teacher, and Members of Other College Departments		Activity Initiated by					Total Number Who Helped Plan	Number of Such Instructors in 25 Schools
	Daily	Twice Weekly	Weekly	Twice Monthly	Monthly	Once a Term	Weekly	Monthly	Once a Term	Monthly	Once a Term	Administration	College Instructor	Critic Teacher	Mutual	Student		
Teaching of History Instructor..........	1		1		1[b]	2		1[b]				2			1[b]	2	5	13
Teaching of Nature Study Instructor.....		1	3		1							1	1		1	1	4	5
Teaching of Reading Instructor..........			1[b]		2[h]			1[b]	1[h]				1[h]	1	1[b]		3	3
Total..........................	10	33	43	5	23	8	8	10	5	1	1	47	20	11	10	36	124	300

[a] One additional category, In joint conference with student teacher and members of other college departments, was included on the questionnaire but received no frequencies.

[b] Same instructor appears under more than one category.

[c] Instructors who teach several different courses in education department.

[d] Educational Psychology and Tests and Measurements instructors from same school.

[e] Educational Psychology, Teaching of Elementary School Science, and Teaching of Reading instructors are in same school.

[f] These two persons are in same school.

[g] These six persons are in three schools.

[h] One official teaches Professional Ethics.

[i] These four persons represent two schools.

[j] Unit planning in college courses prior to student teaching.

[k] This instructor teaches Children's Literature.

[l] One of these officers teaches the professionalized subject matter course in geography; the other represents an institution where two members of the department aid students with lesson planning.

Though expert opinion places it second in importance a trend in practice is observable in conference with the student teacher alone, since 122 of the 124 so report. Of this 122, 44, or 36 per cent, are from the special instructor group who are training school supervisors, and 10 are from the education department instructor group who supervise in the training school.

	Jury I Over 1,000			Jury II 500 to 1,000			Jury III Less than 500			Mean of Juries
	P	D	M	P	D	M	P	D	M	
1. In a joint conference with student teacher and critic teacher..........	1.8	1.2	1.5	1.5	1.3	1.3	1.1	1.5	1.3	1.4
2. With student teacher, alone.................	2.2	2.7	2.5	2.0	2.4	2.2	2.5	2.0	2.3	2.3
3. In a joint conference with student teacher, critic teacher, and members of other college departments.............	2.6	2.7	2.7	2.9	3.0	2.9	3.0	3.3	3.1	2.9
4. In a joint conference with student teacher and members of other college departments..........	3.4	3.4	3.4	3.6	3.4	3.5	3.4	3.3	3.3	3.4

Joint conference as to lesson planning with the student and the critic teacher under whose supervision he is teaching or will teach in future was reported by 23 of 124 college department instructors. The frequency with which these joint conferences are held is recorded as eight, weekly; ten, monthly; and five, once a term.

The questionnaire gave instructors reporting the opportunity to check under an additional category if they helped students plan through joint conference with the student teacher and members of other college departments, the critic teacher not present. Since no listings occurred under this head, it has been omitted from Table V.

Only two instructors' names of the 124 appear under the heading "By helping students plan in joint conference with student teacher, critic teacher, and members of other college departments." One of these, the Children's Literature instructor, is in a small institution where members of the college departments are expected to aid students with such planning. In this institution it is the director of training, who teaches no college courses, who attends this conference. The other individual is instructor in the Teaching of Public School Art, who once a month plans with students in conference with the principal of the training school, who teaches courses in Elementary Education.

Unlike those for whom data are given in Tables III and IV, members of the education department did not report the majority of the frequencies. Ninety-nine of the 124 cases are divided among the subject matter departments.

Of the 21 schools offering a course in Children's Literature taught by a member of the English department, two report that they aid student teachers in planning work. Of the five schools which employ a children's librarian, two report that they help students plan for their teaching by suggesting supplementary books which they may use in connection with various teaching units.

Of the 18 institutions where the fine arts department head does not also offer the course in the Teaching of Public School Art, two schools report that he aids fine arts major students in the planning of their work for the training school. Each of the 18 schools maintains a fine arts critic teacher who teaches no college courses.

Of the 20 schools having a music department head who does not teach the course in the Teaching of Public School Music, only one recorded participation in this activity. This institution maintains a special music critic in the training school who offers no college courses.

The greater number of instances under this category are from the group of special training school supervisors in Physical Education, Public School Art, and Public School Music who also teach college courses. This can be readily understood since they are expected to devote considerable time to the functions of the training school, because of their dual service load.

If the critic teachers from seven schools who offer college courses in the education department were listed in Table V, their participation would augment the frequency count for the education department just as the special subject instructors who supervise in the training school increase the count for their respective departments.

Of the 124 persons appearing in Table V, 25 are members of the education department. The one case of an Educational Psychology instructor who aids students was explained by the fact that this school is conducting an experiment in which every member of the education department, including Psychology, aids students in lesson planning. One of the two General Education instructors, who aid student teachers once a term at the request of the student, is a member of the same institution.

Several authorities have suggested that the units of work to be used in student teaching should be prepared in the professionalized subject matter courses prior to the semester in which the actual teaching is done. Dr. Alexander has given an extended discussion of the value of this activity in an article previously cited.[13] The faculty of the Maryland State Normal School at Towson has reported their plan of this type in concise detail.[14] A third article on this subject has been presented by Miss Edna Neal, the Second Grade Critic Teacher at the State Teachers College, Morehead, Kentucky. She presents her conception of an "ideal" plan of preparing units as a means of coordination between professionalized subject matter instructors and the training school.[15]

A separate section for this method of cooperation was not included in the questionnaire but was considered in the same section with the heading, "By helping student teachers plan work they are teaching in the training school." The extent to which this work was done in the several institutions was ascertained and recorded in Table V under the following two categories: In joint conference with student teacher and critic teacher; In joint conference with student teacher, critic teacher, and members of other college departments.

Since it is not the province of this study to examine the content of college courses unless they are organized with some degree of cooperation from the training school staff, no mention of the planning of units with the college class alone is included in Table V. Only

[13] Alexander, Thomas. "Coordination of the Laboratory Schools With the Subject-Matter Departments in the College." *Cooperative Planning for Teacher Training Standards in Texas*. Bulletin, North Texas State Teachers College, Denton, Texas, May, 1931, p. 141.

[14] Faculty of the Maryland State Normal School at Towson. "A Plan for the Closer Coordination of Professionalized Subject-Matter and Student-Teaching in a Normal School." *Educational Administration and Supervision*, April, 1930, p. 257.

[15] Neal, Edna. "Closer Coordination Between Professionalized Subject-Matter Instructors and the Training School." *Kentucky School Journal*, May, 1933, p. 39.

one of the schools[16] visited reported extensive work along this line, the notations for which appear under the heading "In joint conference with student teacher and critic teacher." Instructors in Children's Literature, Teaching of Public School Music, Teaching of Elementary School Science, and Teaching of Geography indicated participation in this type of cooperative activity. In each case these instructors also record lesson planning with student teachers during their term of teaching in the campus laboratory school.

4. *Aiding the Training School Staff by Giving Student Teachers a Rating or Grade* (*Table VI*)

College Instructors Who Are Not Supervisors. In only five of the 25 teacher training institutions studied, do members of the college faculty, other than those who have been designated as training school supervisors, participate in giving a term rating or grade to the work of student teachers. In two of these five schools it is the Teaching of Reading instructors only who assume this responsibility. In both cases they assign such grades to their own students because these latter have been doing remedial teaching in Reading in the training school under the college instructor's supervision.

The instructors who participate in the third of these schools are the Early and Later Elementary Education instructors.

In the fourth of the five schools, the instructors who so rate the student teachers are those teaching Educational Psychology, Children's Literature, Teaching of English, Teaching of Reading, Teaching of Geography, Teaching of History, and Teaching of Elementary School Science. Each of these participates in this activity because he has observed the teaching of these students at least once a semester. Obviously, the weight of their rating in according final marks to students would be slight since they would have seen but little of the students' teaching.

In the last of these five schools, the instructors in the "teaching" courses who have observed these students weekly and oftener take a major place in the assigning of student teaching grades.

In all of the other cases where college instructors have a part in the grading of student teachers, they do so because it is a part of

[16] See page 87 for a fuller discussion.

TABLE VI[b]

Frequency with Which College Instructors Give a Rating or Grade to Student Teaching*

Faculty Members	Frequency**						
	Only Rating Student Receives	Joint Rating with Critic Teacher	Joint Rating with Critic Teacher and Other College Instructors	Activity Initiated by Admin- istrator	Activity Initiated by Critic Teacher	Total Number Who Give Rating	Number of Such Instructors in 25 Schools
Children's Literature Instructor			1	1		1	9
Director of Training (No Courses)[c]		4	1	5		5	8
Director of Training (Teaches Education Courses)		8	1	9		9	16
Early Elementary Education Instructor		1		1		1	8
Education Department Instructors (Supervisors)[a]	2[d]	8[i]	3[e]	13		13	15[h]
Fine Arts Department Head		1		1		1	18[g]
Later Elementary Education Instructor		1		1		1	4
Music Department Head[f]		1			1	1	20[g]
Principal of Training School (Teaches Education Courses)		3		3		3	5
Special Subject Instructors (Supervisors)							
Teaching of Home Economics		1		1		1	1
Teaching of Industrial Arts	1			1		1	1
Teaching of Penmanship		1	1	2		2	2
Teaching of Physical Education	6	3	1	10		10	16
Teaching of Public School Art	3	5	1	8	1	9	15
Teaching of Public School Music	5	6	2	12	1	13	17
Teaching of Arithmetic Instructor		1	2	3		3	13
Teaching of Elementary School Science Instructor			1	1		1	8
Teaching of English							
English Department Head		1		1		1[j]	7
Teaching of English Instructor		1	2	3		3	15
Teaching of Geography							
Geography Department Head		1		1		1[k]	6
Teaching of Geography Instructor		1	2	3		3	17
Teaching of History Instructor		2	2	4		4	13

TABLE VI[b] (*Continued*)

Faculty Members	Frequency**						
	Only Rating Student Receives	Joint Rating with Critic Teacher	Joint Rating with Critic Teacher and Other College Instructors	Activity Initiated by Administrator	Activity Initiated by Critic Teacher	Total Number Who Give Rating	Number of Such Instructors in 25 Schools
Teaching of Nature Study Instructor......		1		1		1	5
Teaching of Reading Instructor...........	1	1	1	2	1	3	3
Total...........................	18	52	21	87	4	91	242

* No answer received from two schools.

** It seemed unnecessary to record frequencies since grades are assigned at the end of a student teaching period. In such institutions this is six or nine weeks in length. Each instructor in this table participated every time such work was done.

[a] In Tables III, IV, and V, called College department instructor who supervises.

[b] No director of training in this school. This work is in charge of dean of women.

[c] Director of training teaches no college courses.

[d] Educational Psychology and Tests and Measurements instructors from same school.

[e] Educational Psychology, Teaching of Elementary School Science, and Teaching of Reading instructors are in same school.

[f] Instructors who teach several different courses in education department.

[g] In remaining schools head of department is training school supervisor—considered under that title.

[h] Representing seven schools.

[i] Two supervisors from each of four schools—Early and Later Elementary Education.

[j] This instructor teaches Children's Literature.

[k] One of these officers teaches the professionalized subject matter course in geography; the other represents an institution where two members of the department aid students with lesson planning.

their regular work as supervisor or administrator. For instance, of the 87 instructors who participate in assigning grades to student teachers, 68 are training school administrators or supervisors.

Two schools visited reported that no one other than the critic teacher participates in rating or grading student teachers. One of these two has no director of training but the principal of the campus school is also a critic teacher. No one of the college faculty members feels that he is sufficiently intimately acquainted with the work of student teachers to make suggestions as to rating or grading. Many of the college instructors in this school, however, visit the training school often, and through a Saturday morning symposium composed of the entire faculty, keep in touch with the work of the training school. In the other institution, the director of training teaches no college courses but is supervisor of a number of off-campus training schools, in addition to the campus training school. He does not see the work of any given student teacher frequently enough to consider himself able to give an intelligent rating. However, in doubtful cases the critic teachers seek the advice of this director of training and ask him to observe the teaching of these students.

Analysis of Table VI in Terms of Various Ways in Which Faculty Members Aid in Giving Student Teachers a Rating or Grade

	Jury I			Jury II			Jury III			All Juries
	P	D	Both	P	D	Both	P	D	Both	
By giving a joint rating with the critic teacher..	1.8	1.4	1.6	1.7	1.4	1.5	1.4	1.3	1.3	1.5
By giving a joint final rating with critic teacher and members of other college departments.....	1.6	1.8	1.7	1.8	1.9	1.9	1.9	2.3	2.0	1.9
By giving a joint final rating with members of other college departments	2.6	3.1	2.9	2.8	2.9	2.9	3.1	3.1	3.1	3.0
By giving the only rating the student is to receive..	4.0	3.7	3.8	3.6	3.8	3.7	3.6	3.4	3.5	3.7

Fifty-two of the 91 persons of Table VI record that they give a rating jointly with the critic teacher. Under this list there are sixteen special subject instructors who are training school supervisors. These do not have major students but rather are supervising general elementary education students who may happen to be doing directed teaching in these special fields.

Only two institutions are represented in the category of a rating given jointly with the critic teacher and other college instructors. These are the two schools which have been mentioned before in this study as having all members of the faculty cooperate in the work of the training school whether they be designated as supervisors or are instructors in the "teaching" courses, as is the case in one of the schools. In the former school, the three training school supervisors request that the other eight college faculty members who have observed students teach during the semester aid them in assigning grades or make suggestions regarding rating.

One college instructor who is not a training school supervisor indicates that he gives the only rating which the student receives. This is the instructor in the Teaching of Reading who has been discussed above. In another institution where rating is done by members of the college faculty alone, the task is assumed by two college department instructors who are training school supervisors in an institution which uses city schools for student teaching. Here the public school teachers have little part in the supervision of student teachers, since the responsibility of this work is carried by the education department entirely. Except for these two schools, in every case in which instructors give the only rating the student is to receive, such instructors are "Special Subject Instructors who supervise in training school." They are thus supervising their major students and have no reason for consulting critic teachers.

Requested to Participate in the Activity by. In 87 of the 91 instances, instructors participate in assigning grades because the administration of the school has cited that as part of their work. In the other four which represent two schools, two from each, it is done by mutual agreement with the critic teacher. In one of these schools it is the Teaching of Reading instructor and the music department head—the latter indicating mutual agreement with the music critic teacher in the training school.

One may conclude from Table VI that participation in the assignment of grades to student teachers is not a voluntary cooperative function.

Cooperative Effort in Working Out and Revising Manuals or Handbooks to Be Used by Student Teachers in the Training School

In the previously mentioned address delivered at a conference for the study and discussion of teacher training in Texas, Dr. Alexander stressed the following type of cooperative activity which is quoted in full to explain its inclusion in this study.

> There are many schools now carrying on a type of work which coordinates the entire experience of student teachers through the use of student teaching manuals or guide sheets prepared by cooperative effort of the faculty as a whole. These have some disadvantages but they have the advantage of making very concrete the points of view of the various departments with reference to the problems of teaching.[17]

Apparently not a large amount of work in the revision or construction of manuals for student teachers to be used in the training school was being done at the time of this survey, since only eight of the 25 schools make any mention of such an activity. In seven of the schools only a few instructors were engaged in such work, as is evidenced in the following discussion.

School 1. The school discussing this type of work in the greatest detail was the one in which the biology instructor who teaches courses in nature study and hygiene for the elementary grades was working out an extensive manual in health with the cooperation of the school nurse and the critic teachers. This instructor and the school nurse reported that they spent a part of each day in the training school teaching, observing, and making suggestions as to the use of this manual.

School 2. The director of training who teaches a course in Introduction to Teaching recorded the spending of at least one hour a week with student teachers in the construction of a manual to be used for all of the training school subjects.

School 3. Three instructors, who offer courses in Teaching of Arithmetic, Teaching of Reading, and Teaching of Industrial Arts, reported that they confer with the critic teachers and director of training at least once a month regarding a manual in progress.

[17] Alexander, Thomas. "Coordination of the Laboratory Schools with the Subject-Matter Departments in the College." *Cooperative Planning for Teacher Training Standards in Texas.* Bulletin, North Texas State Teachers College, May, 1931, p. 142.

School 4. In an institution which uses city schools for training school purposes, the Teaching of Reading instructor[18] and the Teaching of Art and Home Economics instructors[18] are members of a state course of study committee. This committee includes representatives from each of the other state teacher training institutions. These two instructors recorded monthly meetings with this group on the project of constructing a manual to be used by student teachers in each of the state teacher training institutions. The work is included under the category "Alone" in this study because no critic teachers from their institution were members of the committee. However, these two instructors are supervisors of student teaching and represent the critic teachers who are city school teachers, not paid by the state.

The reader may question the inclusion of this work since it does not represent cooperative work between college and training school staff within the institution. One justification for including it is that critic teachers from other teacher training institutions are members of the state committee; another, that these instructors reported that they conferred with the critic teachers in their own institution regarding the suggestions made in each of the state meetings.

School 5. The music department reported activity in writing a manual to be used by the students majoring in music. In this instance, the head of the music department reported that he spent at least one period a week discussing this manual with the music critic teacher in the training school.

School 6. In school 6, the instructor in Teaching of Music, who also supervises in the training school, reported that she was working with the major student teachers on such a manual. This same school also reported that the kindergarten critic and the head of the kindergarten department were cooperating on a manual to be used in the kindergarten only.

School 7. The entire faculty reported work on such a manual and that monthly meetings were held for this work. Since the head of the education department is directing the work, his reported frequency is listed separately for this school. It is evident that this is the most

[18] These instructors are also designated as training school supervisors by the administration of the school.

extensive cooperative venture which was reported. In addition, this teacher training institution is conducting an experiment in the preparation of units of work which the students will later use in their student teaching. Every member of the faculty of both college and training school confer with students regarding the organization of their units before the student is assigned to his work in directed teaching.

School 8. The director of training who teaches a course in Directed Observation reported that he worked out such a manual as an individual project at the beginning of the year.

Recorded below is the order of importance assigned by the juries to the personnel of groups who engage in cooperative construction and revision of manuals or handbooks used by student teachers:

	Jury I Over 1,000			Jury II 500 to 1,000			Jury III Less than 500			Mean of Juries
	P	D	M	P	D	M	P	D	M	
1. As a joint project with the critic teachers and student teachers*......	2.1	1.9	2.0	2.4	2.0	2.2	2.1	2.7	2.4	2.2
2. As a joint project with student teachers, critic teacher, and members of other college departments................	2.6	2.2	2.4	2.5	1.9	2.2	1.9	1.8	1.9	2.2
3. As a joint project with the critic teachers......	3.1	2.5	2.8	2.6	3.2	2.9	2.8	2.7	2.7	2.8
4. As a joint project with student teachers and members of other college departments...........	4.0	4.4	4.2	4.1	4.5	4.3	4.9	4.4	4.7	4.4
5. As a joint project with members of other college departments...........	5.0	4.9	5.0	4.9	4.9	4.9	5.3	5.4	5.3	5.1
6. By working them out with student teachers ..	4.8	5.8	5.3	5.6	5.2	5.4	5.0	4.6	4.8	5.2
7. By working them out alone.................	6.4	6.3	6.3	6.0	6.3	6.1	6.1	6.4	6.3	6.2

* Refers to an individual member of an academic department who may participate with critic and student teachers.

No central tendency as to personnel was apparent in the reports from the eight schools engaging in this cooperative work.

CHAPTER IV

PARTICIPATION OF MEMBERS OF THE COLLEGE DEPARTMENTS IN THE FUNCTIONS OF THE TRAINING SCHOOL (*CONTINUED*)

B. By Aiding in Carrying on the Training School Curriculum

1. By Constructing and Revising Courses of Study for the Training School

Among the activities which have been suggested as means of coordinating theory and practice in teacher training institutions is the cooperative planning of the training school course of study. Dr. Lester Wilson included such an item in his questionnaire, sent to 100 normal schools in 1919. His returns showed that seven out of 43 institutions answering reported that "Normal school teachers made the course of study for the training school, in whole or in part." [1] In his survey of the articulation of the laboratory school with the college, Dr. Eubank includes a similar item, namely, "A committee made up of college teachers, laboratory school teachers, and training supervisors determine the course of study for laboratory schools." [2]

Reciprocal cooperation in this field was suggested by Miss Lenora E. Johnson in her "Constructive Proposals for Cooperation Between the Training School and Subject-matter Instructors": "The staff as a whole, or as groups, should determine the subject-matter and methods of their training school and of the subject-matter courses." [3]

[1] Wilson, L. M. "Training Departments in the State Normal Schools of the United States." *Normal School Bulletin,* No. 66, October 1, 1919, Chapter IV. Eastern Illinois State Normal School.

[2] Eubank, L. A. *The Organization and Administration of Laboratory Schools in State Teachers Colleges.* Northeast Missouri State Teachers College Bulletin, April, 1931, p. 56.

[3] Johnson, Lenora E. "Constructive Proposals for Cooperation Between the Training School and Subject-Matter Instructors." *The Virginia Teacher,* February, 1931, p. 35.

An examination of the data reported in Table VII indicates that at the time this survey was made very little was being done in the field of construction and revision of courses of study for the training school. Of the two schools reporting to this section of the questionnaire, one gave as a reason the fact that there was practically no cooperation between training school and college staff except in cases where instructors in Directed Observation brought classes to observe scheduled demonstration lessons in the training school. This teacher training institution reported that the course of study used in the laboratory school was one constructed by their own training school faculty. In the other school the courses in Directed Observation (called Technique of Teaching) were taught by the director of training, and no instructors in the education department or other departments signified that they were in close touch with the training school. This institution uses the state prescribed elementary school course of study in the training school.

The questionnaire submitted to the critic teachers in the twenty-five schools visited included a section in which each was asked to list the type of training school course of study in use. These data are listed below:

1. Prescribed by the state—ten schools[4]
2. Prescribed by the city—two schools[5]
3. Constructed by training school faculty—seven schools
4. Prescribed by state and supplemented by training school faculty—five schools
5. Combination of 1, 2, and 3 above—one school

In the light of these data, it is evident that most of the cooperative course of study work reported in Table VII is in supplementing existing courses rather than in construction or revision.

According to the mean jury rankings, the committee plan is preferred for constructing, revising, and supplementing courses of study to be used in the campus training school.

The data from the twenty-five schools being considered in this study are not in complete agreement with this judgment, since a major portion of such cooperative enterprise is effected through indi-

[4] Two of these schools use city schools for laboratory purposes.
[5] One of these schools uses city schools for laboratory purposes.

	Jury I Over 1,000			Jury II 500 to 1,000			Jury III Less than 500			Mean of Juries
	P	D	M	P	D	M	P	D	M	
1. By constructing and revising courses of study for the training school										
a. As members of a general curriculum committee composed of representatives of each college department and the training school which considers all training school courses of study.....	2.0	1.9	2.0	1.5	1.6	1.6	1.4	1.8	1.6	1.7
b. As members of subject committees which confer with the training school faculty on their own subject only	1.5	2.0	1.8	1.5	1.9	1.7	2.0	1.9	1.9	1.8
c. Through individual conferences with the critic teachers.......	2.5	2.1	2.3	2.9	2.5	2.7	2.6	2.3	2.5	2.5
2. By assisting in the application of details and the enrichment of state or city prescribed courses of study which are used by the training school										
a. As members of a general curriculum committee composed of representatives of each college department and the training school which considers all training school courses of study.....	2.0	1.9	2.0	1.9	1.7	1.8	1.6	2.0	1.8	1
b. As members of subject committees which confer with the training school faculty on their own subject only	1.5	2.0	1.8	1.5	1.9	1.7	1.9	1.9	1.9	1.8
c. Through individual conferences with the critic teachers.......	2.6	2.1	2.3	2.5	2.4	2.5	2.6	2.1	2.4	2.4

vidual conferences between critic teachers and college faculty members. However, Table VII indicates that, in many instances, both the

TABLE VII

Frequency with Which College Instructors Construct, Revise, or Supplement Courses of Study for the Training School*

Training School Courses of Study and Faculty Members Who Participate in This Activity	Frequency: As Member of General Curriculum Committee, Including College and Training School Faculty		As Special Subject Committee which Confers with Training School Faculty on Its Own Subject						Through Individual Conference with Critic Teacher					Activity Initiated by					State Department of Education	Total Number Who Participate[i]
	Weekly	Once a Term	Twice Weekly	Weekly	Twice Monthly	Monthly	Once a Term	Yearly	Twice Weely	Weekly	Monthly	Once a Term	Yearly	Administration	College Instructor	Critic Teacher	Mutual	Director of Training		
Arithmetic																				
Director of Training (Teaches Education Courses)			1											1						1
Mathematics Department Head		1					1					1						1		1
Principal of Training School (Teaches Education Courses)			1											1						1
Teaching of Arithmetic Instructor			1[g]				1		1[g]		1	1	2	3			2		1	6
Technique of Teaching											1					1				1
Elementary School Curriculum (Units of Work)																				
Director of Training (No Courses)	1											2		1			1			2
Director of Training (Teaches Education Courses)		1						1			1	1		1	2				1	4
Education Department Instructors (Supervisors)[h]	2[c]							2[c]				2[c]		2[c]	2[c]				2[c]	6[d]
Entire College and Training School Faculty	1																		1	1
Early Elementary Education Instructor						1									1					1
Later Elementary Education Instructor						1									1					1
Music Department Head												1			1					1
Principal of Training School (Teaches Education Courses)					1									1						1
English																				
Education Department Instructors (Supervisors)[h]					1						2[c]				1			2[c]		3
English Committee							1							1						1

TABLE VII (*Continued*)

Training School Courses of Study and Faculty Members Who Participate in This Activity	Frequency: As Member of General Curriculum Committee, Including College and Training School Faculty		As Special Subject Committee which Confers with Training School Faculty on Its Own Subject						Through Individual Conference with Critic Teacher					Activity Initiated by					State Department of Education	Total Number Who Participate[i]
	Weekly	Once a Term	Twice Weekly	Weekly	Twice Monthly	Monthly	Once a Term	Yearly	Twice Weekly	Weekly	Monthly	Once a Term	Yearly	Administration	College Instructor	Critic Teacher	Mutual	Director of Training		
Principal of Training School (Teaches Education Courses)							I					I						I		I
Teaching of English Instructor				I^{g}			I^{f}	I	I^{g}	I	I^{f}	I		3			I		I	5
Director of Training (No Courses)												I				I				I
Fine Arts																				
Director of Training (No Courses)													I			I				I
Fine Arts Department							I											I		I
Fine Arts Department Head													I	I			I			I
Teaching of Public School Art Instructor			I^{g}				I^{f}		3^{g}	2^{f}	I	4	I	3	2	I	4	I		II
Geography																				
Contemporary Life Instructor											I						I			I
Director of Training (No Courses)													I				I			I
Teaching of Geography Instructor			I^{g}			I^{e}			I^{g}	I^{e}	4	3	I	2		3	3	I	I	IO
Teaching of Social Studies Instructor							I										I			I
Education Department Instructors (Supervisors)[h]											2^{c}							2^{c}		2
Health																				
Director of Training (Teaches Education Courses)												I		I						I
Physical Education and Health Department								I						I						I
School Nurse			I^{g}				I		I^{g}					I					I	2
Teaching of Health Instructor							2^{g}		I		I^{g}	2		I	I	I	I		I	5
Teaching of Physical Education Instructor			I^{g}						I^{g}		2			I			I		I	3
Education Department Instructor (Supervises)[h]											2^{c}							2^{c}		2
History																				
Contemporary Life Instructor							I												I	I

TABLE VII (*Continued*)

Training School Courses of Study and Faculty Members Who Participate in This Activity	Frequency: As Member of General Curriculum Committee, Including College and Training School Faculty		As Special Subject Committee which Confers with Training School Faculty on Its Own Subject						Through Individual Conference with Critic Teacher					Activity Initiated by					State Department of Education	Total Number Who Participate[i]
	Weekly	Once a Term	Twice Weekly	Weekly	Twice Monthly	Monthly	Once a Term	Yearly	Twice Weekly	Weekly	Monthly	Once a Term	Yearly	Administration	College Instructor	Critic Teacher	Mutual	Director of Training		
Teaching of History Instructor			1[g]						1[g]		2			2					1	3
Education Department Instructor (Supervises)[h]											2[c]							2[c]		2
Industrial Arts																				
Industrial Arts Instructor									1								1			1
Teaching of Public School Art Instructor											1						1			1
Music																				
Music Department								2							1			1		2
Music Department Head		1[f]				1[f]				1	1[f]	2	1		2	2		1		5
Teaching of Public School Music Instructor			1[g]				1		2[g]	2	3	2	1	4	1	2	3		1	11
Penmanship																				
Teaching of Penmanship Instructor									1		2	2	2	1	1	2	2			6
Physical Education																				
Director of Training (Teaches Education Courses)												1		1						1
School Nurse							1						1	1					1	2
Teaching of Health Instructor							1												1	1
Teaching of Physical Education Instructor		2[f]	1[g]					1[f]	2[g]	2	1	4	1	3	6	1	1	1		12
Woman's Physical Education Department								1							1					1
Science for Elementary Grades																				
Home Economics Instructor											1				1					1
Physical Science Instructor											1							1		1
Science Department Head													1		1					1
Teaching of Elementary School Science Instructor		1[f]		1[g]			2[f]			2[g]	1[f]			2	2[f]				1	5
Teaching of Nature Study Instructor										1	1	1		1			1	1		3

TABLE VII (*Continued*)

Training School Courses of Study and Faculty Members Who Participate in This Activity	Frequency: As Member of General Curriculum Committee, Including College and Training School Faculty		Frequency: As Special Subject Committee which Confers with Training School Faculty on Its Own Subject						Frequency: Through Individual Conference with Critic Teacher					Activity Initiated by					State Department of Education	Total Number Who Participate[i]
	Weekly	Once a Term	Twice Weekly	Weekly	Twice Monthly	Monthly	Once a Term	Yearly	Twice Weekly	Weekly	Monthly	Once a Term	Yearly	Administration	College Instructor	Critic Teacher	Mutual	Director of Training		
Spelling																				
English Department Head											1						1			1
Social Studies																				
Chairman of Curriculum Committee[a]											1						1			1

* No answer from two schools.
[a] The director of research is chairman of the curriculum committee.
[b] This instructor teaches college courses and is a training school supervisor.
[c] These two persons are in the same school.
[d] Instructors who teach several different courses in the education department.
[e] The professionalized subject matter course is taught by another member of the department.
[f] Also supervises in the training school.
[g] The same instructor appears under more than one category.
[h] In Tables III, IV, and V, called College department instructor who supervises.
[i] See Table VI for number bearing each title listed who might have participated.

special subject committee plans and the individual conference technique are used.

Entire Elementary School Curriculum (Units of Work). The questionnaire bore a heading called "Units of Work." The majority of the cases seemed to fall in this field since most of the curriculum construction work was on a coordinated course from the "activities curriculum" viewpoint, rather than on the separate subjects.

The education department acts predominantly in this work since in only two instances did other departments mention such activity. Of the seventeen persons representing nine schools, who list participation in reconstructing the elementary school curriculum as a whole, thirteen are training school supervisors or administrators, as well as college instructors.

One teachers college reported that the entire college and training school faculty met once a week, Saturday morning, to discuss, revise, and supplement the entire training school curriculum. This seems to be the most concerted effort in curriculum construction for the training school shown in any institution included in this survey.

In the other case where work on the entire elementary school curriculum was contributed to by anyone outside of the education department, the music department head explained that once a term he conferred with each critic teacher so that he might better coordinate the music work with the needs of the unified course of study.

The nine schools reporting work by the college departments on the entire elementary school curriculum list infrequent participation. The exception is the one school where the director of training who teaches no courses and the education department instructors who are training school supervisors record weekly cooperation in this work, as members of a general curriculum committee. This school was revising not only its college but its training school curriculum offerings to further an experiment in the training of teachers which has been mentioned elsewhere in this study.[6]

There seems to be no particular trend in the way in which this work was done, since five officials said they participated as members of a general curriculum committee, six as members of a special sub-

[6] See page 59.

ject committee, and seven through individual conference with the critic teacher.

Summarized data gained from Table VII for each training school subject in which curriculum work was reported follow.

Arithmetic. Ten instructors representing nine teacher training institutions mentioned activity in the revision of the course of study in arithmetic, the trend being for the Teaching of Arithmetic instructor to confer individually with the critic teacher.

English. The English course of study for the training school was receiving consideration in ten schools at the time of this survey. In one of these, an English department committee met once a term to work on an experimental course of study for the training school. As in the other courses of study the college instructors who are also training school staff members are prominent in the list. Five of the ten schools report that the Teaching of English instructor participates with varying frequency.

Fine Arts. Thirteen schools record some type of activity in the construction of a training school course in fine arts. In one, the entire fine arts department, in cooperation with the critic teachers as a special subject committee, held conferences each term regarding this phase of work. In another school, the head of the fine arts department conferred individually with the art supervisor and the regular critic teachers once a year to plan the fine arts work in terms of the training school needs. In a third school the director of training planned the fine arts curriculum in conference with the individual critic teachers.

In eight instances, the frequencies are recorded by the Teaching of Public School Art instructor who is also the supervisor of art in the training school. In one instance, the school has a special art critic teacher in the training school with whom this instructor confers weekly. One school, in which the city art supervisor directs this work in the training school, reports that at least twice a week the Teaching of Art instructor plans the work to be taught with this supervisor.

Geography. Fourteen of the schools included in this survey record some degree of cooperation between the training school and college faculty in the construction of a geography course of study to be used in the training school. The Contemporary Life instructor in one of these confers monthly with the critic teachers on this subject. In the same institution, the Teaching of Social Studies instructor reports meetings once a term with the critic teachers, as a subject committee, on the geography course of study. In an institution where the head of the geography department offers the course in the teaching of geography, it was reported that he interviewed critic teachers weekly and directed monthly geography course of study group meetings. This school published a training school course of study in geography as a result of such activity which was initiated by the director of training.

Health. Ten schools recorded work being done on a Health Course of Study for the training school, as separate from the Physical education course.

History. Not a great deal of curriculum construction for the training school was done in the field of history, but six instructors from five schools reported such work. Except for the one Teaching of History instructor who participates in this activity twice weekly as a member of a special history committee and twice weekly through individual conference with the critic teachers, the frequency with which this work is done ranges from once a month to once a term.

Industrial Arts. All but two of the 25 schools offer college courses in Industrial Arts. Seventeen have a department separate from the fine arts department and six call their department Fine and Industrial Arts. One school in the latter group reported that the public school art instructor, who is also a supervisor in the training school, developed an industrial arts course of study through monthly conferences with the individual critic teachers. In one other school which reported activity of this type, the industrial arts instructor conferred with the critic teachers individually at least twice a week in the formulation of this course of study. It is apparent that Industrial Arts as a separate course was not receiving great attention when this survey was made.

Music. Seventeen institutions reported that an instructor from the music department cooperated on a course of study for the training school. The entire music department in two schools reported that they conferred yearly with the critic teachers as a special music course of study committee. Five schools reported that the head of the music department conferred with the music critic teacher or with the music supervisor who taught college courses regarding the course of study to be offered. In one of these schools, special prominence was being given this course of study so that one general curriculum committee meeting a term was conducted for this purpose. In addition, monthly meetings were held by a special music committee which included the critic teachers, as well as monthly conferences between the individual critic teachers and the head of the music department.

Penmanship. Curriculum work in penmanship is confined to individual conferences with critic teachers by the college instructors in that field. Two of seven schools listed penmanship supervisors who also teach college courses. In the other cases, these officials are college instructors only.

Physical Education. Thirteen schools reported curriculum construction in physical education for the training school. One school indicated that the entire women's department, which included the training school supervisor, conferred as a special physical education committee once a year. None of the other schools reported that all members of the department cooperated in this venture.

Table VII shows that, except for the two schools which have given attention to this work through general curriculum and special subject committees, the larger part of such work is done through individual conferences with the critic teachers by the Teaching of Physical Education instructor who is also the training school supervisor.

Science in the Elementary Grades. One school of the nine which reported curriculum construction in this field says that the head of the science department conferred once a year with the individual critic teachers. In another school, the instructor in physical science conferred at least once a month with individual critic teachers at the request of the director of training. A third school mentioned not only the Teaching of Nature Study instructor in this activity, but also a Home Economics instructor.

As has been previously cited,[7] the schools which offer a course in science for the elementary grades term it either Teaching of Elementary School Science, or Teaching of Nature Study. No school

[7] See page 64.

listed both courses. If Teaching of Elementary Science instructors and Teaching of Nature Study instructors are grouped together, the majority of the cases appear under the heading "Through individual conferences with the critic teachers."

Spelling. Only one school made any reference to curriculum construction in spelling, such work being done by the head of the English department through monthly conferences with the individual critic teachers. A culmination of the activity was a published course of study in spelling to which both the head of the English department and an individual critic teacher contributed.

Social Studies. One school was giving considerable time to a social studies course of study at the time of this survey. The chairman of the curriculum committee, who is director of research in this school, conducted meetings once a semester on this subject with the critic teachers as a group including the off-campus critic teachers. He also conferred with them individually as often as once a month. Owing to the large enrollment in this school, it was considered impossible to have all critic teachers from the several off-campus schools and the campus school meet together oftener than twice a year. Therefore, the director of the curriculum committee met not only with the campus school critic teachers but also with the off-campus teachers in an effort to coordinate their suggestions.

2. *By Aiding in the Selection of Materials of Instruction and Equipment*

Questionnaires personally presented to faculty members in twenty-five state teachers colleges and normal schools requested information as to the extent college faculty members aided the training school staff in selecting such materials of instruction and equipment as textbooks, supplementary books, art materials, slides, maps, moving pictures, laboratory equipment, and the like. A comparison of Table VIII with the jury ranking of ways in which such cooperative endeavor should be effected shows that in practice the committee plan (which was preferred by the juries) is seldom used.

Textbooks. As is evidenced by Table VIII, there is a slight trend indicating which college departments give more aid to the training school faculty in the selection of textbooks to be used in the training

	Jury I Over 1,000			Jury II 500 to 1,000			Jury III Less than 500			Mean of Juries
	P	D	M	P	D	M	P	D	M	
1. As members of subject committees which confer with the training school faculty on materials and equipment for only their own subject...........	1.6	2.0	1.8	1.4	1.7	1.6	1.8	1.8	1.8	1.7
2. As members of a general curriculum committee composed of representatives of each college department and the training school which aids in selecting all training school materials and equipment............	2.4	2.2	2.3	2.5	2.1	2.3	1.7	1.9	1.8	2.1
3. Through individual conferences with the critic teachers..............	2.1	1.9	2.0	2.1	2.2	2.2	2.5	2.3	2.4	2.2

school. Eighteen of the 33 persons who report such participation are members of the training school administrative or supervisory staff.

The director of research, who participates in this activity both as a member of a special subject committee and through individual conference with the training school staff, is chairman of the curriculum committee. This committee was engaged in curriculum construction for the training school and the selection of textbooks was a part of this work.

The academic department instructors who participate in the selection of textbooks for the training school are few in number, only 14 individuals, representing 8 departments, indicating this method of participating in the curriculum of the training school.

The head of the English department and the head of the history department who confer with individual critic teachers each term regarding the selection of textbooks represent the school which has been mentioned previously as promoting as much contact as possible between training school staff and all members of the academic departments. Only one librarian in the 25 schools participates in the selection of textbooks, but this officer appears with greater frequency in the selection of supplementary books. The one music department

TABLE VIII

Frequency with Which College Instructors Aid in the Selection of Materials of Instruction and Equipment for the Training School*

Faculty Members	Frequency: As Special Subject Committee Which Confers with Training School Faculty on Its Own Subject		Frequency: Through Individual Conference with Critic Teacher				Activity Initiated by				Total Number Who Select Materials	Number of Such Instructors in 25 Schools
	Once a Term	Yearly	Weekly	Monthly	Once a Term	Yearly	Administration	College Instructor	Critic Teacher	Mutual		
Textbooks												
Director of Research	1			1			1				1	4
Director of Training (No Courses)				1	1	2	4				4	8
Director of Training (Education Courses)			1		2	2	3	1			4	16
Education Department Instructors (Supervise)				1	2[b]			1		2[b]	3	15[e]
English Department Head[g]	1							1			1[d]	18
History Department Head[g]					1					1	1	22
Librarian						1		1			1	25
Music Department Head					1					1	1	20[c]
Principal of Training School (Teaches Education Courses)					1		1				1	6
Teaching of Arithmetic Instructor					2	1	1	1	1		3	13
Teaching of Elementary School Science					1					1	1	8
Teaching of English Instructor				1			1				1	15
Teaching of Geography Instructor					2				2		2	17
Teaching of History Instructor					1			1			1	13
Teaching of Physical Education Instructor[f]		1					1				1	16
Teaching of Public School Art[f]						1	1				1	15
Teaching of Public School Music		1		1	1	1	1	2		1	4	17
Teaching of Reading Instructor		1						1			1	3
Visual Education Instructor		1					1				1	1
Total	2	4	1	5	15	8	15	9	3	6	33	

TABLE VIII (*Continued*)

Faculty Members	Frequency: As Special Subject Committee Which Confers with Training School Faculty on Its Own Subject		Frequency: Through Individual Conference with Critic Teacher				Activity Initiated by				Total Number Who Select Materials	Number of Such Instructors in 25 Schools
	Once a Term	Yearly	Weekly	Monthly	Once a Term	Yearly	Administration	College Instructor	Critic Teacher	Mutual		
Supplementary Books												
Director of Training (No Courses)			1		1		1	1			2	8
Director of Training (Education Courses)			1		4	1	5	1			6	16
Education Department Instructors (Supervise)				1	4[b]		2[b]	1		2[b]	5	15[e]
English Department Head[g]					1			1			1[d]	18
History Department Head[g]					1					1	1	22
Kindergarten Department Head						1			1		1	2
Librarian		1	2		4	1	3	1	1	2	7	25
Music Department Head						1		1			1	20[c]
Principal of Training School (Education Courses)					2		2				2	6
Teaching of Arithmetic Instructor					2		1	1			2	13
Teaching of Elementary School Science					1				1		1	8
Teaching of English Instructor				1			1				1	15
Teaching of Geography Instructor					2				2		2	17
Teaching of History Instructor					1			1			1	13
Teaching of Physical Education Instructor[f]	1						1				1	16
Teaching of Public School Art Instructor[f]	1						1				1	15
Teaching of Public School Music Instructor[f]	1						1				1	17
Visual Education Instructor	1						1				1	1
Total	4	1	4	2	23	4	19	8	5	5	37	

TABLE VIII (*Continued*)

Laboratory Equipment												
Director of Training (No Courses)			2	1			2	1			3	8
Director of Training (Education Courses)			1		3		3	1			4	16
Education Department Instructors (Supervisors)				1	4[b]		2[b]	1		2[b]	5	15[e]
English Department Head[g]					1			1			1[d]	18
Fine Arts Department		1			1					1	1	25
Fine Arts Department Head					1				1		1	18[c]
History Department Head[g]					1					1	1	22
Librarian			1		1		1			1	2	25
Nursery School Director					1					1	1	1
Principal of Training School (Teaches Education Courses)					2		2				2	6
President of Institution					1			1			1	25
Teaching of Arithmetic Instructor					1		1				1	13
Teaching of Elementary School Science Instructor	1				2		1		1		2	8
Teaching of Geography Instructor	1	1			3		1	1	2		4	17
Teaching of History Instructor						1		1			1	13
Teaching of Nature Study Instructor				1	1		1			1	2	5
Teaching of Physical Education Instructor[f]	1	1			3		2	2	1		5	16
Teaching of Public School Art[f]	1		1	2	5		4	3	2		9	15
Teaching of Public School Music[f]	1				2	2	3	2			5	17
Visual Education Instructor	1						1				1	1
Total	6	3	5	5	33	3	24	14	7	7	52	

* No answers were received from six schools.
[a] One additional category, As member of a general curriculum committee composed of representatives of each college department and training school, was included on the questionnaire but received no frequencies.
[b] Two of these persons are in same school.
[c] In remaining schools head of department is training school supervisor and is considered under that title.
[d] This instructor teaches Children's Literature.
[e] Representing seven schools.
[f] Also supervises in the training school.
[g] The professionalized subject matter course is taught by another member of the department.

head who participates in this function does so with the music critic in the training school.

The following four members of academic departments are from the same teacher training institution: English department head, History department head, Teaching of Arithmetic instructor (1) and Teaching of Geography instructor (1); four others represent a second school: Teaching of Arithmetic instructor, Teaching of English instructor, Teaching of History instructor, and Teaching of Reading instructor. Still a third school contributed these instances: Teaching of Public School Art instructor, Teaching of Public School Music instructor, Teaching of Physical Education instructor, and Visual Education instructor.

To summarize, 16 schools of the 25 mention cooperative work in the selection of textbooks to be used in the training school. Nine of these list only an administrative or supervisory officer such as director of training, principal of the training school, or an education department instructor who supervises. Every instance from fourteen of the schools appears under the category "Through individual conference with critic teacher." Only two schools report this activity as carried on by a special subject committee. The director of research represents one of these schools; the other three frequencies represent one other institution.

A trend may be noticed where this is done through individual conference with the critic teacher since three cases do so monthly; twelve, once a term; and five, yearly.

Supplementary Books. Practically without exception, the same faculty members record participation in the selection of supplementary books or selected textbooks with a similar scattering of frequencies. Sixteen schools are represented in this section of Table VIII, five of which report only administrative officers or supervisors. Two others list administrative officers plus the librarian, and one other lists administrative officers, supervisors, and the visual education instructor.

As in the case of textbook selection, the majority of the listings fall under the heading "Through individual conference with critic teachers." The same two institutions report that cooperative selection of supplementary books is done by a special committee appointed to do this work. The only noticeable change is the increase in the number of school librarians who aid in the selection of supplementary books but who did not report such cooperative work under the textbook heading. This can be readily understood since the selection of supplementary books is more generally accepted as a function of the library department.

Laboratory Equipment. The questionnaire gave an opportunity for college instructors to mention the types of laboratory equipment which they helped select, but instructors in art, music, physical education, and science departments said it was obvious that they aided only with the selection of material for their own fields. Seventeen institutions listed some college instructor who cooperated in this activity.

The trend in this type of cooperation is toward once-a-term participation.

To summarize for the entire table:

1. Six schools out of 25 list no cooperation in the selection of textbooks, supplementary books, or laboratory equipment to be used in the training school. In the case of one school this situation was explained by the fact that the institution uses city schools for directed teaching. The room teachers are not paid by the state, and the city directs the selection and purchase of all such materials. In the other five schools it is not the policy for the college and training school faculty to engage in reciprocal relations. In three of these schools the only type of cooperation mentioned throughout the study is in the case of the classes in Directed Observation which observe scheduled demonstration lessons. In the other two schools, even this type of coordination was not evident since Directed Observation is taught by the director of training and the critic teachers.

2. Some college department faculty members aid in the selection of textbooks for the training school in 16 schools, in selecting supplementary books in 16 schools, and in selecting laboratory equipment in 17 schools.

3. By Participating in the Testing of Training School Children

Of the 54 different members of various college departments recorded in Table IX who report some degree of participation in the testing of training school pupils, 40 are members of the education department. Since it is rather generally accepted that the testing of training school children is a part of the work of the Tests and Measurements instructor in a teachers college, we should expect this officer to receive the largest number of frequencies on Table IX. Twenty-four of the 25 schools offer a course in Tests and Measurements, and in the twenty-fifth school, an Educational Psychology instructor includes such work in the content of his courses. Of the 24 schools offering a Tests and Measurements course, 11 of the instructors bearing the title reported participation in the testing of training school children. The Tests and Measurements instructor in seven other schools also participates in this work, but he has been listed on Table IX under another title, as is explained below:

(1). In two of the schools the director of training teaches the course in Tests and Measurements, so the record is given opposite director of training who teaches education courses.

(2). In three other schools such a course is taught by the Educational Psychology instructor, so that the record appears opposite his name (one case appears by head of psychology department).

(3). In two schools the Tests and Measurements course is taught by the Educational Psychology instructor who is a supervisor of student teachers in the training school.

In five of the seven remaining schools, not mentioned in the above data, some members of the education department recorded slight participation in the testing of training school children; for instance, one reported that the nursery school director administered tests in the kindergarten, two that instructors in Elementary Education courses who are also training school supervisors aided with the testing program, and one that the Teaching of Reading instructor listed occasional participation, but in reading only.

Only two schools failed to make any response to this section. The reason given by one school was that the critic teachers who teach college courses direct the training school testing program; in the other, that such work is a training school activity which does not require the aid of the college departments.

The majority of those who recorded some work in the testing of training school children signified that it was both in intelligence

TABLE IX

Frequency with Which College Instructors Participate in the Testing of Training School Children*

Faculty Members	Frequency: Administer Tests Themselves			Frequency: College Students Administer Tests under Guidance of College Instructor			Frequency: Student Teachers Administer Tests under Guidance of College Instructor		Frequency: Critic Teachers Administer Tests under Guidance of College Instructor		Activity Initiated by					Total Number Who Participate	Number of Such Instructors in 25 Schools
	Monthly	Once a Term	Yearly	Monthly	Once a Term	Yearly	Monthly	Once a Term	Once a Term	Yearly	Administration	College Instructor	Critic	Mutual	Director of Training		
Directed Observation Instructor		I			I							I				I	2
Director of Training (No Courses)			I								I					I	8
Director of Training (Teaches Education Courses)		I			2		I	I	I	I	2	3				5	16
Early Elementary Education Instructor		I		I				I				I				I	8
Educational Psychology Instructor	I	I	2	I	I	I					I			I	3	5	19
Education Department Instructor (Supervises)	I	6[c]				4[b]	3[b]	2[a]			4[b]	5[c]				9	15
English Department Head							I					I				I	18
Kindergarten Department Head			I										I			I	2
Later Elementary Education Instructor		I		I				I				I				I	4
Nursery School Director		I													I	I	I
Principal of Training School (Teaches Directed Observation)			I								I					I	4
Psychology Department Head		I			I			I				2				2	2
Teaching of Arithmetic Instructor										I	I					I	13
Teaching of Elementary School Subjects Instructor			I												I	I	4
Teaching of Geography Instructor									2			2				2	17
Teaching of History Instructor									2			2				2	13
Teaching of Physical Education Instructor[d]								I	I		I	I				2	16
Teaching of Public School Art Instructor[d]								I				I				I	15

TABLE IX (*Continued*)

Faculty Members	Frequency: Administer Tests Themselves			College Students Administer Tests under Guidance of College Instructor			Student Teachers Administer Tests under Guidance of College Instructor		Critic Teachers Administer Tests under Guidance of College Instructor		Activity Initiated by					Total Number Who Participate	Number of Such Instructors in 25 Schools
	Monthly	Once a Term	Yearly	Monthly	Once a Term	Yearly	Monthly	Once a Term	Once a Term	Yearly	Administration	College Instructor	Critic	Mutual	Director of Training		
Teaching of Public School Music Instructor[d]	1	1	1					3	2			3		1		4	17
Teaching of Reading Instructor...........				1							1					1	3
Tests and Measurements Instructor.......		3	5		2	3		1	2	2	4	2	2	2	1	11	23
Total.........................	3	17	12	4	7	8	5	12	8	4	16	25	3	4	6	54	

* No answer from one school.
[a] These two persons are in same school.
[b] These four persons represent two schools.
[c] These six persons are in three schools.
[d] These instructors are also training school instructors.

testing and achievement testing. All of the instructors in professionalized subject matter courses, who are recorded in Table IX, stated that their testing was in their specific fields only.

	Jury I Over 1,000			Jury II 500 to 1,000			Jury III Less than 500			Mean of Juries
	P	D	M	P	D	M	P	D	M	
By having critic teachers administer the tests under guidance of the college instructor	2.3	2.3	2.3	2.1	1.6	1.8	2.0	2.1	2.0	2.0
By having student teachers administer the tests under guidance of the college instructor	2.5	2.2	2.3	1.7	2.1	2.0	2.1	2.1	2.1	2.1
By having students in college classes administer the tests under the guidance of the instructor	3.1	2.9	3.0	2.8	3.2	3.0	2.4	3.2	2.8	2.9
By administering the tests themselves	2.1	2.7	2.4	3.4	3.1	3.2	3.5	2.7	3.1	2.9

A comparison of the order in which the juries ranked the four ways in which testing should be done and the findings in Table IX shows them to be in almost reverse order, for 32 administer the tests themselves, 19 report that college students administer tests under their guidance, 17 have student teachers administer tests under their guidance, and 12 have critic teachers administer tests under their guidance.

Practically every instructor said that he was responsible for training school testing in more than one of the four ways; the trend, however, seems to be for the college instructor to administer tests himself once a term or once a year.

Unlike many of the cooperative activities described, this activity was found to be initiated by the college instructor himself more often than he was requested to do so by the administration or by members of the training school staff. The reason given for this in each case was that in order to make a college course in tests and measurements meaningful and practical, it was necessary to use the training school as a laboratory.

Apparently the testing of training school children is left to the authority of the critic teachers and the college instructors in the schools where the director of training does not teach college courses, since only one out of nine of these directors recorded such participation and that only once a year. Of the other eight schools where the director of training does not teach college courses, seven list such work as done by the Tests and Measurements instructors. In the remaining school this work is carried on by individual critic teachers without aid of the college instructors or this director of training.

4. *By Participating in Analyzing the Results of Tests Administered to Training School Children, and Planning Remedial Measures*

Thirty-eight of the 54 college instructors who recorded participation in the testing of training school children also report that they participate in the analysis of the results and in the planning of remedial measures. The following who appear in Table IX do not appear in Table X.

Directed Observation instructor	1
Director of training who does not teach	1
Educational Psychology instructor	4
Elementary Education course instructors who are supervisors	1
Kindergarten department head	1
Principal of training school who teaches Directed Observation	1
Teaching of Elementary School Subjects instructor	1
Teaching of History instructor	1
Teaching of Public School Music instructor	1
Tests and Measurements instructor	4

These 16 instructors who did not participate in analyzing the test returns with the training school staff, though they had engaged in testing training school children, gave the explanation that such tests were administered to training school children to provide material for discussion in the college classes.

The non-teaching director of training who participated in the testing of training school children, as shown in Table IX, refers the analysis of such data and the planning of remedial measures to the education department, which discusses this work with individual critic teachers.

One more frequency for each of the following titles is listed in Table X than in Table IX: instructors in Early Elementary Education, the Teaching of Arithmetic, and the Teaching of Geography.

TABLE X**

Frequency with Which College Instructors Participate in Analyzing the Results of Tests Administered to Training School Children and in Planning Remedial Measures*

Faculty Members	Frequency — With Student Teacher Whose Class Was Tested			With Critic Teacher and Student Teacher Whose Class Was Tested			With Critic Teacher Alone			Activity Initiated by				Total Number Who Participate	Number of Such Instructors in 25 Schools
	Monthly	Once a Term	Yearly	Monthly	Once a Term	Yearly	Monthly	Once a Term	Yearly	Administration	College Instructor	Critic	Mutual		
Director of Training (Teaches)			1	1	2		1	2	1	3	1		1	5	16
Early Elementary Education Instructor					2			1				1	1	2	8
Education Department								1		1				1	25
Educational Psychology								1					1	1	19
Education Department Instructor (Supervises)	5[c]		2[a]	2[a]		2[a]		2[a]		2[a]	4[b]		2[a]	8	15
English Department Head	1										1			1	18
Later Elementary Education Instructor					1								1	1	4
Nursery School Director								1		1				1	1
Psychology Department Head		1							1			1	1	2	2
Teaching of Arithmetic Instructor					2				1	1	1			2	13
Teaching of Geography Instructor		2			1			2			2		1	3	17
Teaching of History Instructor	1												1	1	13
Teaching of Physical Education Instructor[d]	1			1	1					1	1		1	3	16
Teaching of Public School Art Instructor[d]				1									1	1	15
Teaching of Public School Music Instructor[d]		2		1	1						2		1	3	17
Teaching of Reading Instructor	1			1			1				1			1	3
Tests and Measurements Instructor					1	2	1	1	2	3	2	1	1	7	23
Total	9	5	3	7	11	4	3	11	5	12	15	3	13	43	

* No answers received from four schools.

** Two additional categories, With student teacher and members of other college departments, and With student teacher, critic teacher, and members of other college departments, were included in the questionnaire, but received no frequencies.

[a] These two persons are in same school.

[b] These four persons represent two schools.

[c] These six persons are in three schools.

[d] These instructors are also training school instructors.

Each represents a different teacher training institution. In another school, the director of physical education, who is also the training school supervisor, aids in the analysis of health tests but leaves the administration of such tests to the individual critic teachers.

No answer was given by one institution regarding the data recorded in Table IX, nor by four institutions regarding the data recorded in Table X.

No trend is apparent as to frequency or manner in which cooperative analysis of the tests is carried on. Twenty-two discuss the returns with student teacher and critic teacher jointly; 17 with the student teacher whose class was tested; and 19 with the critic teacher alone.

The extent to which these findings compare with expert opinion may be determined from the data given below. No frequencies are recorded in Table IX for the category which shows second rank in the five suggested personnel groups.

	Jury I Over 1,000			Jury II 500 to 1,000			Jury III Less than 500			Mean of Juries
	P	D	M	P	D	M	P	D	M	
With the critic teacher and student teacher whose class was tested	1.4	1.5	1.3	1.4	1.4	1.4	1.5	1.2	1.4	1.3
With the critic teacher alone	3.1	2.7	2.9	3.1	2.5	2.8	3.5	2.6	3.1	2.9
With student teacher, critic teacher, and members of other college departments	2.6	3.0	2.8	3.4	3.0	3.2	2.3	3.4	2.8	2.9
With the student teacher whose class was tested	3.2	3.8	3.5	3.4	3.8	3.6	3.5	3.4	3.4	3.5
With student teacher and members of other college departments	4.7	4.4	4.2	3.8	4.4	4.1	4.2	4.4	4.3	4.2

5. By Participating in Planning and Conducting Such Training School Activities as Assembly Programs, School Publications, Parent-Teacher Association Programs, Field Trips, etc.

The questionnaire listed the following training school activities in which faculty members might list participation: Assembly Programs, School Publications, Parent-Teacher Association Programs, and Field

Trips. In addition, ample space was left with the suggestion that other activities in which they had a part might be listed. This section brought forth the following new groups:

School Dramatics
Pageants
Musical Activities
  Chorus
  Glee Club
  Music Week
  Operettas
  Training School Band
  Orchestra
  Radio Programs
  Song Festivals

Special Day Programs
  Arbor Day
  Christmas
  Commencement
  May Festivals
  Physical Education Play Day

Units of Work
  Fete of Nations Bazaar
  Educational Exhibit
  Flower Club
  Industrial Arts
  School Savings Bank

For ease in tabulation and discussion, all school dramatics and pageants were grouped together. For the same reason, chorus and glee club, band and orchestra were grouped together under musical activities.

The heading "Units of Work" was decided upon for the last section because each of the five activities named seemed to be an outgrowth of something which had occurred in the classroom. For instance, in the case of the Industrial Arts Unit, this work was first done as a part of the classroom instruction, but, owing to its popularity, was expanded to an exhibit of various crafts for the entire training school.

Assembly Programs. Twenty-one schools out of the 25 reported that one or more members of the college faculty participated in the presentation of assembly programs.

In one the entire college faculty and student body meet with the training school children and instructors in a joint assembly program once every month. This study was unable to take into account those cases where children from the training school came to give programs for the college assembly. Every school visited reported that at some time during the year such programs were presented but, since very often a small group of children who were advertising some training school function were the participants, no actual count had been kept

TABLE XI

Frequency with Which Members of the College Department Participate in Planning and Conducting the Extracurricular Activities of the Training School*

Training School Activities in Which College Faculty Members Participate	Frequency: With Student Teacher and Training School Children	With Critic Teacher and Training School Children		With Student Teacher, Critic Teacher, and Training School Children				With Student Teacher, Critic Teacher, Other College Instructors, and Children			Activity Initiated by					Total Number Who Participated[b]
	Once a Term	Monthly	Once a Term	Yearly	Weekly	Monthly	Once a Term	Yearly	Monthly	Once a Term	Yearly	Administration	Director of Training	College Instructor	Critic Teacher	Mutual	
Assembly Programs																	
Director of Training (Teaches)			1			2						3					3
Dramatics Instructor				1				1				1					1
Education Department Head								1					1				1
English Department Head										2		1		1			2
Entire Faculty and Student Body									1			1					1
Fine Arts Department Head			1			1							1	1			2
General Subject Instructors (Supervise)																	
Teaching of Elementary School Science										1					1		1
Teaching of Elementary School Subjects									2[d]				2[d]				2
Home Economics Instructor								1				1					1
Mathematics Department Head	1		1				1					1					1
Music Department	1		1				1										1
Music Department Head			2[a]		1		1								1	3	4
Physical Education and Health Department	1												1				1
Physics Instructor								1					1				1
Psychology Department Head								1					1				1
Religious Education Instructor				1											1		1
Special Subject Instructors (Supervise)																	
Teaching of Physical Education			1			1	2							1		2	3
Teaching of Public School Art										2		1		1			2
Teaching of Public School Music	1				2	1	2			2		2			2	4	8

TABLE XI (*Continued*)

Training School Activities in Which College Faculty Members Participate	Frequency: With Student Teacher and Training School Children	With Critic Teacher and Training School Children			With Student Teacher, Critic Teacher, and Training School Children				With Student Teacher, Critic Teacher, Other College Instructors, and Children			Activity Initiated by					Total Number Who Participated[b]
	Once a Term	Monthly	Once a Term	Yearly	Weekly	Monthly	Once a Term	Yearly	Monthly	Once a Term	Yearly	Administration	Director of Training	College Instructor	Critic Teacher	Mutual	
Teaching of English Instructor								1				1					1
Teaching of Geography Instructor			1				1					1			1		2
Teaching of History Instructor											1			1			1
Teaching of Nature Study Instructor							2	1				1	1	1			3
Teaching of Public School Music Instructor							1						1				1
Teaching of Physical Education Instructor							1	1		1			2			1	3
Teaching of Health Instructor	1		1				1					1					1
Dramatics—Pageants																	
Director of Training (Teaches)								1				1					1
Dramatic Instructor								1							1		1
English Department Head									1			1					1
Fine Arts Department Head								1				1					1
Kindergarten Department Head	1												1				1
Music Department Head								1				1					1
Principal of the Training School								1				1					1
Teaching of History Instructor				1											1		1
Field Trips																	
Biology Instructor	1		1				2							2			2
Director of Training (Teaches)			1													1	1
Teaching of Agriculture Instructor								1							1		1
Teaching of Elementary School Science							2									2	2
Teaching of Geography Instructor			1				2							1	1	1	3
Teaching of History Instructor				1											1		1
Teaching of Nature Study Instructor							5	1				1				5	6
Musical Activities																	
Chorus—Glee Clubs																	
Music Department			1					2				1	1			1	3

TABLE XI (*Continued*)

Training School Activities in Which College Faculty Members Participate	Frequency: With Student Teacher and Training School Children	With Critic Teacher and Training School Children			With Student Teacher, Critic Teacher, and Training School Children				With Student Teacher, Critic Teacher, Other College Instructors, and Children			Activity Initiated by						Total Number Who Participated[b]
	Once a Term	Monthly	Once a Term	Yearly	Weekly	Monthly	Once a Term	Yearly	Monthly	Once a Term	Yearly	Administration	Director of Training	College Instructor	Critic Teacher	Mutual	Parents	
Music Department Head							1									1		1
Teaching of Public School Music Instructor					1											1		1
Music Week																		
Music Department								1				1						1
Music Department Head							1							1				1
Operetta																		
Teaching of Physical Education Instructor								1			1					2		2
Teaching of Public School Music Instructor								1			1			1		1		2
Band—Orchestra																		
Teaching of Public School Instructor					1		1							2				2
Radio Programs																		
Director of Training (Does Not Teach)			1													1		1
Teaching of Public School Music Instructor			1													1		1
Song Festival																		
Teaching of History Instructor											1					1		1
Teaching of Public School Music Instructor								1			1			1		1		2
Parent-Teachers Association																		
Dean of Women										1					1			1
Directed Observation Instructor			1									1						1
Director of Training (Teaches Education Courses)						1											1	1
Director of Training (No Courses)							1					1						1
Dramatics Instructor												1						1
Early Elementary Education Instructor								1				1						1
Education Department Head	1			1													2	2
Educational Psychology Instructor		1		1							1	1	1			1		3

TABLE XI (*Continued*)

Training School Activities in Which College Faculty Members Participate	Frequency: With Student Teacher and Training School Children	With Critic Teacher and Training School Children			With Student Teacher, Critic Teacher, and Training School Children				With Student Teacher, Critic Teacher, Other College Instructors, and Children			Activity Initiated by						Total Number Who Participated[b]
	Once a Term	Monthly	Once a Term	Yearly	Weekly	Monthly	Once a Term	Yearly	Monthly	Once a Term	Yearly	Administration	Director of Training	College Instructor	Critic Teacher	Mutual	Parents	
Elementary Education Instructor (Supervises)			2^{d}			2^{d}			2^{d}						2^{d}	4		6
Home Economics Instructor				1											1			1
Physical Education and Health Department Head				2								1					1	2
President of College				1													1	1
Registrar										1						1		1
Sociology Instructor											1					1		1
Special Subject Instructors (Supervise)																		
Teaching of Physical Education Instructor			1								2	1			1	1		3
Teaching of Public School Art			1								2	1			1	1		3
Teaching of Public School Music	1		1				1			1	1	1			2	2		5
Teaching of Arithmetic Instructor											1					1		1
Teaching of Elementary School Subjects Instructor											1					1		1
Teaching of English Instructor				1				1		1		1			1		1	3
Teaching of Geography Instructor										1	1				1	1		2
Teaching of Health Instructor								1				1						1
Teaching of Nature Study Instructor				1				1							1	1		2
Teaching of Penmanship Instructor				1									1					1
Teaching of Public School Art Instructor							1										1	1
Teaching of Public School Music Instructor							1										1	1
Teaching of Reading Instructor				1									1					1
Tests and Measurements Instructor				1									1					1

TABLE XI (*Continued*)

Training School Activities in Which College Faculty Members Participate	Frequency: With Student Teacher and Training School Children	With Critic Teacher and Training School Children			With Student Teacher, Critic Teacher, and Training School Children				With Student Teacher, Critic Teacher, Other College Instructors, and Children			Activity Initiated by					Total Number Who Participated[b]
	Once a Term	Monthly	Once a Term	Yearly	Weekly	Monthly	Once a Term	Yearly	Monthly	Once a Term	Yearly	Administration	Director of Training	College Instructor	Critic Teacher	Mutual	
Publications																	
Elementary Education Instructors (Supervise)							2[d]	2[d]						2[d]	2[d]		4
English Department Head		1				2									1	1	2
Journalism Instructor					1							1					1
Teaching of English Instructor		1				1			1			1			2		3
Teaching of Public School Art Instructor		1				2	1		1			1			3		4
Teaching of Industrial Arts Instructor						1						1					1
Special Day Programs																	
Arbor Day																	
Teaching of Nature Study Instructor								1							1		1
Christmas Activities																	
English Department Head											1					1	1
Fine Arts Department								1							1		1
Music Department Head				1								1					1
Teaching of Public School Art Instructor											1	1					1
Teaching of Public School Music Instructor	1							1		1		1				2	3
Commencement																	
Music Department Head							1							1			1
Teaching of Public School Music Instructor								1								1	1
May Festival																	
English Department Head											1					1	1
Physical Education and Health Department								2			1			1		2	3
Teaching of Public School Art Instructor											1	1					1
Teaching of Public School Music Instructor								1			3	1		1		2	4

TABLE XI (*Continued*)

Training School Activities in Which College Faculty Members Participate	Frequency: With Student Teacher and Training School Children	With Critic Teacher and Training School Children			With Student Teacher, Critic Teacher, and Training School Children				With Student Teacher, Critic Teacher, Other College Instructors, and Children			Activity Initiated by					Total Number Who Participated[b]
	Once a Term	Monthly	Once a Term	Yearly	Weekly	Monthly	Once a Term	Yearly	Monthly	Once a Term	Yearly	Administration	Director of Training	College Instructor	Critic Teacher	Mutual	
Play Day																	
Physical Education and Health Department								2					1	1			2
Teaching of Physical Education Instructor								1							1		1
Units of Work																	
Fete of Nations Bazaar																	
Teaching of Public School Art Instructor											1	1					1
Educational Exhibit																	
Elementary Education Instructors (Supervise)											2[d]			2[d]			2
Teaching of Public School Art Instructor										1		1		1			2
Flower Club																	
Elementary Education Instructor (Supervises)					1									1			1
Industrial Arts Units																	
Industrial Arts Instructor						1									1		1
School Savings Bank																	
Teaching of Arithmetic Instructor		1										1					1

* No answer was received from two schools.
[a] With a music critic teacher.
[b] For number bearing each title listed, who might have participated, see Table VIII.
[c] Represents three schools (two supervisors in each).
[d] These two cases represent one institution.

of such occurrences. The instructors who have some definite position in the training school, such as director of training who teaches college courses (3 schools), general subject instructors[8] who are training school supervisors (3 schools), special subject instructors who are training school supervisors (13 schools), stand out in participation in this activity.

The music department appears most prominently, probably because of the fact that musical activities comprise the major portion of all assembly programs. In one school the entire music department took charge of this work.

In no case did a member of the college faculty indicate that he attended the assembly program unless he was officially connected in some way with the training school or had helped in the planning of a program or was asked to give a talk to the children. The following faculty members who indicated participation in the training school assembly programs did so through giving an assembly talk at the request of either the director of training or an individual critic teacher. Several of these instances are recorded under the heading "With student teacher and critic teacher jointly," because these latter persons were in attendance on the assembly program where the instructor delivered the address.

Education department head	1
English department head	2
Teaching of Elementary School Science instructor who is supervisor	1
Home Economics instructor	1
Mathematics department head	1
Physics instructor	1
Psychology department head	1
Religious Education instructor	1
Teaching of English instructor	1
Teaching of Geography instructor	2
Teaching of History instructor	1

Dramatics and Pageants. Only five schools of the 25 reported that members of the college departments participated in the presentation of training school dramatics. The following four faculty members represent one institution in which they cooperated on one dramatic

[8] Called college department instructors who supervise, elsewhere in the study.

venture, a school pageant. They are the director of training who teaches education courses; fine arts department head; music department head; and the principal of the training school who teaches Elementary Education courses.

No one of the other four schools mentioned so pretentious an undertaking or one which included more than one member of the college faculty.

Field Trips. It is evident from Table XI that the instructors in the professionalized subject matter courses in Elementary Science, Nature Study, and Agriculture recorded the larger number of the cases —nine of the sixteen. Two of the schools which have no teaching course of this type indicated that the Biology instructor took training school children on field trips. In no case did a college faculty member report that he took members of the training school faculty or training school children on a field trip oftener than once a term.

Musical Activities. Members of the college departments in nine schools recorded participation in the musical activities of the training school. Obviously the majority of these are members of the music department. Radio programs were mentioned by one school only, the two members listed reporting that they cooperated on this venture.

Most of the cases which report cooperation in the musical activities of the training school fall under the heading "With student teachers, critic teachers, other college instructors, and training school children," since these activities require joint participation. The heading which includes "Other college instructors" means another member of the same department except in the school where the Physical Education and Public School Music instructors work together on a training school operetta.

Parent-Teachers Association. Of the 49 persons who mentioned participation in the Parent-Teachers Association, 17 did so only through giving talks once a term or once a year to the members who attended these meetings. Such was true in the following 17 instances:

Dean of Women	1
Early Elementary Education instructor	1
Education department head	1
Educational Psychology instructor	2

Home Economics instructor	1
President of the college	1
Registrar	1
Sociology instructor	1
Teaching of Arithmetic instructor	1
Teaching of Elementary School Subjects instructor	1
Teaching of English instructor	1
Teaching of Geography instructor	2
Teaching of Nature Study instructor	1
Teaching of Reading instructor	1
Tests and Measurements instructor	1

All of the others signify that they helped with the organization of the programs and this with varied frequency.

Publications. Although few people (15 from eight schools) mention any cooperation regarding training school publications, those who do so participate rather frequently, the majority saying that they do so at least once a month. The four Teaching of Public School Art instructors who mentioned this type of activity said their part had to do with the illustrations and cover pages for the training school magazine which was published once a month.

One school lists three people who help training school children with their newspaper, the Teaching of English instructor, the Teaching of Public School Art instructor, and the Teaching of Industrial Arts instructor.

Another school publishes a weekly training school newspaper about which the training school children and student teachers consult the Journalism instructor weekly.

The schools which made no mention of this type of participation said that training school news was included in the regular college newspaper. Since this news was solicited by students from the director of training or various critic teachers, it did not seem to fit into this or any other table.

Special Day Programs. Christmas programs received the greatest number of markings, the larger number of these being from the fine arts and music departments and representing six institutions.

Units of Work. One school mentioned a Fete of Nations bazaar which included contributions of various types of work in the training school, but was largely composed of work from the fine arts classes. An educational exhibit, which included material from every part of the training school's curriculum for the entire year, was reported by one institution. This work was directed by the supervisor of student teaching who worked with critic teachers, demonstration teachers, and student teachers in the three schools which cooperated in the program.

The Flower Club was an individual project worked out by one of the education department instructors who supervised students in an off-campus training school. This instructor has been mentioned before as being responsible for practically all the supervision of students in this training school where critic teachers are not paid by the state. The Flower Club was an outgrowth of the language classes, this supervisor having worked directly with the children, student teachers, and the room teachers. One school described industrial arts units which became exhibits of the training school work in this field. Although the college Industrial Arts instructor was not a training school supervisor, his help was solicited by the student teachers and critic teachers. A school savings bank activity was being furthered by the Teaching of Arithmetic instructor in one school. The project had been suggested by the administration of the school.

To summarize for Table XI, only two schools made no reply to this section of the questionnaire, but in many cases participation in the activity listed included so few faculty members that participation in the extracurricular activities of the training school could hardly be said to be a significant means of cooperation between training school and college faculty. The personnel of groups engaged in these cooperative enterprises seems to be in accord with the judgment of authorities on teacher training.

	Jury I Over 1,000			Jury II 500 to 1,000			Jury III Less than 500			Mean of Juries
	P	D	M	P	D	M	P	D	M	
With student teacher and critic teacher jointly....	1.6	1.3	1.5	1.8	1.4	1.6	1.6	1.3	1.5	1.5
With student teacher, critic teacher, and members of other college departments................	2.1	2.4	2.3	1.8	2.6	2.3	1.9	2.9	2.4	2.3
With the critic teacher alone................	3.0	2.6	2.8	2.9	2.6	2.7	2.8	2.4	2.6	2.7
With the student teacher alone.................	3.3	3.7	3.5	3.5	3.3	3.4	3.8	3.3	3.6	3.5

6. By Participating in Planning and Conducting the Community Activities of the Training School

The community activities of the training school were considered as a separate section on the questionnaire since they seemed to include a larger group of people with whom the college department instructors might cooperate. Such activities as Health Clinics, Community Chests, Clean-Up Campaigns, Safety Projects, Boy and Girl Scout Activities, and Story Telling at the Library were given as suggestive headings. In addition, space was allowed for other community activities not listed by the questionnaire.

Few frequencies under any heading were listed by members of the college departments and no new types of activities were added.

The thirty cases of participation in the community activities of the training school recorded in Table XII were given by 16 schools. There is no trend with respect to departments participating, manner of participation, or frequency of participation, except that most of the frequencies appear under the category which indicates participation "With student teachers, critic teachers, and training school children jointly." This is in agreement with the jury rankings since 13 report that they participate in community activities with the student teachers, critic teachers, and training school children jointly; 6 that they do so with these three last mentioned and other college instructors; 5 that they participate with the critic teacher and training school children only; 8 that they participate with student teachers and training school children only.

These data are not too unlike the judgment of experts.

	Jury I Over 1,000			Jury II 500 to 1,000			Jury III Less than 500			Mean of Juries
	P	D	M	P	D	M	P	D	M	
With student teacher and critic teacher jointly....	1.7	1.2	1.4	1.6	1.6	1.6	1.6	1.3	1.5	1.5
With student teacher, critic teacher, and members of other college departments................	2.0	2.6	2.4	2.5	2.2	2.3	1.6	2.4	2.0	2.7
With the critic teacher alone................	2.9	2.5	2.7	2.8	2.7	2.7	3.0	2.6	2.8	2.8
With the student teacher alone................	3.3	3.7	3.5	3.1	3.5	3.4	3.8	3.7	3.7	3.5

TABLE XII

Frequency with Which College Instructors Participate in Planning and Conducting Community Activities of the Training School[a]

Faculty Members	Frequency: With Student Teacher and Training School Children				With Critic Teacher and Training School Children			With Student Teacher, Critic Teacher and Training School Children				With Student Teacher, Critic Teacher, Training School Children, and Other College Instructors		Activity Initiated by								Total Number Who Participated[b]
	Weekly	Monthly	Once a Term	Yearly	Monthly	Once a Term	Yearly	Weekly	Twice a Term	Once a Term	Yearly	Once a Term	Yearly	Administration	College Instructor	Critic Teacher	Mutual	Community	Director of Training	Reading Instructor	Scout Leader	
Boy and Girl Scout Activities																						
Director of Training (Teaches)					1	1											1	1				2
Education Department Instructor (Supervises)		1													1							1
Physical Education Director		1																			1	1
Teaching of Physical Education Instructor				1	1						1			1								1
Community Chest																						
Director of Training			1		1[a]									1			1[a]					2
Fine Arts Department Head													1		1							1
Music Department Head													1		1							1
Community Entertainments																						
Dramatics Instructor											1							1				1
Music Department											1							1				1
Teaching of Public School Music Instructor			1								1	1			2			1				3
Health Clinic																						
School Nurse					1					1		1		1			1					2
Teaching of Elementary Science Instructor			1														1					1
Teaching of Physical Education Instructor							1			1	2				1		2		1			4

TABLE XII (*Continued*)

Faculty Members	Frequency: With Student Teacher and Training School Children				With Critic Teacher and Training School Children			With Student Teacher, Critic Teacher and Training School Children				With Student Teacher, Critic Teacher, Training School Children, and Other College Instructors		Activity Initiated by								Total Number Who Participated[b]
	Weekly	Monthly	Once a Term	Yearly	Monthly	Once a Term	Yearly	Weekly	Twice a Term	Once a Term	Yearly	Once a Term	Yearly	Administration	College Instructor	Critic Teacher	Mutual	Community	Director of Training	Reading Instructor	Scout Leader	
Patriotic Pageants																						
Teaching of Physical Education Instructor											1								1			1
Teaching of Public School Art Instructor									1						1							1
Safety Project																						
Teaching of Elementary Science Instructor													1				1					1
Story Telling at the Library																						
Children's Librarian	1							2							1	2						3
Librarian		1						1						1	1							2
Speech Instructor													1							1		1

* No answer was received from nine schools.
[a] Director of training teaches courses in education department.
[b] For number bearing each title listed, who might have participated, see Table VI.

There is no trend as to who initiated this participation in community activities, since eight different titles are listed under the heading "Activity initiated by."

According to the weight assigned this type of cooperative activity by the juries, Table X should receive fewer frequencies than most of the other items in the score card, but should receive at least as many as Table IX.

7. *By Aiding in Planning and Conducting Experiments and New Techniques in the Training School*

Most of the writers who have proposed an ideal plan of coordination between the campus training school and college faculties suggest cooperative planning and conducting of training school experiments in such fields as types of teaching, use of new materials, course of study units, and the content of student teaching. Notable among these suggestions is one made by Dr. Evenden: "Normal school instructors should be encouraged to 'try out' various methods of instruction (conduct simple experiments) in cooperation with the training school teachers. In such experiments the actual teaching involved should be done by the 'teaching specialists.' "[9]

The Louisiana Survey[10] recommends that "differences of opinion as to method can be made the center of experimentation."

One of the fifteen constructive proposals for cooperation between the training school and subject matter instructors made by Miss Lenora Johnson is "The training school should be considered the central department of the institution and the testing laboratory of every other department." [11]

The Garrison and Eubank questionnaire studies regarding experimentation as a cooperative training school function further validate the inclusion of this item in the present study. Dr. Eubank found that "Members of the college faculty do research work regularly in

[9] Evenden, E. S. "Cooperation of Teachers of Academic Subjects with the Training School." *Supervisors of Student Teaching Yearbook*, 1925, pp. 5–8.

[10] Bagley, W. C., Alexander, T. and Foote, J. *Report of a Special Commission on the Professional Education of White Public School Teachers in Louisiana*, p. 191, 1923.

[11] Johnson, Lenora E. "Constructive Proposals for Cooperation Between the Training School and Subject-Matter Instructors." *The Virginia Teacher*, February, 1931, p. 35.

the laboratory schools in 14.7 per cent of the colleges, occasionally in 50.7 per cent, and never in 34.6 per cent."[12]

Table XIII of the present study shows that 19 of the schools visited listed one or more cooperative training school experiments. These have been grouped together as to subjects since the majority were related to some one field of study in the training school. English, reading, fine arts, and music experiments seem to predominate in this subject list.

Three ways in which these experiments might have been conducted were listed on the questionnaire but only two received frequencies, the majority appearing under the category, "Through individual conference with critic teacher."

	Jury I Over 1,000			Jury II 500 to 1,000			Jury III Less than 500			Mean of Juries
	P	D	M	P	D	M	P	D	M	
As members of a general curriculum committee composed of representatives of each college department and the training school............	2.1	2.0	2.0	2.1	1.9	2.0	1.8	1.8	1.8	1.9
As members of subject committees which confer with the training school faculty on their own subject only..............	1.8	1.7	1.8	1.8	2.0	1.9	1.9	2.0	1.9	1.9
Through individual conferences with the critic teachers..............	2.1	2.3	2.2	2.1	2.1	2.1	2.4	2.2	2.3	2.2

The tendency was for these conferences to be held as often as once a week or once a month, rather than once a term or once a year. Another noticeable trend is that the college instructor usually initiated the activity instead of the college administration directing them to do so.

Certain of these experiments were considered of such importance in the work of these schools that they deserve special discussion. An example is the third English experiment listed, which involved the use of a mimeographed textbook in each grade in the training school.

[12] Eubank, L. A. *The Organization and Administration of Laboratory Schools in State Teachers Colleges.* Northeast Missouri State Teachers College Bulletin, April, 1931, p. 60.

TABLE XIII[a]

Frequency with Which Members of the College Department Aid in Planning and Conducting Experiments or New Techniques in the Training School*

Experiments or New Techniques Which College Faculty Members Helped Plan and Conduct in the Training School	College Faculty Members Who Participated with Critic Teachers[b]	Through Individual Conference with Critic Teacher				Activity Initiated by				
		Weekly	Monthly	Once a Term	Yearly	Administration	College Isntructor	Critic Teacher	Director of Training	Mutua
Arithmetic Experiments[g]										
Error control in number material	Director of Training[c] and Third Grade Critic	1							1	
Use of cards for problem solving	Teaching of Arithmetic Instructor				1					1
English Experiments										
Correction of speech defects with Training School children[i]	Dramatics Instructor, Kindergarten Critic	1								1
Creative writing in the elementary grades	English Department Head and Student Teachers		1				1			
Experimental use of data to be included in a new textbook for elementary grades	Teaching of English Instructor and Grade Supervisors[e]	1					1			
Stimulation of verse and prose writing	Elementary Education Instructor (Training School Supervisor)	1					1			
Poetry clubs in elementary grades	Teaching of English Instructor		1							1
Teaching of grammar in the seventh grade	Teaching of English Instructor, Seventh Grade Critic	1					1			
Use of the Training School as a laboratory for dramatics class	Dramatics Instructor, Second and Sixth Grade Critic	1					1			
Fine Arts Experiments										
Art activities related to geography, history, and literature	Teaching of Public School Art Instructor[d]		1				1			
Art appreciation through picture study and music correlation; free illustration with crayon and paint	Teaching of Public School Art Instructor,[d] Critic Teachers Grades 1 to 4	1					1			
Correlated activities in the arts	Teaching of Public School Art Instructor, Teaching of Public School Music Instructor, Head of Manual Training Department		1				1			
Handmade Training School yearbook by children	Teaching of Public School Art Instructor,[d] and Seventh Grade Critic Teacher		1					1		
New uses of art materials with Training School children	Fine Arts Department Head		1				1			

TABLE XIII[a] (*Continued*)

Experiments or New Techniques Which College Faculty Members Helped Plan and Conduct in the Training School	College Faculty Members Who Participated with Critic Teachers[b]	Through Individual Conference with Critic Teacher				Activity Initiated by				
		Weekly	Monthly	Once a Term	Yearly	Administration	College Instructor	Critic Teacher	Director of Training	Mutual
"Under Sea Life" project	Art Department, and Fifth Grade Critic Teacher			1						1
Geography Experiments[f]										
Geography tests for finding children's interests; constructed and used to check the new Units of Work Course of Study in Geography[i]	Geography Department Head; Fourth to Eighth Grade Critic Teachers				1		1			
Seventh grade geography experiment[i]	Teaching of Geography Instructor and Seventh Grade Critic	1					1			
Units of work in the Teaching of Geography	Geography Department	1								1
Use of mimeographed textbook built around units of work	Teaching of Geography Instructor; Director of Training		1							1
Materials of Instruction Experiments										
Use of recent textbooks in reading and social studies, etc.	Director of Training			1					1	
Music[f]										
Christmas vesper service by Training School children[j]	Director of Training;[c] Principal of Training School[e]				1		1			
Creative music in the elementary grades	Teaching of Public School Music Instructor[d]		1				1			
Creative music through original song writing	College Music Classes, Teaching of Public School Music Instructor,[d] Student teachers[d]		1				1			
Improvement of music instruction in the Training School	Teaching of Public School Music Instructor[d]		1				1			
Intermediate grades boys' chorus[j]	Teaching of Public School Music Instructor[d]		1				1			
Rhythm band in third and fourth grades	Teaching of Public School Music Instructor[d] Third and Fourth Grade Critic Teacher	1								1
Teaching children to read music without using syllables	Music Department Head, Music Critic Teacher, student teachers	1					1			
Teaching songs with aid of piano to those incapable of learning without much aid	Teaching of Public School Music Instructor[d]		1				1			
Physical Education Experiment										
New method in teaching rhythm to children	Teaching of Physical Education Instructor,[d] Student Teachers	1					1			

TABLE XIII[a] *(Continued)*

Experiments or New Techniques Which College Faculty Members Helped Plan and Conduct in the Training School	College Faculty Members Who Participated with Critic Teachers[b]	Through Individual Conference with Critic Teacher				Activity Initiated by				
		Weekly	Monthly	Once a Term	Yearly	Administration	College Instructor	Critic Teacher	Director of Training	Mutual
Reading Experiments[kf]										
Diagnostic and remedial work in reading and arithmetic	Teaching of Reading Instructor, Director of Training, Principal of the Training School	I					I			
Extensive primary reading program for individual pupils	Elementary Education Instructor (Training School Supervisor) First Grade Critic Teacher	I					I			
Improvement in methods of teaching reading at differentiated levels	Teaching of Reading Instructor (Training School Supervisor)	I					I			
Reading tests	Educational Psychology Instructor	I							I	
Reading experiment in grades 4 to 8 conducted by Psychology of Reading class in college	Psychology of Reading Instructor, Tests and Measurements Instructor, and Fourth to Eighth Grade Critic Teachers		I						I	
"Library corners" in each room of the Training School	Director of Training[e]; Librarian			I					I	
Science for Elementary Grades										
Experimental course of study in elementary science	Science Department Head	I					I			
Experimental use of science units in the elementary grades[i]	College Science Instructor		I				I			
Method of teaching nature study to primary children	Teaching of Nature Study Instructor	I					I			
Science experiments in the use of microscopes with children, and in the feeding of rats	Biology Instructor, Student Teachers		I							I
Science project—"Aquarium," and "Bees"	Science Department, Art Department, Fifth and Sixth Grade Critic Teachers, English Department	I								I
Teaching units in physical science to primary children	Teaching of Physical Science Instructor, and Student Teachers		I				I			
Social Studies[kf]										
An attempt to measure character development	Social Science Instructor, Intermediate Grade Critic Teachers		I				I			
Correlation of various social studies	Social Science Instructor, and Grade Supervisors[e]		I				I			
Student Teaching										
Correlation between grades in technique of teaching, and student teaching[i]	Technique of Teaching Instructor				I		I			

TABLE XIII[a] (*Continued*)

Experiments or New Techniques Which College Faculty Members Helped Plan and Conduct in the Training School	College Faculty Members Who Participated with Critic Teachers[b]	Through Individual Conference with Critic Teacher				Activity Initiated by				
		Weekly	Monthly	Once a Term	Yearly	Administration	College Instructor	Critic Teacher	Director of Training	Mutual
Having students in methods classes teach children in the training school prior to the student teaching period[i]	Early Elementary Education Instructor and Primary Critic Teachers		I				I			
Laboratory plan of student teaching	President of College, Director of Training, Education Department, Student Teachers	I				I				
Reorganization of the content of student teaching	Director of Training[e]; all departments			I		I				
Types of advanced observation	Director of Training[e]; Psychology Instructor			I		I				
Types of freshman observation	Director of Training[e]; Psychology Instructor				I				I	
Teaching Children "How to Study" Experiments										
Group study plan	Director of Training[e]	I							I	
Program for training in how to study	Director of Training[e]			I					I	
Socialized recitation—group study plan	Teaching of Geography Instructor; Sixth and Seventh Grade Critic Teachers	I						I		
Units of Work Experiments[h]										
Puppet show	Art, English, History, Music Departments and Sixth Grade Critic Teacher			I						I
Units of work organization in the training school: farm unit, health unit, library unit	Director of Training; Librarian; Teaching of Public School Art Instructor[d]; President of Institution			I					I	

* No experiments listed by six institutions; six other institutions listed only one experiment.

[a] Another category, As a member of a special subject committee, was included on the questionnaire, but since it received no frequencies, has been omitted from this table.

[b] Unless otherwise noted, each training school critic teacher participated in this work.

[c] This training school staff member teaches courses in the education department.

[d] This instructor is also designated as a training school supervisor in this field.

[e] Called grade supervisors because they carry a heavy teaching load of college courses, in addition to doing the work of critic teachers.

[f] See Fine Arts Experiments.

[g] See first listing in Reading Experiments.

[h] See also sixth Fine Arts Experiments, third and fourth Geography Experiments, and fifth Science Experiments.

[i] This is the only cooperative experiment listed by this institution.

[j] Cooperative experiments in music only were listed by this institution. Two were listed.

[k] See listing under Materials of Instruction Experiment.

One series of English textbooks published by this college instructor was in general use throughout the United States. The experimental data being used at the time of this survey were to be incorporated in a revision of these textbooks. After two or three years' trial, the revised textbook, which would incorporate the suggestions of the critic teachers, was to be published by the Teaching of English instructor.

Another experiment which was described in detail to the writer was one in which the Teaching of Public School Art instructor was correlating her fine arts course of study with the units in geography, history, and literature. This experiment was an attempt to unify all the fine arts work of the training school with the activities curriculum.

The geography department in one of the teachers colleges visited had spent the entire year in the construction of a new textbook in geography built around the units of work plan. This textbook was being used in mimeographed form in the campus training school under the guidance of the critic teachers and the head of the geography department who offered the professionalized subject matter course in that field. This latter instructor directed the construction and administration of a battery of geography tests for finding children's interests in this field. These tests were a check against the new course of study mentioned above and were the product of mutual suggestions given by the critic teachers and the geography department.

Another institution which stressed experimental work in geography between the training school and the college department listed a seventh grade geography experiment. This was an attempt to stress the units of work organization rather than the separate subject emphasis which had formerly been characteristic of the work of that grade.

Every instructor in one of the institutions visited made some mention of the extensive reading experiment which had been inaugurated in the campus training school. This institution offers several courses in the Teaching of Reading, and the director of this work had been conducting a remedial clinic in which his advanced major students were giving individual instruction to children with a specific reading disability. This experiment is the first one listed under the reading group, weekly participation by the college instructor in it being recorded.

Science, as a separate subject in the elementary school curriculum, seemed to be the center of interest in several of the schools, as is evidenced by the number of experiments in this field.

Various plans of conducting student teaching were described under this section. Each of these experiments was also listed in the section which asked for cooperative college department experiments. Since the work is done in the training school rather than in college classes, the experiments have been included here. Notable among these is one in which student teaching is entered upon before the completion of major courses in Early and Later Elementary Education. These college students have no contact with the training school until the last year of their course. They then begin directed teaching and, as questions regarding technique arise, they go to the Early and Later Elementary Education instructors for guidance. These instructors also observe the teaching of these student teachers, as has been described in Chapter II in the discussion of Table III. This is an education department experiment although it was suggested by the administration of the school and the details were worked out by a general curriculum committee.

A teacher training institution which limits its enrollment to from 700 to 800 students contributed the last three of the student teaching experiments listed. One of these was a reorganization of the content of student teaching as to length, units to be stressed, and gradual induction from participation to responsible room teaching. The content of the observation courses for freshmen and advanced students was being reorganized in this institution under the guidance of the director of training who taught several sections of these courses, entitled Introduction to Teaching and Technique of Teaching.

A detailed explanation of the second student teaching experiment in Table XIII was given to the writer both in discussion and in manuscript form. The Early Elementary Education instructor in the institution represented was inaugurating participation teaching in the methods class for the term before the student enrolled for the course in Directed Teaching. Briefly, the formula for this work was:

1. The critic teacher in the training school taught for observation by this class a lesson which had been planned in a joint conference with the college instructor, the college class, and the critic teacher.

2. At the next meeting of the class, the critic teacher was present for the discussion of the outcome of the lesson.

3. After a lapse of several days, the college instructor again took the class to the training school to observe. All were prepared to teach a lesson similar in type to the one observed previously. One student was selected at the beginning of this meeting to teach for the observers.

4. After this experimental lesson, a third joint meeting was held which the critic teacher attended.

To summarize, no attempt has been made to include similar experiments under one title but rather to list each one separately under a subject heading. This is particularly evident in experiments regarding elementary school science. This technique was used in Table XIII because the writer felt that the reader would prefer a specific list of the titles as given by the various institutions and because the group of instructors participating in a given experiment differed for each experiment.

CHAPTER V

PARTICIPATION OF MEMBERS OF THE COLLEGE DEPARTMENTS IN THE FUNCTIONS OF THE TRAINING SCHOOL (*CONTINUED*)

C. By Having College Classes Observe Teaching Done by Critic Teachers in the Training School

Having college classes observe the teaching of critic teachers in the training school is a rather generally accepted method of cooperation between the departments of theory and practice in a teacher training institution.

The following quotations from the professional literature of the field substantiate this statement:

1. Have all special demonstration lessons arranged for through the director of practice. The details of the lesson should be worked out at a conference between the subject-matter teacher desiring the lesson, the demonstration teacher and the director of practice.[1]

2. Every subject-matter and every theory course in a teachers' college should contribute to the training of teachers and should be closely related to the training school through observation, demonstration, and participation. . . .

   The teaching of children in the training school for observation, demonstration, and regular classroom work should be done by "expert teachers of children."[2]

3. The observation and demonstration work that is done for college (theory and subject-matter) classes should be a cooperative undertaking of the training supervisor and the college instructor concerned.[3]

[1] Evenden, E. S. "Cooperation of Teachers of Academic Subjects with the Training School." *Supervisors of Student Teaching Yearbook,* 1925, p. 8.

[2] Johnson, Lenora E. "Constructive Proposals for Cooperation Between the Training School and Subject-Matter Instructors." *The Virginia Teacher,* February, 1931, p. 35.

[3] Garrison, N. L. *Status and Work of the Training Supervisor,* pp. 76-98. Contributions to Education, No. 280. Bureau of Publications, Teachers College, Columbia University, 1927.

1. By Preparing for Observation in the Training School

A great variety of titles was given to the courses in Directed Observation, but for purposes of condensing the table these have been included under headings which would make the content of the course obvious. For instance, the title Directed Observation includes courses with the following titles:

Observation and Teaching
Technique of Teaching and School Management
Observation and Participation
Directed Observation
Directed Observation and Practice Teaching
Technique of Teaching for Elementary Teachers
Observation; Demonstration
Fundamentals of Method
Preparation for Teaching in Elementary Schools

Every school reported some cooperative preparation for observation in the training school under this section of the questionnaire, although such preparation varied greatly as to frequency. Table XIV shows that a large number of these instructors are members of the education department. Eight of this group are directors of training who teach courses in the education department and ten others are training school supervisors as well as college instructors of education courses. Three schools report that the principal of the training school, who teaches Directed Observation, participates in the activity being discussed. Each of these institutions also employs a director of training who offers college courses.

One school, which was a notable exception to the above statement, requires that every college instructor who offers a course in professionalized subject matter must observe in the training school each semester. Consequently, instructors in the following courses report that they engage in cooperative planning for observation under the second category: Introduction to Teaching,[4] Teaching of Arithmetic, Teaching of English, Teaching of Geography, Teaching of Health, Teaching of History, Teaching of Reading.

The majority of the college faculty members who report that they engage in some definite preparation for observation with their college

[4] This instructor is head of the education department.

TABLE XIV

Frequency with Which College Instructors Prepare for Observation When They Bring Their College Classes to Observe Teaching Done by Critic Teachers in the Training School

Faculty Members	Frequency: Plans for Observation with College Class Only[g]					Plans for Observation with Both College Class and Critic Teacher in Separate Conference							Plans for Observation with Critic Teacher and College Class in a Joint Conference					Activity Initiated by			Total Number Who Reported
	Twice Weekly	Weekly	Twice Monthly	Monthly	Once a Term	Twice Weekly	Weekly	Twice Monthly	Four per Quarter	Monthly	Twice a Term	Once a Term	Daily	Twice Weekly	Weekly	Monthly	Once a Term	Administration	College Instructor	Mutual	
Children's Literature Instructor										2								2			2
College Department Instructors (Supervisors)																					
Psychology of Elementary School Subjects[c]										1									1		1
Teaching of Elementary School Subjects							2[a]		2[a]	4[b]								4[b]	4[b]		8
Tests and Measurements[c]								1											1		1
Director of Training (Teaches Education Courses)																					
Directed Observation	1[d]											1							2		2
Directed Observation (Advanced)						1												1			1
Elementary Curriculum															1				1		1
Introduction to Teaching										1							1	1	1		2
Teaching of Elementary School Subjects				1															1		1
Technique of Teaching							1												1		1
Fine Arts Department Head										1[k]		1							1	1[k]	2
General Education Course Instructor																					
Classroom Management				1															1		1
Directed Observation						2		1										1	2		3
Directed Observation (Advanced)							1												1		1
Early Elementary Education							2[h]			1					1[h]			1	2[h]		3
Educational Psychology					1		1			1							1	1	3		4
Introduction to Teaching							1	1										1	1		2
Kindergarten Education												1							1		1
Later Elementary Education		1					1											1	1		2
Principles of Education				1						2[e]							1	1[e]	3		4
Professional Adjustment																	1		1		1
Psychology of Elementary School Subjects												1						1			1
Rural Education				1						1		1						1	1		2
Supervision of Instruction																			1		1

TABLE XIV (*Continued*)

Faculty Members	Frequency: Plans for Observation with College Class Only[g]					Plans for Observation with Both College Class and Critic Teacher in Separate Conference							Plans for Observation with Critic Teacher and College Class in a Joint Conference					Activity Initiated by			Total Number Who Reported
	Twice Weekly	Weekly	Twice Monthly	Monthly	Once a Term	Twice Weekly	Weekly	Twice Monthly	Four per Quarter	Monthly	Twice a Term	Once a Term	Daily	Twice Weekly	Weekly	Monthly	Once a Term	Administration	College Instructor	Mutual	
Teaching of Elementary School Subjects						2		1			1	1				1		2	4		6
Teaching of the Common Branches[i]				1														1			1
Technique of Teaching								1		1								1	1		2
Tests and Measurements																	1	1			1
Industrial Arts Instructor												1						1			1
Music Department Head							1												1		1
Principal of Training School (Teaches Directed Observation)	1			1[j]			1											2	1		3
Teaching of Arithmetic Instructor				1			3	1				2						4	3		7
Teaching of English Instructor			1				2			3		2						3	5		8
Teaching of Geography Instructor							1	1		3		3					1	3	4	2	9
Teaching of Health Instructor							1			1								2			2
Teaching of History Instructor			1							1		2						2	2		4
Teaching of Nature Study Instructor										1		1		1				3			3
Teaching of Penmanship Instructor												1						1			1
Teaching of Public School Art Instructor							1		1	2						1		3	2		5
Teaching of Public School Music Instructor										1						1		2			2
Teaching of Reading Instructor		1	1		1		1			3				1				4	4		8
Total	2	2	3	7	2	5	20	7	3	30	1	18		2	2	3	6	51	58	3	112

[a] These two persons are in same school.
[b] These four persons represent two schools.
[c] Educational Psychology and Tests and Measurements instructors from same school.
[d] This instructor prepares for observation three times per week.
[e] This instructor teaches Principles of Teaching.
[f] These college instructors who are training school supervisors do the teaching for their classes to observe.
[g] Arrangements for observation made with the director of training.
[h] One Early Elementary Education instructor plans for observation under categories 2 and 3. See Experiment, Table XIII.
[i] This course taught by five instructors in one school (each instructor teaching several sections of the course).
[j] The college class observes the teaching of student teachers.
[k] Plans with the art supervisor in the training school.

classes, indicate that they do so with both the college class and the critic teacher, but in separate conferences. Eighty-four of the 112 total cases make such a report. This manner of preparing for observation was ranked second by the juries; such planning in a joint conference was ranked first. Twelve instructors indicated that they planned for observation in a joint conference with the critic teacher and the college class, rather than with each separately.

The Early Elementary Education instructor in one institution described a plan of preparation for observation which has also been listed in Table XIII as a student teaching experiment. This instructor checked a frequency under each of the two above-mentioned categories because she planned with the critic teacher and her college class separately once a week and, in addition, held a joint conference with these two regarding a proposed demonstration lesson.

Sixteen out of the total 112 cases reported that their method of planning for observation was with the college class, except when arranging for such observation through the office of the director of training. One institution gave a detailed reason for this type of planning. A course called The Teaching of the Common Branches is required of all students who are completing work for a one-year certificate. Many sections of this course are taught each semester but, because only one training school is available for observation purposes, this work must be arranged to accommodate large groups. The head of the education department and the director of training plan a series of observations when several sections of this college course may observe at one time. Various critic teachers do this teaching; consequently it is impossible for each individual college instructor to plan in advance with the individual critic teachers.

Two of the directors of training who teach college courses report that their only method of planning is with their college class and through notifying the critic teacher that a demonstration lesson is expected at a scheduled hour. The details of the lesson are not planned cooperatively with a critic teacher in one case because the director of training, who offers courses in the Teaching of Elementary School Subjects, usually does the teaching himself or observes the work of student teachers. This institution uses a city school for practice purposes; the room teachers are not paid by the state and hence do no demonstration teaching for the teachers college.

Two training school principals who offer courses in Directed Observation reported that they planned for this observation with the college class only. One school explained the lack of any other type of preparation as due to the fact that no critic teachers are employed in this institution, student teachers in their senior year doing responsible teaching in the training school under the supervision of Early and Later Elementary Education instructors. This meant that the Directed Observation classes observed the teaching of student teachers rather than of critic teachers.

The other training school principal reported that he was so closely in touch with what was being taught in each room of the training school that it was unnecessary to plan for special demonstration work.

A course in Directed Observation is taught by the critic teachers in three of the schools. No record was made in this table for these cases since the planning and follow up of this work would not be a cooperative enterprise between the college and training school faculties. In like manner, the observation work done in Early and Later Elementary Education courses which are taught by critic teachers is not recorded. Many college instructors from the special departments of fine arts, music, and physical education, who are also training school supervisors, indicated that they took college classes to the training school to observe. Since these college classes would be observing the teaching of this instructor or of major students in these fields, no cooperative planning could be done and therefore no record of this type of observation is recorded in Tables XIV, XV, and XVI.

In cases where the college instructors in fine arts, music, and physical education observe the work of the special critic teacher, the record of cooperative planning is included in Table XIV. Of the eight institutions which have an art critic teacher in the training school, five report that the Teaching of Public School Art instructor plans for observation with this critic teacher. In one additional school, the fine arts department head plans with this critic teacher. Only one institution reported that the fine arts department head planned for observation with the special supervisor who is both a member of the college art department and teaches training school children for demonstration purposes.

TABLE XV

Frequency with Which College Instructors Who Have College Classes Observe Teaching Done by Critic Teachers in the Training School

Faculty Members	Frequency: Sends Classes to Do Undirected and Unscheduled Observation in Training School			Sends Classes Unaccompanied to Observe Scheduled Demonstration Units						Accompanies Classes When They Observe							Activity Initiated by			Total Number Who Observed
	Weekly	Monthly	Once a Term	Daily	Twice Weekly	Weekly	Twice Monthly	Monthly	Once a Term	Twice Weekly	Weekly	Twice Monthly	Four per Quarter	Monthly	Twice a Term	Once a Term	Administration	College Instructor	Mutual	
Children's Literature Instructor		1[i]						1[i]				1[i]		1			2[i]			2
College Department Instructors (Supervisors)																				
Psychology of Elementary School Subjects[f]							1											1		1
Teaching of Elementary School Subjects								2[d]			2[d]		2[d]	2[d]			6[a]	2[d]		8
Tests and Measurements[f]												1						1		1
Director of Training (Teaches Education Courses)																				
Directed Observation			1							1[b]							1	1		2
Directed Observation (Advanced)					1[i]					1[i]							1[i]			1
Elementary Curriculum											1						1			1
Introduction to Teaching					1[i]									1		1[i]	1[i]	1		2
Teaching of Elementary School Subjects												1						1		1
Technique of Teaching											1						1			1
Fine Arts Department Head			2[ib]											1[i]		1[b]		2		2
General Education Course Instructor																				
Classroom Management						1[g]		1										2		2
Directed Observation										2		1					3			3
Directed Observation (Advanced)											1							1		1
Early Elementary Education	1[i]							1[i]		1[i]	1[e]					1	2[e]	1		3
Educational Psychology	1[i]							1[i]			1	1				2	3[i]	2		5
Introduction to Teaching					1[i]						1[i]	1					1[i]	1		2
Kindergarten Education																1		1		1
Later Elementary Education	1[i]							1[i]		1[i]	1						1[i]	1		2
Principles of Education														3[c]		1	3	1		4
Professional Adjustment																1		1		1
Psychology of Elementary School Subjects																1	1			1
Rural Education		1[i]						1[i]	1					2[i]			2[i]	1		3
Supervision of Instruction														1				1		1
Teaching of Elementary School Subjects								1[i]		2	1	1		1[i]	1	1	4	3[i]		7
Teaching of the Common Branches														1			1			1

TABLE XV (*Continued*)

Faculty Members	Frequency																Activity Initiated by			Total Number Who Observed
	Sends Classes to Do Undirected and Unscheduled Observation in Training School			Sends Classes Unaccompanied to Observe Scheduled Demonstration Units						Accompanies Classes When They Observe										
	Weekly	Monthly	Once a Term	Daily	Twice Weekly	Weekly	Twice Monthly	Monthly	Once a Term	Twice Weekly	Weekly	Twice Monthly	Four per Quarter	Monthly	Twice a Term	Once a Term	Administration	College Instructor	Mutual	
Technique of Teaching												1		1			1	1		2
Tests and Measurements			1[i]						2[i]							2[i]	1	2[i]		3
Industrial Arts Instructor																1	1			1
Music Department Head											1							1		1
Physical Education and Health Department Head					1												1			1
Principal of Training School (Teaches Directed Observation)	1[i]			1[b]		1[i]					2[ib]			1			2[ib]	1		3
Teaching of Arithmetic Instructor								1			4				1	2	6	2		8
Teaching of Elementary School Science Instructor											1					1	2			2
Teaching of English Instructor	3[ib]				1[i]					1[b]	2			1	1	1	5[b]	3[i]		8
Teaching of Geography Instructor			1			1[i]			1		1	1		3[i]	1	2	4[i]	5[i]	1	10
Teaching of Health Instructor		1[i]						1[i]	1		1			1[i]			3[i]			3
Teaching of History Instructor											1			1	1	2	4	1		5
Teaching of Nature Study Instructor										1				1		1	3			3
Teaching of Penmanship Instructor																1	1			1
Teaching of Public School Art Instructor		2[h]						2[h]			1		1	3[h]			3[h]	2		5
Teaching of Public School Music Instructor		1[i]						1[i]						2[i]			2[i]			2
Teaching of Reading Instructor	1[i]	1								1	2[i]			4		1	6[i]	3		9
Teaching of Social Studies Instructor											1						1			1
Teaching of Spelling Instructor																1		1		1
Total	8	7	5	1	5	3	1	14	5	11	27	9	3	31	5	25	80	47	1	128

[a] These six cases represent three institutions.
[b] Observes three times a week.
[c] One instructor teaches Principles of Teaching.
[d] These two cases represent one institution.
[e] One Early Elementary Education instructor plans for observation under categories 2 and 3. See Experiment, Table XIII.
[f] Educational Psychology and Tests and Measurements instructors from same school.
[g] This instructor did not record any type of preparation for observation. See Table XIV.
[h] Two cases under more than one category.
[i] One case appears under more than one category in this table.

Of the seven schools which have a music critic teacher, three college department instructors in Music plan cooperatively for observation. Again, of the six schools which have a critic teacher in physical education, no member of the college department reports cooperative planning for observation.

A summary seems necessary for these three departments in schools which have no special critic teachers but a supervisor who is also a member of the college department. With but one exception (fine arts department head mentioned above), no member of these college departments planned with the special supervisor for observation in the training school. This was explained by the fact that in every case the special supervisor taught the college course in Professionalized Subject Matter and therefore was the only one who conducted observation work in the training school.

The section, "Activity initiated by" in Table XIV reveals no trend, since 51 of the cases say that the administration is responsible for this type of preparation and 59 say that it was initiated by the college instructor. Only three cases report the preparation as the outcome of mutual agreement.

2. *By Taking College Classes to Observe Teaching Done by Critic Teachers in the Training School*

Although three methods by which college classes might observe the teaching done by critic teachers have been indicated, the third category, "Accompanies classes when they observe," was the one receiving the most frequencies. The majority of the schools indicated that the number of observations of this type per term was worked out at the beginning of each term and ranged from twice a week to once a term.

The following instructors indicated that, though they accompanied their classes for scheduled demonstration units, they also sent them unaccompanied to observe scheduled demonstration units and to do undirected and unscheduled observation in the training school.

*Children's Literature instructor	1
*Early Elementary Education instructor	1
*Later Elementary Education instructor	1
Principal of the training school who teaches Directed Observation	1

*Rural Education instructor	1
*Teaching of Health instructor	1
*Teaching of Public School Art instructor	2
*Teaching of Public School Music instructor	1
Tests and Measurements instructor	1

* The instructors who are starred represent the same institution in which it is the policy for observation to be conducted in the three ways listed. The star by the Teaching of Public School Art instructor refers to only one case of the two listed.

The nine instructors who report that, in addition to accompanying their classes for scheduled demonstration units, they send them to observe by means of one or the other of the other two methods listed in Table XV are:

First Category in Table XV	*Second Category in Table XV*
Fine arts department head 2 cases	†Director of training who teaches Advanced Directed Observation
*Teaching of English instructor	Director of training who teaches Introduction to Teaching
*Teaching of Reading instructor	Kindergarten Education Instructor
	†Principal of training school who teaches Directed Observation
	Teaching of Geography instructor

* These two instructors represent the same institution.
† These two instructors represent the same institution.

Instructors from 14 different schools record that they never accompany their students when they observe. They are listed below showing whether their students do undirected and unscheduled observation or observe scheduled demonstration units.

First Category Only	*Second Category Only*	*Both First and Second Categories*
Director of training who teaches Directed Observation	Classroom Management instructor (2 cases)	Educational Psychology instructor
Teaching of English instructor	Physical education department head	Teaching of English instructor
Teaching of Geography instructor	Psychology of Elementary School Subjects instructor who is a training school supervisor	
Teaching of Reading instructor	Rural Education instructor	
	Teaching of Arithmetic instructor	
	Teaching the Elementary School Subjects instructor who is a training school supervisor (2 cases)	
	Teaching of Geography instructor	
	Teaching of Health instructor	
	Tests and Measurements instructor	

The following instructors are listed in Table XV who did not appear in Table XIV. These instructors mention no definite type of cooperative preparation for observation because they feel free to go to the training school at any time to observe, without previously notifying the training school staff. It follows that no change in the work of the training school would be made for the benefit of these instructors and classes.

*Classroom Management instructor	1
*Educational Psychology instructor	1
*Physical Education department head	1
*Rural Education instructor	1
Teaching of Arithmetic instructor	1
Teaching of Elementary School Science instructor	2
Teaching of Elementary School Subjects instructor	1
*Teaching of Geography instructor	1
Teaching of History instructor	1
Teaching the Social Studies instructor	1
Teaching of Spelling instructor	1
*Tests and Measurements instructor	2
*Teaching of Health instructor	1
Teaching of Reading instructor	1

* The cases which are starred represent instructors who do not accompany their college classes when they observe in the training school. Only one Tests and Measurements instructor is starred.

Some conclusions which may be drawn from Table XV are:

1. The college instructors who have their students observe the teaching of critic teachers in the training school usually accompany the class when such observation is done. The frequency with which they accompany their classes in such observation ranges from twice weekly to once a term; 31 of the 128 cases recording once a month; 27, once a week; and 25, once a term.

2. The majority of the instructors who participate in this type of observation are members of the education department.

3. The administration of the school was responsible for this observation in 80, or 62 per cent, of the total cases. The college instructor initiated the activity in 47, or 37 per cent, of the cases. Only one case reported that it was due to mutual suggestion between critic teacher and college instructor.

4. The findings in Table XV are in close agreement with expert judgment as to the rank importance of the three categories across the top of the table.

	Jury I Over 1,000			Jury II 500 to 1,000			Jury III Less than 500			Mean of Juries
	P	D	M	P	D	M	P	D	M	
1. By accompanying classes when they observe.....	1.3	1.1	1.2	1.2	1.0	1.1	1.0	1.1	1.0	1.1
2. By sending classes unaccompanied to observe scheduled demonstration units................	1.8	2.1	2.0	1.8	2.1	2.0	2.0	2.0	2.0	2.0
3. By sending classes to do undirected and unscheduled observation in the training school.........	2.9	2.8	2.9	3.0	2.9	2.9	3.0	2.9	2.9	2.9

3. By Following Up Observation in the Training School

A study of the total number of college instructors who follow up observation in the training school in the four ways mentioned in Table XVI shows that the greatest number, 66 of 122 cases, or 54 per cent, say they discuss the work privately with the critic teacher, the college class not being present at the conference.

Forty-six of 122, or 38 per cent, report that they discuss the work observed in a joint conference with critic teacher and college class, and 28, or 23 per cent, that they discuss the work observed with the college class only, unaided by the critic teacher. One person from this last-named group, the principal of the training school who teaches Directed Observation, reported that he also arranged for the college class to discuss the work observed with the critic teacher, though he, the instructor, was not present at this conference.

Six individuals out of the 122, representing four schools, report that the critic teacher and the college class discuss the work observed in a conference which the college instructor does not attend. Five of these cases also registered some additional type of follow-up under one or more of the other categories. The one case where observation was followed up in the above manner only was due to the fact that the college instructor (who was a training school supervisor) did not accompany the students when they observed.

The following instructors, representing 11 schools, follow up observation in a joint conference only, with the critic teacher and the college class:

	Case
Directed Observation instructor	1
Educational Psychology instructor	2
Director of training who teaches Elementary Curriculum	1
Early Elementary Education instructor	1
Later Elementary Education instructor	1
Principal of training school who teaches Directed Observation	1
Principles of Education instructor	1
Professional Adjustment instructor	1
Teaching of Elementary School Science instructor	1
Teaching of Elementary School Subjects instructor (who is a training school supervisor)	2
Teaching of Elementary School Subjects instructor	1
Teaching of English instructor	2
Teaching of Health instructor	1
Teaching of History instructor	1
Teaching of Nature Study instructor	1
Teaching of Public School Art instructor	1
Teaching of Reading instructor	4
Teaching of Social Studies instructor	1
Teaching of Spelling instructor	1
Technique of Teaching instructor	1

Many of the instructors listed in Table XVI signified that they followed up observation in more than one of the ways listed at the top of the table. The majority of these signified that they discussed the observation in an individual conference with the critic teacher, but, in addition, requested that the critic teacher attend the class discussion. Eight of these instructors invite the critic teacher to the class meeting as frequently as he confers individually. Six others invite the college instructor to the class discussion less frequently than they confer individually regarding the work observed.

Four of the cases who report participation under both the second and third categories in Table XVI indicate that the joint meeting of the college class and critic teacher occurs more frequently than the individual conference between college instructor and critic teacher. These instructors are:

Director of training who teaches Technique of Teaching
Music department head
Principal of training school who teaches Directed Observation
Teaching of Reading instructor

Judgment of the educational authorities favors observation follow-up at a meeting attended by the critic teacher.

	Jury I Over 1,000			Jury II 500 to 1,000			Jury III Less than 500			Mean of Juries
	P	D	M	P	D	M	P	D	M	
By discussing the work observed in the training school with the critic teacher and college class in a joint meeting......	1.4	1.2	1.3	1.1	1.2	1.2	1.0	1.0	1.0	1.1
By allowing the class and critic teacher to discuss the work observed without the aid of the college teacher...............	2.7	2.7	2.7	2.7	2.7	2.7	2.8	2.9	2.9	2.8
By discussing the work observed with the college class only, unaided by the critic teacher.......	3.4	2.8	3.1	3.4	3.1	3.2	3.4	2.8	3.1	3.1
By discussing the work privately with the critic teacher...............	3.4	2.8	3.1	3.4	3.1	3.2	3.4	2.8	3.1	3.1

A comparative analysis of Tables XV and XVI shows that the following six instructors from four schools who sent their college classes unaccompanied to observe the teaching of critic teachers in the training school did not report any type of follow-up work in Table XVI.

Educational Psychology instructor
Physical education department head
Teaching of English instructor
Teaching of Geography instructor
Teaching of Health instructor
Tests and Measurements instructor

Further comparison of the two tables shows that 80 of the 93 instructors who engage in some type of cooperative follow-up work with the critic teacher do so after each training school observation. The thirteen who do so less often are:

TABLE XVI

Frequency with Which College Instructors Follow Up Observation Done by College Classes in the Training School

Faculty Members	Frequency: Discusses Work Observed with College Class Only					Discusses Work Observed with Critic Teacher in a Conference at Which College Class is Not Present						Discusses Work Observed with Critic Teacher and College Class in a Joint Meeting					Allows Class and Critic Teacher to Discuss Alone			Activity Initiated by			Total Number Who Reported
	Weekly	Twice Monthly	Four per Quarter	Monthly	Once a Term	Twice Weekly	Weekly	Twice Monthly	Four per Quarter	Monthly	Once a Term	Twice Weekly	Weekly	Twice Monthly	Monthly	Once a Term	Twice Weekly	Monthly	Once a Term	Administration	College Instructor	Mutual	
Childrens' Literature Instructor		1								1										1	1		2
College Department Instructors (Supervisors)																							
Psychology of Elementary School Subjects[m]																		1				1	1
Teaching of Elementary School Subjects									2[p]	4[q]			2[p]							2[p]	6[o]		8
Tests and Measurements[m]		1																		1			1
Director of Training (Teaches Education Course)																							
Directed Observation					1		1[i]						1[i]						1[i]		2		2
Directed Observation (Advanced)							1[a]										1[a]				1		1
Elementary Curriculum													1								1		1
Introduction to Teaching										1	1[b]					1[b]					2		2
Teaching of Elementary School Subjects		1																			1		1
Technique of Teaching										1[c]			1[c]							1			1
Fine Arts Department Head				1	1																2		2
General Education Course Instructor																							
Classroom Management	1			1																	2		2
Directed Observation						1[b]				1		1		1[b]						1	2		3
Directed Observation (Advanced)											1[d]								1[d]		1		1
Early Elementary Education						1[b]					1		1[n]			1[b]				1	2[n]		3
Educational Psychology								1[j]			1		1		1[j]	1				2	2		4
Introduction to Teaching		1																		1	1		2
Kindergarten Education											1[e]					1[e]					1		1

TABLE XVI (*Continued*)

Faculty Members	Frequency: Discusses Work Observed with College Class Only					Frequency: Discusses Work Observed with Critic Teacher in a Conference at Which College Class is Not Present						Frequency: Discusses Work Observed with Critic Teacher and College Class in a Joint Meeting					Frequency: Allows Class and Critic Teacher to Discuss Alone			Activity Initiated by			Total Number Who Reported
	Weekly	Twice Monthly	Four per Quarter	Monthly	Once a Term	Twice Weekly	Weekly	Twice Monthly	Four per Quarter	Monthly	Once a Term	Twice Weekly	Weekly	Twice Monthly	Monthly	Once a Term	Twice Weekly	Monthly	Once a Term	Administration	College Instructor	Mutual	
Later Elementary Education						1[b]							1			1[b]				1	1		2
Principles of Education				1[r]						1[r]	1[f]					1					4[r]		4
Professional Adjustment																1					1		1
Psychology of Elementary School Subjects											1									1			1
Rural Education				1						1	1										3		3
Supervision of Instruction				1																	1		1
Teaching of Elementary School Subjects						2[k]		1		1	2[f]		1		2[k]					1	5	1	7
Teaching the Common Branches				1																	1		1
Technique of Teaching								1							1						2		2
Tests and Measurements											2										1	1	2
Industrial Arts Instructor											1										1		1
Music Department Head								1[c]					1[c]								1		1
Principal of Training School (Teaches Directed Observation)	1[l]										1[c]		1[c]		1		1[l]			1	2		3
Teaching of Arithmetic Instructor				1	1		2[g]	1[c]			2[e]		2[g]	1[c]					1[f]	4	4		8
Teaching of Elementary School Science Instructor					1								1								2		2
Teaching of English Instructor	1			1	1					1	1		2							2	5		7
Teaching of Geography Instructor				1	3		1	1[c]		2	1				1[c]					2	7		9
Teaching of Health Instructor							1[g]						1[g]			1					1	1	2
Teaching of History Instructor					1					1	2			1						1	4		5
Teaching of Nature Study Instructor										1	1	1									3		3
Teaching of Penmanship Instructor											1										1		1
Teaching of Public School Art Instructor			1	1						2[g]			1		1[g]						5		5

TABLE XVI (*Continued*)

Faculty Members	Frequency: Discusses Work Observed with College Class Only					Discusses Work Observed with Critic Teacher in a Conference at Which College Class is Not Present						Discusses Work Observed with Critic Teacher and College Class in a Joint Meeting					Allows Class and Critic Teacher to Discuss Alone			Activity Initiated by			Total Number Who Reported
	Weekly	Twice Monthly	Four per Quarter	Monthly	Once a Term	Twice Weekly	Weekly	Twice Monthly	Four per Quarter	Monthly	Once a Term	Twice Weekly	Weekly	Twice Monthly	Monthly	Once a Term	Twice Weekly	Monthly	Once a Term	Administration	College Instructor	Mutual	
Teaching of Public School Music Instructor										2											2		2
Teaching of Reading Instructor					1					3[g]	1[h]	1	1	1	3[gh]					3	5	1	9
Teaching of Social Studies Instructor													1							1			1
Teaching of Spelling Instructor																1					1		1
Total	3	4	1	10	10	5	7	6	2	23	23	3	20	4	10	9	2	1	3	27	90	5	122

[a] One individual appears under both second and fourth categories, observed twice weekly.
[b] One individual appears under both second and third categories, observed twice weekly.
[c] One individual appears under both second and third categories, observed once a week.
[d] One individual appears under both second and fourth categories, observed weekly.
[e] One individual appears under both second and third categories, observed once a term.
[f] This instructor observed once a month.
[g] One individual appears under both second and third categories.
[h] One individual appears under second and third categories, observed once a month.
[i] One individual appears under second, third and fourth categories, observed three times a week.
[j] One individual appears under second and third categories, observed twice monthly.
[k] Both individuals appear under second and third categories, observed twice weekly.
[l] One individual appears under first and fourth categories, observed with students weekly, and had them observe unaccompanied daily.
[n] One Early Elementary Education instructor plans for observation under categories 2 and 3. See Experiment, Table XIII.
[o] These six cases represent three institutions.
[p] These two cases represent one school.
[q] These four cases represent two schools.
[r] This instructor teaches Principles of Teaching.

Director of training who teaches Directed Observation	1
Director of training who teaches Introduction to Teaching	1
Directed Observation instructor	1
Directed Observation instructor (advanced)	1
Principles of Education instructor	1
Teaching of Elementary School Subjects instructor	1
Teaching of Arithmetic instructor	1
Teaching of English instructor	1
Teaching of Geography instructor	2
Teaching of Health instructor	1
Teaching of History instructor	1
Teaching of Reading instructor	1

Table XVI shows that 90 of the 122 cases initiated their own method of following up observation in the training school. Twenty-seven out of the 122 reported that the administration was responsible for this activity and five that it was due to a mutual agreement between the critic teacher and the college instructor.

D. By Personally Teaching Children in the Training School

A controversial issue in the field of cooperation between the training school and college departments is evidenced by the following quotations:

In case of campus training schools coordination can be best brought about by interlocking college and training school staff, requiring members of subject matter departments to teach and supervise in their own fields from time to time in the training school and allowing the supervisors to teach as members of some departments. Naturally the first objection raised against this proposal is one of teacher load. Instructors in the subject matter fields say they cannot do a regular college schedule and teach in the laboratory school too. This objection seems valid. It can be surmounted by the authorities of the institution in assignment of work. Upon employment laboratory work can be explained as part of one's work and not an extra burden. However, I personally have done laboratory teaching as a part of my work, over and above a regular college schedule, merely considering it a more valuable type of course preparation than any other. I have always looked upon teaching or supervising in the training school as legitimate preparation for my college classes, preferring it to some other form of preparation, which usually consists merely of reading.

Now I have not said that each college instructor ought to teach in the laboratory schools or supervise each quarter or semester. That is a matter which depends upon the circumstances and needs of the case. I merely maintain that a teacher in a professional school cannot expect his courses to function if he continually remains away from the laboratory where he expects them to be practically applied.[5]

Demonstration teaching of children in a normal school (or teachers college) requires a degree of specialization on the part of the demonstration teacher comparable to that of the subject-matter teacher in extent but differing materially in nature. These "instruction specialists" must have as their professional equipment: . . .[6]

The main contention of Evenden is opposed vigorously by W. C. Bagley and Thomas Alexander who insistently point out that teaching in the laboratory school by theory and subject-matter teachers is not only desirable but is an accomplished fact in many places in the United States and foreign countries.

. . . We should not overlook the fact that there are cases of cooperation, that there are teachers who do an expert job of teaching their subject to college students and also to laboratory pupils. These facts the writer cheerfully recognizes. At the same time there is the existing overload of the supervising teacher and the lack of preparation of many of these teachers for their specific work. Moreover, the number of directors of laboratory schools who can train supervising teachers in service, and do it well, is not large. These are the "impedimenta" in the situation. The writer believes, from his observations of such teachers, that there are often difficulties encountered, because of different levels of teaching involved, when the cooperation is teaching in laboratory school and subject-matter (or theory) classes. When these levels are not too far removed and when the practices have become skills for the teachers in both situations, the possibility is no longer a question. In other words, the writer holds that Evenden's proposals are not sound in 100 per cent of the cases; nor are the proposals of his opponents. To secure sufficient specialized mastery to do the technical work of demonstration teaching, supervision of student-teaching, teaching of professionalized subject-matter and theory courses, we shall be compelled to forego some of the interdepartmental teaching by a supervising teacher and his colleagues in other departments. There is also a legitimate need that teachers of related subject-matter fields do interdepartmental teaching; this would add to a burden already onerous.

. . . Exactly where the different levels of teaching are enough alike to allow successful work by the average teacher is an open question. Just how much the unlikeness of the two situations can be overcome by the teacher of more than average adaptability is also unknown. But it is clear that there are many supervising teachers who can do the two things and that there are many who cannot. The writer believes strongly in Evenden's demand for greater specialization of function, for

[5] Alexander, Thomas. "Coordination of the Laboratory Schools with the Subject-Matter Departments in the College." *Cooperative Planning For Teacher Training Standards in Texas.* North Texas State Teachers College Bulletin, May, 1931, pp. 139–140.

[6] Evenden, E. S. "Cooperation of Teachers of Academic Subjects With the Training School." *Supervisors of Student Teaching.* Cincinnati, Ohio, February, 1925, p. 7.

this will mean greater specialization and intensification of preparation. However, to fix a regulation that none may teach in the laboratory school and also in the theory classes carries the matter too far. Those who can do these things should be encouraged to do them and be rewarded for their services. Such service will secure some of the integration needed. The controversy on this matter should continue until the valid practices and limitations of both sets of practices are more thoroughly understood and the better ones obtain.[7]

The teaching of children in the training school for observation, demonstration, and regular classroom work should be done by "expert teachers of children." (All teachers in a teacher-training institution should be qualified for this work.)[8]

1. *Returns from Selected Published Questionnaire Studies*

Other questionnaire studies of cooperation between college and training school faculty have ascertained the extent to which academic college teachers teach classes of children in the training school. The returns from two of these are quoted below:

It is quite customary for normal school instructors in music, physical education, fine arts, domestic science, domestic arts, manual training and science to teach classes of children in the training school. This teaching is almost entirely done as part of the regular instruction in these fields and for demonstration purposes. Teachers in practically every other field in one or more schools teach classes of children, largely for demonstration purposes as often as once or more times per week. A total of 64 such teachers were reported from the 72 schools. Even with this number of normal school instructors teaching classes of children, only 21 per cent of the schools list normal school instructors as being the ones who ordinarily give demonstration lessons.[9]

Academic college teachers teach classes in the laboratory schools regularly in 22.7 per cent of the colleges, occasionally in 29.3 per cent, and never in 48 per cent. Again it is reported that teachers in special departments teach more frequently in the laboratory schools than do the teachers in other departments. From the table it is seen that a much higher percentage of college teachers supervise than teach in laboratory schools.[10]

[7] Meade, A. R. *Supervised Student-Teaching*, pp. 624–626. Johnson Publishing Company, 1930.

[8] Johnson, Lenora E. "Constructive Proposals for Cooperation Between the Training School and Subject-Matter Instructors." *The Virginia Teacher*, February, 1931, p. 35.

[9] Evenden, E. S. "Cooperation of Teachers of Academic Subjects with the Training School." *Supervisors of Student Teaching*. Cincinnati, Ohio, February, 1925, p. 5.

[10] Eubank, L. A. *The Organization and Administration of Laboratory Schools in State Teachers Colleges*. Kirksville, Missouri, April, 1931, p. 59.

The present study of faculty members other than critic teachers who teach classes of children in the training school found a total of 74 cases in 22 of the schools visited. Three schools made no answer to this section of the questionnaire.

Table XVII shows that 24 of the 74 total cases are members of the special departments of fine arts, home economics, industrial arts, music, and physical education, who are training school supervisors; seven others are education department instructors who are training school supervisors; and two are directors of training who teach education department courses.

Three of the 22 schools signified that only college faculty members from departments other than the special subjects listed above teach children in the training school; and eight others list only faculty members from the special departments.

The mean jury rankings of ways in which college instructors may teach training school children show little preference in the minds of the experts.

	Jury I Over 1,000			Jury II 500 to 1,000			Jury III Less than 500			Mean of Juries
	P	D	M	P	D	M	P	D	M	
By teaching without observers to try out experimental units	1.7	1.7	1.7	1.7	1.9	1.8	2.1	1.6	1.9	1.8
By teaching occasional units in fields where more of an authority than the critic teacher	1.9	2.3	2.1	2.0	1.9	2.0	1.4	2.1	1.7	1.9
By teaching for college classes to observe	2.4	2.0	2.2	2.3	2.1	2.2	2.6	2.3	2.5	2.3

2. Teaches for College Classes or Student Teachers to Observe

A study of Table XVII shows that many instructors teach children in the training school for more than one reason, i.e., under more than one category. This is especially true of the special subject instructors who are training school supervisors. Forty-nine of the 74 cases, or 66 per cent, select the first category as their method of teaching children in the training school. This heading refers not only to teaching for college classes to observe but for student teachers to observe. Many of these instructors reported infrequent rather than fre-

TABLE XVII

Frequency with which College Instructors, Other than Critic Teachers, Personally Teach Children in the Training School*

Faculty Members	Frequency — Teaches for College Classes to Observe							Teaches Without Observers to Try Out Experimental Units				Teaches Occasional Units in Fields Where More Competent Than Critic Teacher					Activity Initiated by				Total Number Who Teach
	Daily	Twice Weekly	Weekly	Twice Monthly	Monthly	Twice a Term	Once a Term	Weekly	Monthly	Once a Term	Yearly	Daily	Twice Weekly	Weekly	Monthly	Once a Term	Administration	College Instructor	Critic Teacher	Mutual	
Directed Observation Instructor (Advanced)							1											1			1
Director of Training (Teaches Education Courses)				1	1													2			2
Dramatics Instructor																1			1		1
Educational Psychology Instructor																1			1		1
English Department Head[c]						1											1				1
Fine Arts Department Head							1										1				1
College Department Instructors (Supervisors)																					
Educational Psychology[a]					1												1				1
Teaching of Elementary School Subjects			2[b]				2[b]										2[b]	2[b]			4
Teaching of Reading							1								1			1			1
Tests and Measurements[a]						1									1			1			1
Kindergarten Department Head								1										1			1
Music Department Head						1					1							1			1
School Nurse							1							1			1	1			2
Special Subject Instructors (Supervisors)																					
Teaching of Home Economics														1			1				1
Teaching of Industrial Arts	1							1									1	1			2
Teaching of Physical Education	1				6				3		1		1	3	1		6	4			10
Teaching of Public School Art		1			1			1	3			1	2	3	1	1	5	3			8
Teaching of Public School Music	1	1	4		3		2	1	2		1			5	1	1	8	6			14
Teaching Courses																					
Teaching of Arithmetic Instructor	1					1											1	1			2
Teaching of Elementary School Science Instructor									2								1	1			2
Teaching of English Instructor					1		1		1									1		1	2

TABLE XVII (*Continued*)

Faculty Members	Frequency: Teaches for College Classes to Observe							Teaches Without Observers to Try Out Experimental Units				Teaches Occasional Units in Fields Where More Competent Than Critic Teacher					Activity Initiated by				Total Number Who Teach
	Daily	Twice Weekly	Weekly	Twice Monthly	Monthly	Twice a Term	Once a Term	Weekly	Monthly	Once a Term	Yearly	Daily	Twice Weekly	Weekly	Monthly	Once a Term	Administration	College Instructor	Critic Teacher	Mutual	
Teaching of Geography Instructor							4		1	1						2	1	2	1	1	5
Teaching of History Instructor							1									1				1	1
Teaching of Nature Study Instructor			1	1					1					1	1		1	2			3
Teaching of Public School Art Instructor					2			1									1	2			3
Teaching of Public School Music Instructor										1								1			1
Teaching of Reading Instructor							1								1			1	1		2
Total	4	2	7	2	15	4	15	5	13	2	3	1	3	14	7	7	32	35	4	3	74

* No answer from three schools.
[a] Educational Psychology and Tests and Measurements instructors are from the same school.
[b] These two persons are in same school.
[c] This instructor teaches Childrens' Literature.

quent participation in the teaching of training school children. Fifteen indicate that they do so once a month; 15, once a term; 7, once a week; 4, twice a term; 4, daily; 2, twice monthly; and 2, twice weekly.

The four individuals who record daily teaching of this type represent three schools. The two from the same institution are instructors in Teaching of Physical Education and Teaching of Public School Music. Both of these are training school supervisors who supervise major students in these fields and in addition teach classes for these students to observe. A similar explanation was given by the Industrial Arts instructor who reported daily teaching in the training school. The remaining one of these four, the Teaching of Arithmetic instructor, was attempting to illustrate a new technique in teaching mathematics to upper grade children and had assumed the instruction of an eighth grade class for the entire semester. His college class observed this teaching each day and at the end of the period met for a discussion of the work accomplished.

The two persons who report twice-weekly teaching in the training school under the first category represent the same institution and are both special department instructors who supervise in the training school. One of these also indicated participation under the second and third categories.

The two college department instructors in Educational Psychology and Tests and Measurements represent the institution which uses city schools for practice purposes but does not expect the room teachers to do demonstration teaching for their classes. Instead, these college instructors teach for classes to observe or take them to observe student teaching. The director of training from this institution who teaches courses in elementary education also signified that twice each month he also taught children for college classes to observe.

One institution contributed seven of the cases listed under the first category, namely:

Director of training who teaches Technique of Teaching (monthly)
English department head (twice a term)
Fine arts department head (once a term)
Teaching of Arithmetic instructor (twice a term)

Teaching of History instructor (once a term)
Teaching of Nature Study instructor (twice monthly)
Teaching of Public School Music instructor (training school supervisor) (once a month)

One of the three Teaching of Nature Study instructors indicated that she taught classes of training school children in each of the three ways mentioned, because she wished to illustrate techniques she recommended to her college classes, and because the critic teachers were interested in her manner of developing certain units for which the training school children evidenced a need.

3. Teaches Experimental Units Without Observers

Twenty-three of the total 74, or 31 per cent, report that they teach children without observers. The larger number are from the group of special subject instructors who are training school supervisors. Six of this number indicate that this is their only way of teaching children in the training school. They are:

Kindergarten department head
Teaching of Industrial Art instructor
Teaching of Elementary School Science instructor—2 cases
Teaching of Public School Art instructor
Teaching of Public School Music instructor

Thirteen of the 23 instructors under the second category indicate that they teach experimental units without observers with a frequency of once a month.

4. Teaches Occasional Units in Fields Where More Competent Than the Critic Teacher

Thirty-two of the 74 total number of cases, or 43 per cent, report that they teach occasional units to training school children where they are better able to teach this subject than is the critic teacher. As would be expected, the majority of these (20 cases) are from the group of special subject instructors who are training school supervisors. No one of these 20 indicated that he did so at the request of the critic teacher but rather because the administration had designated this as one of his official duties or because the college instructor himself had initiated the activity. Except for the special supervisors mentioned above, no one reports that he engages in this type of training school teaching oftener than once a week.

The trend in the third category is toward weekly participation, but this is due to the inclusion of the special supervisors. If we disregard this group who teach training school children because it is one of their duties, there is only a slight trend, since 3 cases report weekly teaching, 4 monthly, and 7 once a term.

Requested to Participate in the Activity by: Teaching children in the training school is participated in by 32 of the 74 total cases because the administration favors this activity. Thirty-five report that the activity was self-initiated; four that it was at the request of the critic teacher; and three that it was due to a mutual agreement between the critic teacher and the college instructor. If we disregard the group of special supervisors, the administration total becomes 11 instead of 32 and the college instructor total becomes 21 instead of 35, which would show that the administration is not responsible for this teaching in the majority of the cases where the non-supervising college instructors participated in the activity.

Attention should be redirected to the one institution which has a modified Oswego plan whereby the critic teachers teach several college classes in addition to supervising student teachers. The frequency with which they personally teach children in the training school has been omitted from Table XVII since we have considered them as critic teachers throughout the study. These instructors indicated that they taught children only under the first category and that with a frequency of once a term.

E. By Assisting in Adjusting Personality Problems in the Training School

The extent to which college instructors were consulted by or aided critic teachers in adjusting personality problems of training school children and of student teachers is shown in Tables XVIII and XIX. Each will be discussed separately.

1. By Aiding in Adjusting Personality of Training School Children

Though 52 instructors who teach college courses indicated some degree of participation in the adjustment of personality problems of training school children, 25 of the total 52 are also training school officials. They are grouped on page 168:

TABLE XVIII

Frequency with Which College Instructors Aid in Adjusting Personality Problems of Training School Children*

Faculty Members	Frequency — Through Individual Conference with Critic Teacher in Whose Charge Child Is			Through Individual Conference with Student Teacher in Whose Class the Child Is					Through Individual Conference with the Child Concerned			Through Joint Conference with Critic Teacher and Student Teacher		Through Joint Conference with Critic Teacher and Child		Through Joint Conference with Student Teacher and Child		Activity Initiated by					Total Number Who Aid
	Weekly	Monthly	Once a Term	Twice Weekly	Weekly	Monthly	Once a Term	Yearly	Weekly	Monthly	Once a Term	Twice Monthly	Once a Term	Monthly	Once a Term	Weekly	Monthly	Administration	College Instructor	Critic Teacher	Mutual	Student	
College Department Instructors (Supervisors)																							
Educational Psychology[a]		1								1										1			1
Teaching Elementary School Subjects		2[e]	2[e]	2[e]		3[d]				2[e]				2[e]						1	4[d]		5
Tests and Measurements Instructor						1					1											1	1
Director of Training[f] (Teaches Education Courses)	4	2			2	2			4	1								1	2	4			7
Early Elementary Education Instructor		1		1	1	1				1									1	1		1	3
Education Department Head			1															1					1
Educational Psychology Instructor	1	5			1	3					3		1		2			1	1	4	1		7
Exceptional Children's Department Head		1					1				1							1					1
Fine Arts Department Head		1				1													1				1
Kindergarten Department Head		1																		1			1
Later Elementary Education Instructor		1			1	1				1										1		1	2
Nursery School Director			1																		1		1
Principal of Training School (Teaches Education Courses)	3				3	1		1	2	2		1		1		1		2		1	1	1	5

TABLE XVIII (*Continued*)

Faculty Members	Frequency: Through Individual Conference with Critic Teacher in Whose Charge Child Is			Through Individual Conference with Student Teacher in Whose Class the Child Is					Through Individual Conference with the Child Concerned			Through Joint Conference with Critic Teacher and Student Teacher		Through Joint Conference with Critic Teacher and Child		Through Joint Conference with Student Teacher and Child		Activity Initiated by					Total Number Who Aid
	Weekly	Monthly	Once a Term	Twice Weekly	Weekly	Monthly	Once a Term	Yearly	Weekly	Monthly	Once a Term	Twice Monthly	Once a Term	Monthly	Once a Term	Weekly	Monthly	Administration	College Instructor	Critic Teacher	Mutual	Student	
Research Department Head			1								1									1			1
School Physician		1				1					1							1					1
Special Subject Instructors (Supervisors)																							
Teaching of Industrial Arts						1				1									1				1
Teaching of Physical Education		1			1			1			1								2				2
Teaching of Public School Music		1	1	1	1				1	1							1		2				2
Teaching of Arithmetic Instructor					1					1									1				1
Teaching of Geography Instructor		1				1							1							1			1
Teaching of History Instructor		1																		1			1
Teaching of Nature Study Instructor		1			1					1	1				1				2				2
Teaching of Physical Education Instructor															1		1			2			2
Teaching of Public School Music Instructor							1															1	1
Tests and Measurements Instructor		1				1					1							1					1
Total	8	22	6	4	12	17	2	2	7	12	10	1	2	3	4	1	2	8	13	19	7	5	52

* No answer from four schools.
[a] The Educational Psychology and Tests and Measurements instructors are from same institution.
[b] Same instructor appears under more than one category.
[d] These four cases represent two institutions.
[e] These two cases represent one institution.
[f] Three directors of training, who teach no college courses, indicated participation in this work.

College department instructors who are supervisors.... 7
Director of training who teaches education department courses.. 7
Nursery school director............................. 1
Principal of the training school, who teaches education department courses............................. 5
Special subject instructors who are training school supervisors:
Teaching of Industrial Arts.................... 1
Teaching of Physical Education................ 2
Teaching of Public School Music............... 2

Clearly, this suggested type of reciprocal relation between the two faculties is not considered of major importance in the schools visited for this study. The mean weight of the combined juries assigned 10 points to this activity as against 20 points to the adjustment of such problems with student teachers.

The majority of the participants tabulated in Table XVIII report that they aid in this problem in more than one way, the first three categories being indicated most often.

	Jury I Over 1,000			Jury II 500 to 1,000			Jury III Less than 500			Mean of Juries
	P	D	M	P	D	M	P	D	M	
Through individual conference with the critic teacher in whose class the child is...........	2.6	3.1	2.9	2.5	2.2	2.3	2.5	2.1	2.3	2.5
Through joint conference with critic teacher and student teacher........	2.4	2.6	2.5	3.0	2.8	2.9	2.4	2.3	2.3	2.6
Through individual conference with student teacher working with the group...............	4.1	5.1	4.7	4.2	3.6	3.9	3.8	3.7	3.7	4.1
Through joint conference with critic teacher and child.................	4.4	3.2	3.8	3.9	4.6	4.3	4.1	4.3	4.2	4.1
Through joint conference with critic teacher, student teacher and child..	4.6	3.2	3.9	4.8	3.7	4.2	5.5	4.4	5.0	4.4
Through joint conference with student teacher and child.................	5.0	4.9	4.9	5.1	5.6	5.0	5.5	5.4	5.4	5.1
Through individual conference with the child concerned................	4.9	5.9	5.4	4.6	5.4	5.0	4.3	5.8	5.0	5.2

Since the juries ranked the third category in Table XVIII as the least desirable method of participation, practice and expert opinion are not in perfect accord. It should be explained that each instructor who reported that he talked with the individual child also reported that he first conferred with either the student teacher or critic teacher and talked to the child at their request. Further, 17 of the total 29 reported in category three in the table are training school officials. The juries rated this method low in rank because they were considering college instructors only. It is evident that it would be a vicious practice for every college instructor to talk with each problem child in the training school.

Thirty-five of the total of 52 replying engage in the solution of such personality problems through individual conference with the critic teacher who has the child in charge, 11 of the 35 instances listing this as their only way of aiding with the adjustment of personality problems with the training school children, 22 of this 35 indicate monthly participation, 10 weekly, and 6 once a term.

The second category in Table XVIII, "Through individual conference with student teacher in whose class the child is," was checked by 36 of the 52 instructors who indicated some degree of participation in the activity, eight of whom indicated this as their only manner of cooperation in this work. Seventeen of the above 36 reported monthly conferences with the student teacher chiefly concerned with the problem child.

A summarizing statement relative to Table XVIII would include the following:

1. Twenty-five of the 52 instructors who aid in adjusting personality problems of training school children are education department instructors who have been assigned definite work in the training school by the administrator of the school. Ten other members of the education department and 7 instructors in Educational Psychology would bring the total for education department instructors to 42 of the total 52. Such tabulation indicates that the education department assumes this cooperative responsibility in a larger degree than do other college departments.

2. The first three categories in Table XVIII were most frequently selected by the 52 total participants, 35 selecting the first, 36 the

TABLE XIX[g]

Frequency with Which College Instructors Aid in Adjusting Personality Problems of Student Teachers

Faculty Members	Frequency: Through Individual Conference with Critic Teacher with Whom Student is Working				Through Individual Conference with Student Teacher					Through Joint Conference with Critic Teacher and Student Teacher		Through Joint Conference with Critic Teacher and Other Faculty Members		Activity Initiated by					Total Number Who Aid
	Weekly	Monthly	Once a Term	Yearly	Twice Weekly	Weekly	Monthly	Once a Term	Yearly	Monthly	Once a Term	Monthly	Once a Term	Administration	College Instructor	Critic Teacher	Mutual	Director of Training	
College Department Instructors (Supervisors)																			
Educational Psychology[a d]			1					1[d]							2				2
Teaching Elementary School Subjects	2[b]	2[b]	4[c]			2[b]	2[b]	2[b]			2[b]		2[b]			4[c]	4[c]		8
Tests and Measurements[a]							1								1				1
Director of Training[h] (Teaches Education Courses)	2	7	2	2	1	2	4	4	2	1	2		2	3	2	5	4		14
Early Elementary Education Instructor		2				2								2					2
Educational Psychology Instructor		4	1			1	3			1	3	1		1	2	2			5
English Department Head[j]							1							1					1
Fine Arts Department Head	1					1				1			1		1				1
Later Elementary Education		2					2										2		2
Music Department Head[i]								1						1					1
President of College								1										1	1
Principal of Training School (Teaches Education Courses)	1	3	1		1		2	1		1	2		2			4	1		5
Registrar								1									1		1
Scholarship Committee								1					1	1					1
Special Subject Instructors (Supervisors)																			
Teaching of Home Economics				1				1								1			1
Teaching of Industrial Arts							1								1				1
Teaching of Physical Education		1	1	1			1	1	1				1	1	1		1		3
Teaching of Public School Art	1	1				1	1								1		1		2
Teaching of Public School Music		1	1		1			1			1				3				3

TABLE XIX[g] (*Continued*)

Faculty Members	Frequency													Activity Initiated by					Total Number Who Aid
	Through Individual Conference with Critic Teacher with Whom Student is Working				Through Individual Conference with Student Teacher					Through Joint Conference with Critic Teacher and Student Teacher		Through Joint Conference with Critic Teacher and Other Faculty Members							
	Weekly	Monthly	Once a Term	Yearly	Twice Weekly	Weekly	Monthly	Once a Term	Yearly	Monthly	Once a Term	Monthly	Once a Term	Administration	College Instructor	Critic Teacher	Mutual	Director of Training	
Speech Instructor									1							1			1
Teaching of Arithmetic		1	1			1	1								2				2
Teaching of Geography Instructor	1	1				1	2					1			2	1			3
Teaching of Health Instructor			1					1								1			1
Teaching of History Instructor		1					1			1					1				1
Teaching of Public School Art			1												1				1
Teaching of Reading Instructor				1											1				1
Technique of Teaching Instructor	1					1											1		1
Tests and Measurements Instructor			1												1				1
Total	9	26	15	5	3	12	22	16	4	5	10	2	9	10	22	19	15	1	67

[a] The Educational Psychology and Tests and Measurements instructors are from the same institution.
[b] These two persons are in same school.
[c] These four persons represent two schools.
[d] Educational Psychology, Teaching of Elementary School Science, and Teaching of Reading instructors are in same school.
[e] These eight cases represent four institutions.
[g] One additional category, Through conference with student teacher and other faculty members, was included on the questionnaire, but received no frequencies.
[h] Four non-teaching directors of training reported participation.
[i] This school maintains a special music critic teacher in training school.
[j] Head of English department teaches Childrens' Literature.

second, and 29 the third. It can be seen from this table that a large proportion of the instructors who aid in adjusting personality problems of training school children, do so in several ways.

3. Initiation of cooperative effort in adjusting such personality problems was taken by the critic teacher in 19 instances; by the college instructor in 13 instances[11]; through mutual agreements between the two foregoing faculty groups in 7 instances; and at the request of the student teacher in 5 instances.

2. *By Aiding in Adjusting Personality Problems of Student Teachers*

Only a summarizing paragraph will be given regarding the trends evidenced in Table XIX as to cooperative efforts in adjusting personality problems which handicap the student teacher's efficiency. A comparison of Tables XVIII and XIX, both of which relate to cooperative adjustment of personality problems, the former with training school children, the latter with student teachers, shows that with few exceptions the same instructors participated in each problem. Forty of the total 67 participants in Table XIX are members of the education department who have been assigned work in the training school by the administration of the school.

The work was accomplished more frequently through individual conferences with the critic teacher under whose supervision the student was teaching, or through individual conference with the student. The major portion of the total 67 indicated participation in both types of conference. Such cooperative work in a training school problem was initiated by 22 of the college instructors; the critic teacher concerned requested help from 19 others; and 15 college instructors reported it as due to a mutual agreement between themselves and the critic teacher.

The findings in Table XIX agree with the ranking of the categories by the juries.

F. By Aiding in Determining the Policies of the Training School

Each writer who has proposed an organized plan of cooperation between the college faculty and the training school staff, has sug-

[11] Seven of these 13 are training school officials.

	Jury I Over 1,000			Jury II 500 to 1,000			Jury III Less than 500			Mean of Juries
	P	D	M	P	D	M	P	D	M	
Through individual conference with the critic teacher with whom the student teacher is working	2.4	1.9	2.1	2.2	1.9	2.0	2.0	1.7	1.9	2.0
Through joint conference with critic teacher and student teacher	2.6	2.1	2.3	2.4	2.4	2.4	2.6	2.1	2.4	2.3
Through individual conference with the student teacher	2.3	3.0	2.7	1.9	2.2	2.1	2.4	2.5	2.4	2.4
Through joint conference with critic teacher and other faculty members	3.2	3.3	3.3	3.8	3.8	3.8	3.5	4.1	3.8	3.6
Through joint conference with student teacher and other faculty members	4.6	4.8	4.7	4.7	4.8	4.8	4.6	4.7	4.6	4.7

gested that the former group should aid in determining the various policies which govern the work of the training school. In the Missouri Survey[12] Dr. Bagley proposed that this be effected through a training school cabinet:

The desired interlinking of all normal school departments with the training school is certainly not to be realized by turning over the practice teaching to the control either of the general normal school faculty or of a committee representing the various academic departments. The training school must be under the direct control and supervision of an expert administrator fitted by experience and by specialized training for this type of work, and this director or superintendent must have under his immediate charge, a corps of carefully selected and specifically trained critics or supervisors. The supervisory staff should include many, if not most, of the members of the so-called academic departments, and the entire group should form what might be termed a training school "cabinet." This body should legislate upon all matters concerning the organization of the training school curriculum and questions of educational policy; the superintendent or director, as the officer in whom administrative responsibility is lodged, should have authority to make decisions upon all matters of administration, with the provision that any other member of the cabinet may appeal from his decisions to a higher administrative authority.

[12] Learned and Bagley. *The Professional Preparation of Teachers for American Public Schools*. Bulletin No. 14, Carnegie Foundation for the Advancement of Teaching, 1920, pp. 179–204.

A plan of this sort would ensure:

1. the administrative autonomy of the practice school under a responsible head.
2. the responsible cooperation of all academic departments, all members of the critic staff in the organization of the school, the construction of the curriculum, and the oversight of the student-teachers.

The chief difficulty in carrying out this plan under present conditions is serious but not insurmountable. It would require that appointments to all important positions in the academic departments be limited to persons who are qualified by personality, experience, and training to participate in the responsibilities that it is proposed to delegate to the members of the practice school cabinet. It would mean, in other words, that there would be but a very subordinate place in the normal school organization or none at all, for the teacher who is merely a specialist in his subject matter. The requirement of the special abilities needed for intelligent cooperation is after all nothing but the characteristic differentia of a professional school for teachers and should be faced as frankly as similar restrictions are faced in all other genuinely professional institutions.

Needless to say, the relationship between the department of education and the training department should be particularly close and intimate, and to this end it is advisable, we believe, to combine the headship of the department of education and the directorship of the training department in one and the same person. The other members of the staff in education should also have definite responsibilities in the administration and supervision of the training school to the end that every class in educational theory may be in charge of a teacher who is in daily touch with the actual problems of teaching and management in an elementary or a second school.

1. Deciding Which Students Are Prepared to Begin Student Teaching Using Previously Set-up Standards As to Who Shall Be Admitted to Student Teaching

Several authors, Dr. Alexander,[13] Dr. Garrison,[14] Miss Johnson,[15] and others, have indicated that the college faculty members should cooperate in deciding which students are prepared to begin student teaching by using standards which have been arrived at through

[13] Alexander, Thomas. "Coordination of the Laboratory Schools with the Subject-Matter Departments in the College." *Cooperative Planning for Teacher Training Standards in Texas.* North Texas State Teachers College Bulletin, May, 1931, pp. 139-140.

[14] Garrison, Noble L. *Current Practice in Coordination of College and Training School Work.* Michigan State Normal College, 1929. p. 11.

[15] Johnson, Lenora E. "Constructive Proposals for Cooperation Between the Training School and Subject-Matter Instructors." *The Virginia Teacher,* February, 1931, p. 35.

some type of conference which included either all or representatives of each college department and the training school. When this question was submitted by the investigator to the schools visited, practically no such cooperative work was reported. Nine of the 25 schools failed to give any answer to it as a suggested type of cooperation. The reason given was that a certain prescribed number of courses were required before any student could enroll for Directed Teaching. Each of these nine schools indicated that the registrar's office was the only agency for admitting students to the course in Directed Teaching.

Seven schools reported that in addition to fulfilling certain prerequisite courses each student is required to meet with the director of training.[16] If, as a result of this conference, the director feels that the student is prepared to enter upon student teaching, an assignment is made. Since the professional literature indicates that something in addition to fulfilling course requirements should be the basis for cooperative decision as to which students were prepared to begin student teaching, the following data are submitted for the nine individual schools in which a definite plan of cooperative action was in progress.

School 1. An advisory committee, composed of the director of training in the campus school, the supervisor of training in the off-campus schools, and a representative from each college department, meets each semester to discuss the qualifications of the various students applying for entrance to the course in Directed Teaching the following semester. No student may undertake the responsibility of student teaching until he has received the sanction of the advisory committee and in addition has made units of work in certain subjects to be used during his student teaching period. The standards used for judging a student's readiness are not only completion of prerequisite courses but also personal qualifications and scholarship.

This institution provides student teaching facilities in the campus training school, off-campus city schools, and off-campus rural schools. Students are assigned to these schools by the advisory committee in terms of the type of school in which such students will probably begin their first in-service teaching. Each student in this institution

[16] This director teaches courses in the education department in five of the schools.

must spend two nine-week terms in one or more of the training schools for which he is best fitted. One of these nine-week terms of student teaching occurs in the second year of the student's training and the other in the third year, and, in addition, each student must complete a participation course in either a city or a rural training center.

School 2. Another teacher training institution which provides ample facilities for student teaching in campus, off-campus rural, and off-campus city and village schools reported that the faculty council meets once a term to sanction the group of students who are to enter student teaching the following term. The faculty council includes the same staff members as the advisory committee mentioned above for School 1. In addition to meeting once a term with the faculty council, the non-teaching director of training in the campus school and the supervisor of the off-campus training schools confer once a month with the members of the college departments regarding progress of the students who are applying for admission to student teaching for the following term.

In addition each of these above-mentioned administrative officers confers with individual students as a consultant advisor to determine whether or not such students are prepared to begin student teaching.

School 3. The dean of instruction spends one period a week in conference with prospective student teachers, as a consultant advisor, to determine whether or not such students are prepared for the work in other ways than the completion of prescribed courses. The non-teaching director of training meets with these students once a term to advise them as to necessary preparation for the student teaching work the following semester.

School 4. The dean of the college, the principal of the training school, and the director of training, all three of whom teach college courses in the education department, meet in joint conference once a semester to determine which students are prepared to enter student teaching in terms of scholarship and completion of prerequisite courses; and to assign each student to the grade or subject in which he is best prepared to teach in the training school.

The head of the music department in the same institution, who teaches the professionalized subject matter courses and supervises in the training school, reported that once a semester she meets with individual critic teachers to assign certain students to the teaching of music in each grade. There are no students majoring in music at this school, therefore this music instructor meets with the critic teacher after the quota of student teachers has been assigned for a semester, and from this group selects those best prepared to assume the teaching of music.

School 5. Once a semester the dean of the college and the registrar meet with individual critic teachers to assign students in directing teaching for the following semester. In these conferences an attempt is made to place students in the grade or subjects for which they are best suited.

School 6. The early and later elementary education departments act as consultant advisors to students majoring in these fields and not only assign them to the training school work, but consult with them throughout their student teaching period. This institution has been cited before[17] in connection with a laboratory experiment in student teaching.

It is the administrative policy in this institution for the head of each college department to confer with individual critic teachers once a semester regarding such of their students as are prepared to begin directed teaching in the training school. This applies to students majoring in elementary and secondary, or specialized fields of music, art, and physical education.

School 7. The supervisor of training and the Early Elementary Education instructor, both of whom teach courses in the education department and in addition supervise their students during the student teaching period, meet in a monthly conference with the director of training to suggest the list of student teachers for the following six weeks' period.

School 8. The director of training, who teaches courses in the education department, meets with representatives of each college department once a term, to determine which of their students are prepared to begin direct teaching and from this list to select those who fulfill the requirements established. After securing this list, he meets with individual critic teachers to assign students to the work for

[17] See Chap. IV, p. 136.

which they are best fitted. In addition, this director of training acts as a consultant advisor to the students on the list, meeting each one to direct his preparation for the work in student teaching to which he has been assigned. In this school, the head of the education department meets once a term with each major student in the education department. The list of possible candidates for directed teaching which he submits to the director of training is an outgrowth of these conferences.

School 9. The instructor in the education department who offers the courses which are concerned with specialized methods in elementary education acts as a consultant advisor to students majoring in elementary education. Once a term she holds a final conference with these students to determine whether or not they fulfill the standards set up for a student to enter the student teaching course. The director of teaching, who teaches General Education courses, meets with the individual critic teachers once a term to delegate qualified individual students to definite teaching assignments.

2. By Determining the Length and Content of Student Teaching (e.g., Time and Content of Observation, Participation, Responsible Teaching, Conferences, Lesson Planning, etc.)

Seven teacher training institutions reported effort expended in determining the content of student teaching as a faculty group project during the year in which this study was made. One school reported that the curriculum committee, at one large meeting in the fall, outlined the general content. At another meeting, attended by critic teachers, the details of this outline were worked out. Later during the year, individual members of the committee interviewed individual critic teachers in an effort to clarify the recommendations made in the large group meetings. This is the only institution reporting cooperative activity of this type under each of the three categories suggested by the questionnaire. A second institution reported that the supervisor of training schools, who also supervised in a city off-campus school, and the Early Elementary Education instructor presented recommended to the faculty at a group meeting units which should be included in the student teaching course. These findings were based upon monthly conferences with individual critic teachers. During the year of this survey, two additional schools spent one faculty meeting in hearing the presentation of suggested changes in the length and content of student teaching, recommended by the director of training and the dean of instruction. One of the larger institutions visited reported progress in planning a wider extension of the content of student teaching, worked out in a meeting each semester attended by the education department and the campus training school faculty. This school maintains such a large teaching personnel that it is not feasible to work out training school policies in a meeting of the faculty. Therefore, the findings of the above mentioned group were reported to the heads of each department by the director of training.

At a faculty meeting in the institution which is conducting an experiment in the content of student teaching, mentioned elsewhere in this study, the head of each department presented his conception of the necessary units which should be incorporated in the experimental course for student teachers.

The seventh institution reported one meeting of the entire faculty given over to a discussion of the length and content of the student teaching.

The curriculum committee in two institutions not mentioned in the above discussion engaged in this form of policy, determining it at a meeting attended by heads of departments and the director of training. Each term, in one of the schools, the dean of the college and the director of training jointly planned the details of the suggestions made by the larger group.

The advisory committee, discussed in the preceding section relative to the participation of the college faculty in determining policies of the training school, also convened once each term to revise the units which student teachers were expected to fulfill during their student teaching period.

A state course of study committee conducted a meeting on this subject, attended by one representative of each college department (including the director of training) from each state teacher training institution. While this may not be considered cooperation within a school, it does represent participation of college faculty members in determining content of student teaching. The findings of this course

TABLE XX

By Aiding in Determining Policies of the Training School

	Jury I More than 1,000			Jury II 500 to 1,000			Jury III Less than 500			All Juries
	P	D	Both	P	D	Both	P	D	Both	
1. Deciding which students are prepared to begin student teaching, using previously set-up standards as to who shall be admitted to student teaching										
a. As members of a committee including critic teachers, director of training, and representatives of each college department...	1.5	2.0	1.8	1.6	1.6	1.6	1.6	1.8	1.7	1.7
b. As members of a committee including the director of training and representatives of each college department............	2.1	1.7	1.9	1.9	2.1	2.0	2.1	2.0	2.0	2.0
c. Through individual conference with members of the training school staff..	3.1	3.1	3.1	3.1	3.2	3.2	2.9	3.3	3.1	3.1
d. By assigning each student to a consultant advisor who makes the decision..	3.3	3.2	3.3	3.5	3.1	3.3	3.4	2.9	3.2	3.2
2. By determining the length and content of student teaching (e.g., time and content of observation, participation, responsible teaching, conferences, lesson planning, etc.)										
a. As members of a committee including critic teachers, director of training, and representatives of each college department...	1.1	1.6	1.4	1.1	1.5	1.3	1.1	1.3	1.2	1.3
b. As members of a committee including the director of training and representatives of each college department............	1.9	1.6	1.8	2.2	2.0	2.0	2.1	1.8	2.0	1.9
c. Through individual conference with members of the training school staff..	3.0	2.8	2.9	2.7	2.5	2.6	2.9	2.8	2.9	2.8
3. By determining the kind and amount of contacts the students should have with the training school throughout their training courses prior to student teaching										
a. As members of a committee including critic teachers, director of training, and representatives of each college department...	1.2	1.6	1.4	1.3	1.6	1.5	1.1	1.4	1.3	1.4
b. As members of a committee including the director of training and representatives of each college department............	2.0	1.8	1.9	2.0	1.8	1.9	2.0	1.8	1.9	1.9
c. Through individual conference with members of the training school staff..	2.8	2.6	2.7	2.7	2.6	2.6	2.9	2.8	2.9	2.7

of study committee were printed in a mimeographed bulletin, which was tried out experimentally in each of the state institutions.

Ten of the 25 schools visited reported some effort in the cooperative activity being discussed, through conferences between individual members of training schools and college departments.

Four of the 25 schools made no mention of this type of cooperative policy formation; and four others reported that it had been done the previous year. This type of policy formation is carried out by large groups more than by individuals, and on the recommendation of the administration of the school.

3. *By Determining the Kind and Amount of Contacts Students Should Have with the Training School Throughout Their Training Courses Prior to Student Teaching*

Similar groups, which reported participation in the above two types of training school policy recommendations, also reported effort expended in determining the kind and amount of contacts students should have with the training school prior to entering upon student teaching. However, members of the college departments met with critic teachers, individually or in groups, to work out such contacts for their own courses in professionalized subject matter. Eleven of these participants were from the education department. The trend is toward individual contacts rather than large groups, but all on the recommendation of the administration of the school. See Table XX.

In one institution the dean of the college conducted such a meeting each semester, attended by the Methods Course instructor from each department. The purpose of the meeting was to outline a course in Participation Teaching and Observation to be carried out rather uniformly by each instructor concerned.

Five schools made no answer to this section of the questionnaire; six others reported that it had been done previously and the findings were in progress during the year of this survey. Though the judgment of experts recommends that this work be done in a committee attended by critic teachers, the director of training, and members of each college department, it is apparent that this is not the policy in practice.

CHAPTER VI

PARTICIPATION OF THE TRAINING SCHOOL STAFF IN FUNCTIONS OF TEACHER TRAINING INSTITUTIONS, OTHER THAN THOSE CONCERNED WITH THE LABORATORY SCHOOL

Since there are fewer suggested cooperative functions in Parts II and III of the questionnaire than in Part I, and participation in any of such activities was infrequent, both sections will be discussed briefly in this chapter. Tables XXI-XXXII are self-explanatory and exhibit the paucity of reciprocal relations between college and training school faculties other than in the immediate work of the laboratory school.

Part II. Participation of Members of the Training School Staff in the Functions of the Other College Departments

Professional literature pertaining to the problem of coordination of college and training school faculties suggests many more ways in which the college departments may participate in the functions of the training school than ways in which the latter may participate in functions of the former. This seems justified since there are more college departments than accessible training schools, and the cooperative responsibilities may be shared by the former group. The difference in number of suggested activities may be further justified if we accept the thesis that "the training school should be considered the central department of the institution and the testing laboratory of every other department."[1]

The questionnaires used in obtaining information concerning coordination of the two groups contained twenty-one ways in which

[1] Johnson, Lenora. "Cooperation Between Training School and Subject-Matter Instructors." *The Virginia Teacher*, February, 1931, p. 35.

college departments might participate in the functions of the training school and eight ways in which the training school staff might participate in the functions of the college departments. Since these questionnaires were submitted to well-qualified groups[2] for suggestions and additions, we may consider the difference in number to be warranted.

A. By Aiding in Formulating the College Curriculum

1. By Participating in Determining the Content of College Courses

In the judgment of teacher training specialists, the courses of instruction in teachers colleges and normal schools should be organized to serve the purpose of the student teacher in the training school. One of the suggested ways for accomplishing this policy was that members of the training school staff should aid in determining the content of college courses. Table XXI shows the extent to which this policy is in effect in the 25 teacher training institutions visited. Since this is a study of cooperation between faculty members, individual courses taught by training school supervisors and critic teachers have been omitted from the list because in no case was it reported that other critic teachers, supervisors, or college instructors aided them in determining the content of such courses.

It is evident that little cooperative activity of this type reported in Table XXI was in progress at the time of this survey, only eleven of the 25 schools making any report. The juries of experts selected the first category at the top of the table as of first importance, but this practice was being observed in only four schools. Two reported the revision of the entire college curriculum through weekly and twice monthly meetings attended by the entire faculty. In a third institution the course content in Educational Psychology and in Later Elementary Education had been determined in monthly meetings of a curriculum committee. It was the plan in this school to revise all course offerings in a similar manner. A fourth school reported that the professionalized subject matter courses in Language Arts and in Social Studies were being reorganized in group meetings of the faculty. A fifth institution reported that the courses in Principles of Education and Introduction to Teaching were being re-

[2] Chap. I, page 8.

TABLE XXI

Frequency with Which Members of the Training School Staff Participate in Determining the Content of College Courses Which They Do Not Teach*

College Course	Frequency: As Member of a General Curriculum Committee Composed of Representatives of Each College Department and Training School							Frequency: As Member of Subject Committee Composed of Members of the Department Concerned and the Training School Staff		Frequency: Through Individual Conference with the College Instructor			Activity Initiated by						Critic Teachers Who Participated					
	Weekly	Twice Monthly	Monthly	Six Times per Year	Twice a Term	Once a Term	Three times a Year	Once a Term	Yearly	Twice Monthly	Once a Term	Yearly	Administration	College Instructor	Mutual	Head of Department	State Department	All General	Intermediate Grade	Fifth Grade	Fine Arts	Music	Physical Education	Primary Grade
Children's Literature								1						1										1
Educational Psychology			1										1					1						
Entire College Curriculum	1	1											2					2						
Fine Arts Curriculum								1								1					1			
Introduction to Teaching							1										1	1[a]						
Investigations in English									1					1				1						
Later Elementary Education Curriculum			1								1		2					1	1					
Music Curriculum								1								1						1		
Principles of Teaching				1													1	1[a]						
Teaching of Language Arts						1[c]					1[c]		1					1						
Teaching of Physical Education								1				2[b]	1		1[b]	1							3[b]	
Teaching of Public School Art									1			1				2					2			
Teaching of Public School Music											1[b]	1	1[b]		1	2						4[b]		
Teaching of Reading										1				1						1				
Teaching of Social Studies						1[c]					1[c]		1					1						
Physical Education for Women Curriculum								1								1							1	

* No answer from fourteen schools.

[a] These courses were worked out by a state committee which included representatives from each teachers college faculty. The instructors who reported this work were training school supervisors as well as college instructors.

[b] This instructor is a training school supervisor as well as a college instructor (one instance).

[c] Reported under two categories.

vised in meetings called by the State Department of Education, representatives of each college department and the training school from each state teacher training institution being in attendance.

The category ranked second by the juries, "As members of subject committees," was checked for six courses by four schools. One institution reported such type of curriculum revision in both Later Elementary Education and Music; another, in both English and Fine Arts. The third category, "Through individual conferences with the college instructor," received nine frequencies reported by six schools.

One institution reported this type of work in these courses, the Teaching of Physical Education, the Teaching of Public School Art, and the Teaching of Public School Music; another in Language Arts and Social Studies.

Table XXI shows no trend as to frequency with which this type of cooperative endeavor was carried on, since it ranged from one meeting a week to one a year.

2. By Participating in the Selection of Such College Materials as Text-Books, Supplementary Books, Laboratory Equipment, etc.

Table XXII shows that training school faculty members have little part in the selection of the materials of instruction used in college courses. Seven schools report cooperative selection of textbooks for certain college courses. Only one of these reports that it is done in a general curriculum committee meeting attended by representatives from each college department and the critic teachers. In another institution the instructors in Early and Later Elementary Education request such aid from the several critic teachers representing those grade levels.

Four of the schools visited reported some cooperative selection of supplementary books to be used in college courses; and three, cooperative selection of laboratory equipment.

3. By Participating in Planning New Experiments and Techniques for the College Departments (e.g., Size of College Classes, Having Consultant Advisors for Students, etc.)

A brief but significant group of cooperative experiments are listed in Table XXIII, the greater number being reported by the educa-

TABLE XXII

Frequency with Which Members of the Training School Staff Participate in the Selection of Materials of Instruction to Be Used in the College Departments

College Instructors Who Were Aided by the Training School Staff	Frequency: As Member of a General Curriculum Committee Composed of Representatives of Each College Department and Training School	Frequency: As Member of Subject Committee Composed of Members of the Department Concerned and the Training School Staff		Frequency: Through Individual Conference with the College Instructor		Activity Initiated by			Which Critic Teachers Participated					Number of Schools Not Answering
	Yearly	Once a Term	Yearly	Once a Term	Yearly	Administration	College Instructor	Head of Department	All General	Primary Grade	Intermediate Grade	Music	Physical Education	
Textbooks for College Courses														18
Early Elementary Education Instructor[b]		1			1		2			2				
Later Elementary Education Instructor[b]		1					1				1			
Music Department Head					3			3				3[a]		
Physical Education Department Head			1			1							1	
Teaching of Arithmetic Instructor[c]	1			1			1		1					
Teaching of Geography Instructor[c]	1			1				1	1					
Teaching of History Instructor[c]	1							1	1					
Teaching of Language Arts Instructor				1			1		1					
Supplementary Books														21
Early Elementary Education Instructor[b]		1					1			1				
Later Elementary Education Instructor[b]		1					1				1			
Music Department Head					2			2						
Physical Education Department Head					1	1							1	
Laboratory Equipment														22
Early Elementary Education Instructor[b]		1					1			1				
Later Elementary Education Instructor[b]		1					1				1			
Music Department Head					1			1				1		
Physical Education Department Head			1			1							1	

[a] One of these is a training school supervisor who teaches college courses.
[b] One school represented.
[c] Two schools represented.

TABLE XXIII

College Department Experiments and New Techniques Which Training School Staff Members Share in Planning and Conducting*

Experiments and New Techniques	Faculty Members Who Cooperated	Activity Initiated by: Administration	College Instructor	College Department	Head of Department	Art Critic Teacher	Mutual	Curriculum Committee
Education Department Experiments								
Block observation experiment—college students observe in one grade for several days, then repeat in another grade[b]	All critic teachers and the education department	I						
Course of study in educational psychology[c]	College instructor; second grade critic teachers							I
Developing skill in a list of classroom activities through participation teaching	Director of training who teaches technique of teaching; all critic teachers		I					
Education department questionnaire sent to training school faculty for suggestions and points of emphasis in education courses	Education department and training school faculty			I				
Laboratory Plan for student teaching[ac]	Education department and training school faculty	I						
Later Elementary Education instructor finds what units will be used in the training school and has college students work them out tentatively the semester before doing student teaching[b]	Later Elementary Education instructor and intermediate grade critic teachers		I					
Students in Primary Methods and Materials teach in the training school during the college courses*	Early Elementary Education instructor and critic teachers		I					
English Department Experiments								
Correction of speech defects in training school children[a]	Dramatics instructor; kindergarten critic teachers						I	
Fine Arts Department Experiments								
Effect of size of art classes on achievement	Fine arts department head; art supervisor; director of training			I				
Planning of an art notebook (general setup and content)[c]	Fine arts department head; art critic teacher				I			
New Poster Methods developed by the art department adopted by the art critic teacher for the training school	Fine arts department head; art critic teacher					I		

TABLE XXIII (*Continued*)

Experiments and New Techniques	Faculty Members Who Cooperated	Activity Initiated by: Administration	College Instructor	College Department	Head of Department	Art Critic Teacher	Mutual	Curriculum Committee
Music Department Experiment								
Teaching without syllables in Public School Music Course[ac]	Music department head; music critic teacher, and college students				1			
Physical Education Department Experiment								
Swimming Experiment	Physical education department head; physical education critic teacher				1			

* No experiments listed for eighteen schools. Only one experiment listed by four schools.
[a] This experiment has been listed in Table XIII and discussed in Chapter IV.
[b] One school represented.
[c] Two schools represented.

tion department. Though assigned heavy weight by the juries,[3] this suggested phase of coordination is not recognized as feasible in the majority of the 25 schools.

B. By Participating in the Teaching of College Courses

1. Through Offering Occasional Units in College Courses Where the Training School Faculty Member Is More of an Authority than Is the Regular College Instructor (e.g., Lesson Planning, Units of Work)[4]

Table XXIV shows that only a few instructors, representing ten schools, report that critic teachers offer units formally or informally in college courses. The majority of those who invite such assistance do so once a term. It is the policy of the education department in one of the schools to have each critic teacher visit classes and participate in the discussion when technique for a grade is being studied.

2. By Aiding Students Who Are Preparing Work for Their College Classes (e.g., Obtaining Data for Case Studies, Conferences Regarding Routine Details of Classroom Management, etc.)

When critic teachers aid students in preparing work for their college classes, it is usually done through individual conferences, at the request of the college instructor, and by each critic teacher within a given school. Table XXV shows that this type of cooperative activity was reported by 29 college instructors in 15 schools, and that in 11 instances, it was at the request of the college student.

3. Through Teaching Entire College Courses

Campus school critic teachers offer education department courses during the academic year in six of the twenty-five schools. Because it was necessary to use this information in the interpretation of Part I of the questionnaire, some of the details of such teaching are given in Chapter III, pp. 55, 56. The types of courses taught by these critic teachers are discussed by schools as follows:

School 1. All courses in Early and Later Elementary Education

[3] See Chap. II.

[4] This does not include preparation for or follow-up of training school observation which is included in Chap. V, pp. 149 ff.

are taught by critic teachers (called training school supervisors) who have entire supervision of student teaching. This school was described in Chapter III as having a modified Oswego plan in which student teachers are given full responsibility in the training school under the supervision of these supervisors.

School 2. The kindergarten critic teacher conducts a morning kindergarten and teaches two Early Elementary courses each semester.

School 3. During the summer session only, the first grade and sixth grade critic teachers offer college courses in Children's Literature and in the Teaching of Language Arts, respectively.

School 4. Each of the three elementary grade critic teachers offers a course in Directed Observation every semester.

School 5. During the summer session only, the fifth and sixth grade critic teacher offers Child Psychology and Intermediate Grade Methods.

School 6. Each semester the kindergarten critic teacher offers Kindergarten-Primary Education courses, and the first grade critic teacher offers a course in Primary Methods. During the summer three other critic teachers each offers a course in Primary or Intermediate Grade Methods.

School 7. The intermediate grade critic teacher offers Intermediate Grade Education each semester.

School 8. Each critic teacher offers a course in training school observation each semester; in addition, the kindergarten critic teacher offers two Kindergarten-Primary Education courses.

School 9. All critic teachers in the campus school are responsible for freshman observation, the students spending four days a week in this activity. The fifth day is given over to class discussion with the principal of the campus training school.

The questionnaire included a category, "During the summer session at another institution," but no frequencies were recorded.

All of the above report refers to critic teachers in elementary school grades. Certain of the critic teachers in the special subjects reported that they offered college courses.[5] Four of the eight[6] in

[5] These faculty members are not members of the college department, who also supervise in the training school, but are definitely called critic teachers.

[6] Eight schools employ an art critic teacher; six, a music critic teacher; and six, a physical education critic teacher.

TABLE XXIV

College Courses in Which Members of the Training School Staff Offer Occasional Units When More of an Authority Than the Regular College Instructor*

College Courses	Frequency: By Teaching Definite Sections of the College Course Which Were Assigned to Training School Staff Members When Course was Organized this Year			Frequency: By Visiting the College Course and Participating in the Discussion When Asked		Activity Initiated by		Critic Teachers Who Offer Units						
	Monthly	Twice a Term	Once a Term	Weekly	Once a Term	College Instructor	Head of College Department	All General	Kindergarten	Primary	Intermediate Grade	Art	Music	Physical Education
Early Elementary Education Curriculum	1[b]				1[c]	2				2				
Educational Psychology				1	1[c]	2		2						
Fine Arts Curriculum			1				1					1		
Fine Arts Principles			1[c]				1					1		
Introduction to Teaching[a]			1		1[c]	2			1	1				
Kindergarten Theory for Primary Teachers					1[c]	1			1					
Later Elementary Education Curriculum					1[c]	1					1			
Music Principles			1				1						1	
Principles of Education					1[c]	1		1						
Teaching of History			1				1			1				
Teaching of Public School Art			1				1					1		
Teaching of Public School Music		1					1						1	
Teaching of Reading	1[b]		1			2		1		1				

* No answer from fifteen schools.
[a] This course taught by the director of training in both schools represented.
[b] This instructor is director of training in this institution (both courses).
[c] These frequencies reported by two schools.

TABLE XXV

College Courses for Which Training School Faculty Members Aid College Students in Preparing Work*

College Courses	Frequency: By Individual Conferences with the Students at Other Than Scheduled Class Hours				Frequency: By Group Meetings with the Students at Other Than Scheduled Class Hours		Activity Initiated by		Critic Teachers Who Participate						
	Weekly	Monthly	Once a Term	Yearly	Once a Term	Yearly	College Instructor	Students	All General	Kindergarten	Primary	Intermediate	Art	Music	Physical Education
Classroom Management		1						1	1						
Early Elementary Education Courses	1		2[b]		1		3[b]	1			4				
Educational Psychology		1	2	1[a]		1[a]	2[a]	2	4						
History of Education			1				1		1						
Kindergarten Theory for Primary Teachers[d]			1					1		1					
Later Elementary Education Courses	1						1					1			
Rural Education Courses[d]		1					1		1						
Teaching of Arithmetic[d]			1					1	1						
Teaching of the Elementary School Subjects	1	1						2	2						
Teaching of English			1					1	1						
Teaching of Geography[d]	1		1				1	1	1			1			
Teaching of Health[d]		1					1		1						
Teaching of Nature Study[d]	1						1				1				
Teaching of Physical Education[d]			1				1								1
Teaching of Public School Music	1						1							1	
Teaching of Reading	1	1					2		2						
Technique of Teaching		1[c]	1		1[b]		2[b]	1[c]	3						
Tests and Measurements[d]	1			1			2		1			1			

* No answer was received from ten schools.
[a] This same case appears under more than one category.
[b] This course is taught by a college instructor who is a training school supervisor.
[c] This course is taught by the director of training.
[d] Reported by two schools.

fine arts taught a college course in Art Education; and a fifth, Art Theory courses; three of the six in music taught a course in Public School Music; and three of the six in physical education, a course in the Teaching of Physical Education. Each of the above offered these courses during the academic year.

C. By Being Cognizant of the Content of College Courses

1. By Visiting College Courses [7]

Though teacher training authorities recommend intervisitation as a device for coordinating theory and practice in a teacher training institution, the investigator found but few instances of critic teachers visiting college classes. In 17 of the 25 schools no report of such activity was made. The data concerning the remaining 8 are as follows:[7]

College Courses Observed	*Frequency*	*Initiated by*	*Critic Teachers Who Visited*
Educational Psychology..	Weekly	College instructor	Second and sixth
Investigations in Reading.	Daily for 3 weeks*	College instructor	All
Teaching Elementary School Science.........	Once a year	Critic teacher	Third and fourth
Teaching Elementary School Subjects........	Monthly	College instructor	All
Teaching of Geography...	Monthly	Critic teacher	Fifth and sixth
Teaching of Penmanship..	Once a term	Critic teacher	All
Teaching of Public School Music................	Twice a term	Critic teacher	Music
Visual Education........	Weekly	Critic teacher	All

* This visitation extended through the semester so that different critic teachers attended during each three weeks' period.

2. By Having Recent Outlines of the College Courses

Table XXVI displays the fact that critic teachers receive outlines for few college courses, only one school reporting that such outlines were available for each college course. The remaining 20 instances are divided among 11 schools.

[7] This does not refer to or include cooperative preparation for or follow up of training school observation.

TABLE XXVI

Frequency with Which Critic Teachers Receive Outlines of the Content of College Courses*

College Courses	Frequency			Activity Initiated by						Critic Teachers				
	Twice a Month	Once a Term	Yearly	Administration	College Instructor	Critic Teacher	Mutual	Head of Department	State Department	All General	Kindergarten	Primary Grade	Third and Seventh Grade	Physical Education and Primary	Music
Children's Literature			2		1				1	2					
Directed Observation[a]			1	1						1					
Early Elementary Education Curriculum	1						1					1			
Entire College Curriculum		1		1						1					
Introduction to Teaching			2[b]	1	1[b]					2					
Kindergarten Curriculum			1						1		1				
Physical Education Curriculum			1					1						1	
Principles of Education			1	1						1					
Teaching of Arithmetic			1					1		1					
Teaching of Elementary School Science			1		1								1		
Teaching of the Common Branches			1	1						1					
Teaching of Geography[c]															
Teaching of Physical Education			2		2					1				1	
Teaching of Public School Music			1			1									1
Teaching of Reading		1	1			2				2					
Technique of Teaching			2		2					2					
Visual Education			1	1						1					

* No answer from thirteen schools.
[a] This course taught by the principal of the training school.
[b] In one school this instructor is also a training school supervisor.
[c] On file in college office.

To summarize for Part II[8] of this present practice survey, we may say that, though the eight suggested activities were heavily weighted by the juries as being important ways of effecting cooperation between training school and college faculties, little participation in any one of them was reported by the 25 schools. In no case was such cooperation recorded between members of the training school faculty and a college instructor who taught no professional, only subject matter, courses.

Table XXVII is included here to show the jury ranking of various personnel groups who might cooperate in the activities of Part II.

Part III. Participation of the Entire Faculty in Activities Which Concern the Teacher Training Institution as a Unit

The cooperative activities grouped in Part III differ from those in Parts I and II because they apply to the school as a unit rather than to college departments or training school individually. The relative importance of various types of personnel groups through which the activities may be accomplished are tabulated in Table XXXIV.[9] The reader should refer to this table in comparing present practice as exhibited in Tables XXVIII to XXXIII, with the estimate of experts.

A. By Determining the Policies of the Institution Relative to Such Matters as Entrance Requirements, Attendance Regulations, Graduation Requirements, etc.

When questionnaires were personally presented in the visits to 25 schools, the investigator found that without exception members of the college departments were placed on faculty committees, and were always invited to attend group faculty meetings. Since there was not equal participation of critic teachers in such activities, Table XXVIII lists only those committee or group meetings to which critic teachers contributed as members.

It was reported in eleven of the 25 schools that critic teachers

[8] Participation of members of the training school staff in the functions of the other college departments.

[9] Table XXXIV, pages 209–211, shows the ranking of activities in Part III by the three juries.

TABLE XXVII

Rank Value Which Three Juries Assigned to Methods for Carrying out the Cooperative Activities Which Were Given a Weighted Evaluation in Table I A*

	Jury I More than 1,000			Jury II 500 to 1,000			Jury III Less than 500			All Juries
	P	D	Both	P	D	Both	P	D	Both	
II. *Participation of Members of the Training School Staff in the Functions of the Other College Departments*										
A. By aiding in formulating the college curriculum										
1. By participating in determining the content of college courses										
a. As members of a general curriculum committee composed of representatives of each college department and the training school	1.8	1.5	1.6	1.9	1.2	1.5	1.3	1.2	1.2	1.5
b. As members of subject committees	1.8	2.0	1.9	1.8	2.0	1.9	1.9	2.2	2.0	2.0
c. Through individual conferences with the college instructors	2.4	2.6	2.5	2.3	2.8	2.6	2.8	2.7	2.7	2.6
2. By participating in the selection of such college materials as textbooks, supplementary books, laboratory equipment, etc.										
a. As members of subject committees which select materials for their own subjects	1.5	1.9	1.8	1.8	2.0	1.9	1.7	1.8	1.7	1.8
b. As members of a general committee for selecting materials, composed of representatives of each college department and the training school	2.4	1.6	2.0	2.2	2.0	2.1	1.7	1.6	1.7	1.9
c. Through individual conferences with the college instructors	2.1	2.5	2.3	2.0	2.1	2.0	2.6	2.7	2.6	2.3
3. By participating in planning new experiments and techniques for the college departments (e.g., size of college classes, having consultant advisors for students, etc.)										
a. As members of a general curriculum committee composed of representatives of each college department and the training school	2.0	1.5	1.7	2.1	1.6	1.8	1.6	1.5	1.6	1.7
b. As members of subject committees	2.0	1.9	2.0	1.8	2.1	1.9	1.9	2.1	2.0	2.0
c. Through individual conferences with the college instructors	2.0	2.6	2.3	2.2	2.4	2.3	2.5	2.4	2.5	2.4

TABLE XXVII (*Continued*)

	Jury I More than 1,000			Jury II 500 to 1,000			Jury III Less than 500			All Juries
	P	D	Both	P	D	Both	P	D	Both	
B. By participating in the teaching of college courses										
1. Through offering occasional units in college courses where the training school faculty member is more of an authority on that unit than is the regular college instructor (e.g. lesson planning, units of work)										
a. By teaching definite sections of college courses which are assigned to them when the course is set up.......	1.4	1.3	1.3	1.3	1.4	1.3	1.4	1.3	1.4	1.3
b. By sitting in on college courses and participating in the discussion when asked........................	1.6	1.7	1.8	1.7	1.6	1.7	1.6	1.7	1.7	1.7
2. By aiding students who are preparing work for their college classes (e.g., obtaining data for case studies, conferences regarding routine details of classroom management, etc.)										
a. By individual conferences with the students at other than scheduled class hours.......................	1.3	1.3	1.3	1.3	1.4	1.4	1.3	1.3	1.3	1.3
b. By group meetings with the students at other than scheduled class hours............................	1.7	1.7	1.7	1.7	1.6	1.6	1.7	1.7	1.7	1.7
3. Through teaching entire college courses										
a. During the academic year........................	2.0	1.7	1.7	1.7	1.9	1.8	1.5	1.5	1.5	1.7
b. During the summer session at their own institution..	2.0	1.6	1.7	1.9	1.5	1.7	2.0	2.2	2.1	1.8
c. During the summer session at another institution....	2.0	2.7	2.6	2.4	2.6	2.5	2.5	2.3	2.4	2.5
C. By being cognizant of the content of college courses										
1. By visiting college courses..........................	1.6	1.4	1.5	1.4	1.6	1.5	1.4	1.8	1.5	1.5
2. By having recent outlines of the college courses.........	1.5	1.6	1.5	1.6	1.4	1.5	1.6	1.3	1.5	1.5

* In this table, the subitems have been rearranged in order of preference according to the combined rating of the three juries, for example, of the three subitems, item II A 1. *a*, As members of a general curriculum committee composed of representatives of each college department and the training school, is considered most important by the combined juries, and II A I *c*, Through individual conferences with the college instructors, is considered least important. Therefore the former is listed first in the table, and the latter is listed last.

The numerals at the right of this table represent the relative values assigned subitems by the group of professors of education and directors of training within a jury, the mean ranking of a jury, and the mean of the three juries combined. The numeral 1 would represent a perfect score for any subitem, and the numeral represented by the number of subitems (in this case, 3) would represent the lowest possible rank of a subitem.

When ranking the three subitems under item II A 1, it is clear that the professors and directors, when considered as juries, give subitem 1 first rank; but it is also clear that the vote was not unanimous by the three juries and that the vote of Jury III was more favorable than that of Juries I and II. A fuller explanation of the technique used in this connection may be found on pages 30–31.

Jury I was composed of 11 professors of education and 13 directors of training. Jury II was composed of 11 professors of education and 14 directors of training. Jury III was composed of 14 professors of education and 12 directors of training.

were never invited or required to attend faculty meetings. Two of these institutions use city schools for laboratory purposes, which may account for the absence of this type of cooperative endeavor. Only nine of the schools reported that critic teachers were appointed as members of committees to consider school policies. No trend is evident in Table XXVIII as to type of policy determining committee of which critic teachers were members or as to frequency of meeting. It shows, however, that if critic teachers so participate usually the entire campus school staff contributes rather than selected members.

B. By Agreeing upon the Methods by Which Common Equipment May Be Made Accessible to Faculty Members, Students, and Training School Children

Table XXIX displays the extent to which the use of common equipment may be a basis for coordinating the training school and college staff. It is evident that this suggestion is not in force to any noticeable degree since 15 schools made no report concerning it. A materials bureau, described by Dr. Alexander[10] in the following quotation, was reported by three schools.

> I have recommended for a good many years another type of cooperative effort which I called the Materials Bureau. The Bureau should be an adjunct of the main library on the campus, a bureau in which the materials of teaching, as books, papers, clippings, slides, films, and the like, are kept. This Materials Bureau should be organized with the same system as used in the library, the same captions being used as are generally found in the course of study. It is thus possible for students planning to teach various units of work to find materials which each has to find with the least possible loss of time. This Bureau is cooperative in that all members of the staff could be employed in contributing materials to it and seeing that books and pamphlets and the like which students need in planning elementary or secondary school work in their respective fields would be on hand and well organized.

C. By Participating in Planning Such College Activities as College Assembly, Social Program, Departmental Clubs, School Publications, Special Day Programs, Commencement, etc.

A second type of faculty committee organization to which the

[10] Alexander, Thomas. "Coordination of the Laboratory Schools with the Subject-Matter Departments in the College." *Cooperative Planning for Teacher Training Standards in Texas.* 1931 Conference Proceedings, p. 138.

TABLE XXVIII[a]

Faculty Committees or Groups of Which Critic Teachers Are Members and Which Determine Policies of the Institution Relative to Such Matters as Entrance Requirements, Attendance Regulations, Graduation Requirements, Scholarships, etc.*

Faculty Policy Committees or Groups of Which Critic Teachers Are Members	Frequency: As Member of Temporary Committee Appointed to Consider Individual Policy		Frequency: As Member of Standing Faculty Committee for Specific Activity					Activity Initiated by	Critic Teachers Who Participated				
	Twice Monthly	Yearly	Weekly	Twice Monthly	Monthly	Once a Term	Yearly	Administration	All General	First Grade	Second Grade	Third Grade	Sixth Grade
Certification and Degrees		1						1	1				
Chapel Attendance Committee[c]			1					1					1
Curriculum Committee					2		2	4	2	1	1	1	
Educational Exhibit							1	1[b]	1				
Group Faculty Meetings				5	9			14	14				
Personnel Program	1							1	1				
Philosophy of Institution		1						1	1				
Placement and Follow-up					1	1		2[b]	2				
Planning for Faculty Meetings					1			1				1	
Student Teaching Experiment Committee			1					1	1				
Total	1	2	2	5	13	1	3	27	23	1	1	2	1

* No answer from committees in sixteen schools. No answer from faculty meetings in eleven schools.

[a] One additional category, Through individual conferences with various faculty members, appeared on questionnaire, but received no frequencies.

[b] Supervisor of training in one school.

[c] Checking on student attendance.

TABLE XXIX

Cooperation between Training School and College Staff Through Agreement upon the Methods by Which Common Equipment May Be Made Accessible to Faculty Members, Students, and Training School Children

Types of Cooperative Endeavor and Personnel of Groups	Frequency by Schools							Activity Initiated by			
	Daily	Weekly	Twice Monthly	Monthly	Once a Term	Yearly	Never	Administration	College Instructor	Mutual	Critic Teacher
College faculty members with whom critic teachers hold conferences concerning equipment....							15				
Costume room director..........				1							1
Curator of museum regarding historical material................				2							2
Director of materials bureau.....	3							2			1
Geography department..........				1						1	
Home economics department.....		1								1	
Librarian......................				2						1	1
Music department regarding college musical instruments used by training school children........		1							1		
Science department.............		1								1	
Teaching of Geography instructor				1	1						2
Teaching of Nature Study instructor..........................				1					1		
Teaching of Physical Education instructor[a]				1	1					2	
Teaching of Public School Art instructor[a]..................			1							1	
Teaching of Public School Music instructor[a]				1	1					2	
Textbook librarian	1							1			
Agreement through group meetings which include the entire faculty							25				
Agreement as a member of a temporary committee which is appointed for this purpose.......							25				
Agreement as a member of a standing committee which has this work in charge....................							25				

[a] These instructors are also training school supervisors.

training school staffs contribute as members is reported in Table XXX. It is apparent that critic teachers from 14 of the 25 schools participate in planning and conducting a variety of student activities.

D. By Cooperating on the Placement of Graduates

The last two categories at the bottom of Table XXXI can hardly be described as cooperation between training school and college faculty but rather as participation in a cooperative function of a teachers college or normal school. Critic teachers in 15 of the schools reported that they contributed records of students to the placement bureau or placement committee. College department instructors made such a report in each of the 23 schools. Critic teachers in 9 schools indicated that they conferred with employers regarding students while college instructors in 24 of the schools made such a report. Training school and college faculty members in 12 schools jointly confer with respect to the qualifications of individual students for specific positions, 9 of the 34 frequencies being reported by one school.

E. Follow-up Work with Graduates

Table XXXII shows that very little faculty cooperation through follow-up work with graduates was reported. Only one critic teacher indicated that she visited such graduates in the field, in company with another faculty member, and in this instance it was with the director of training who was a member of the education department. Critic teachers in two schools reported the findings of a questionnaire study to the faculty at a group meeting; and in a third school the report of visitations was placed on file in the education department office for reference. One school reported a committee technique for answering written appeals for teaching aids in which the members met once a term to outline definite forms to be used in answering appeals of various types. Extensive cooperative effort was reported by four schools through conferences for graduates. In one of these institutions a different college department directs the conference each year. Table XXXII so clearly presents the findings concerning this type of cooperative function that further discussion does not seem necessary.

TABLE XXX

Faculty Committees or Groups Through Which Critic Teachers Participate in Planning College Activities

Faculty Policy Committees or Groups of Which Critic Teachers Are Members	Frequency: As Member of a Standing Committee for the Specific Activity				Frequency: Casual or Irregular Participation in the Activity as Requested by Faculty and Students Individually				Activity Initiated by				Critic Teachers Who Participated								
	Weekly	Monthly	Once a Term	Yearly	Weekly	Monthly	Once a Term	Yearly	Administration	Chairman of Committee	Head of Department	Students	All General	Second Grade	Third Grade	Fifth Grade	Art	Music	Physical Education	Primary Grades	Intermediate Grades
Adviser to Literary Society					1	1				1		1		1		1		1			
Alumni Committee								1		1			1								
Athletic Committee		2							2					1							
Choral Activities (Accompanist)	2										2							2			
College Assembly Address								1	1					1							
College Assembly Committee			1	1			1		3				3								
College Club Tea Committee			1							1				1							
College Operetta Committee				2							2							2			
Commencement Program			1	1			1	3	4	2			3	1	1[c]				1	1	
Decoration Committee						1			1								1				
Dramatic League Adviser						1						1					1				
Early Elementary Education Club		1				2			1	2										3	
Floral Committee							2		2						3						
Homecoming Committee				1					1									1			
Kindergarten Club						1					1									1	
Later Elementary Education Club		1							1												1
Library Committee			1						1							1					
Mothers' Day Program						1		1	1					1							
School Publications Committee		1					1		2						2						
Social Programs Committee	1	1	1		1	2	3	1	6	2			6				1			1	
Special Day Programs Committee		1		1				1	3				3								

TABLE XXX (*Continued*)

Faculty Policy Committees or Groups of Which Critic Teachers Are Members	Frequency: As Member of a Standing Committee for the Specific Activity				Frequency: Casual or Irregular Participation in the Activity as Requested by Faculty and Students Individually				Activity Initiated by				Critic Teachers Who Participated								
	Weekly	Monthly	Once a Term	Yearly	Weekly	Monthly	Once a Term	Yearly	Administration	Chairman of Committee	Head of Department	Students	All General	Second Grade	Third Grade	Fifth Grade	Art	Music	Physical Education	Primary Grades	Intermediate Grades
Student Social Functions[d]							I		I				I								
Student Societies (or Clubs)			2			I			2			I	I			I[b]	I				
Student Welfare Committee		I							I					I		I					
Y. W. C. A. Adviser					I							I						I			
Total	3	8	7	6	3	10	9	8	33	9	5	4	18	7	4	4	4	7	I	6	I

* No answer was received from committees in eleven schools.

[a] One additional category, As a member of general faculty committee which determines all such activities, appeared on questionnaire, but received no frequencies.

[b] Fifth and sixth grade critic teacher.

[c] Third and fourth grade critic teacher.

[d] Chaperon.

TABLE XXXI

Coordination of Training School and College Staff by Cooperating on the Placement of Graduates

Faculty Member	Frequency by Schools			Activity Initiated by				
	On Request	Each Term	Never	Director of Placement	Administration	Employer	College Instructor	Director of Training
College faculty members with whom critic teachers confer concerning qualifications of individual students for definite teaching positions[b]			13					
Dean of College[b]	1			1				
Dean of Women[ab]	1	1		1	1			
Director of Placement Bureau	1	2		1	2			
Director of Training[b] (teaches Education Courses)	3	4		1	2		1	3
Early Elementary Education Instructor		1					1	
Education Department		1			1			
English Department		1						1
History Department		1						1
Later Elementary Education Instructor		1					1	
Music Department Head		1					1	
President of the College	1	1			1			1
Principal of Training School[b] (teaches Education Courses)	2	1		1	1			1
Registrar	1	1		1	1			
Teaching of Elementary School Subjects Instructor (Training School Supervisor)		3			2		1	
Teaching of Physical Education Instructor[b]	1			1				
Teaching of Public School Art Instructor[b]	1			1				
Teaching of Public School Music Instructor[b]	1	1		1			1	
Schools which maintain a placement service to which critic teachers contribute records of students	4	11	10	4	7			4
Schools in which critic teachers confer with employers regarding students	9		16	1	3	4		1

[a] In one school this officer is coordinator of instruction.
[b] Seven frequencies reported by one school.

TABLE XXXII

Members of the Training School Faculty Who Engage in Follow-Up Work with Graduates

Types of Work	Frequency by Schools				Activity Initiated by				Critic Teachers Who Participated				
	When Asked	Once a Term	Yearly	Never	Graduate	Director of Training	Administration	Director of Placement	Second Grade	Fourth Grade	Fifth Grade	Intermediate	All General
1. *By visiting graduates in the field to supervise their first year of teaching experience and to gain material for revising and improving the training curricula*													
a. By visiting these teachers alone		1		24			1						1
b. By visiting in company with other faculty members Director of Training (teaches Education Courses)		1		24		1				1			
c. By visiting in company with college students			1	24			1					1[e]	
2. *By presenting the findings of visits to students in-service, to the other faculty members*													
a. To the entire faculty in a group meeting[a]			2	23			2						2
b. To committees of the faculty who are most concerned				25									
c. To individual members of the faculty who are most concerned[b]	1			24			1						1
3. *By considering the written appeals for teaching helps from graduates*													
a. As a project for individuals who are most competent on the problem concerned	9			16	9								9
b. As member of subject committees which consider problems concerning own subject				25									
c. As in a general faculty meeting where all such problems are considered[c]			1	24			1						1
d. As a member of a committee which is appointed to answer such appeals				23									
Bureau of service and aid	1							1					1
College Mimeograph Service	1							1					1
Follow-up committee: three critics, 2 subject matter teachers, supervisors of training		1					1		1	1	1		

TABLE XXXII (*Continued*)

Types of Work	Frequency by Schools				Activity Initiated by				Critic Teachers Who Participated				
	When Asked	Once a Term	Yearly	Never	Graduate	Director of Training	Administration	Director of Placement	Second Grade	Fourth Grade	Fifth Grade	Intermediate	All General
4. *By holding conferences with graduates who return to the institution to visit*													
a. By individual conferences with such students	25				25								25
b. By departmental conferences with such students. Educational conference and exhibit committee (different departments each year)			1	24			1[g]						1
c. By attending meetings of the entire faculty as a group to which students are invited. Educational conference—entire faculty[d]			3	22			3[f]						3

[a] Findings of a questionnaire study reported at a faculty meeting.
[b] Findings of a questionnaire study on file in the education department office, and accessible to all faculty members.
[c] At a training school faculty meeting only, each offers courses in the education department.
[d] Yearly educational conference called "Alumni Week-End," to which entire faculty contributes—group meetings on teachers' problems.
[e] This critic teacher offers a course in Intermediate Grade Methods.
[f] One official is head of education department.
[g] Supervisor of training.

F. By Publishing as a Joint Enterprise Such Professional Literature as: Courses of Study, Rating Scales, Textbooks, Reports of Cooperative Activities, News Bulletins, Reports of Experiments, and Student Teaching Manuals.

Cooperative publication of professional literature by critic teachers and college instructors was reported in twelve schools. The list includes textbooks, workbooks, reports of training school visits, standardized tests, rating scales, and reports of experiments. Though not a long or exhaustive list, it is evident from Table XXXIII that this type of activity is an effective method for crystallizing cooperative professional enterprise. The mean judgment of the juries assigned 71 out of a possible 251 points (divided among six subdivisions) to this activity.

To summarize for Part III of the present practice we may say that though few schools report cooperative pursuits in activities concerning the school as a unit, those which do, present challenging and meritorious achievement.

Part IV. Administrative Devices Which May Facilitate Cooperation

One section of the score card and of the questionnaire was devoted to the achievement of cooperative endeavor through status of the faculty personnel and through status of the training schools. Throughout the present study the presence or absence of these administrative devices is constantly evident. Certain of the items have been discussed in Chapter III to explain the present practice reports.[11] No attempt will be made here to justify their inclusion as devices for facilitating cooperation, since this has been done by Alexander,[12] Bagley,[13] Evenden,[14] Garrison[15]; and others. Their rela-

[11] Pages 51–60.

[12] Alexander, Thomas. "Coordination of the Laboratory Schools with the Subject-Matter Departments in the College." *Cooperative Planning For Teacher Training Standards in Texas.* Bulletin, North Texas State Teachers College, Denton, Texas, May, 1931, p. 138.

[13] Bagley, W. C., Alexander, T., and Foote, L. *Report of a Special Commission on the Professional Education of White Public School Teachers in Louisiana*, pp. 177–203.

[14] Evenden, E. S. "Cooperation of Teachers of Academic Subjects with the Training School." *Supervisors of Student Teaching Yearbook*, 1925, pp. 5–8.

[15] Garrison, Noble L. *Status and Work of the Training Supervisor.* Contribution to Education, No. 280, pp. 10, 76–98. Bureau of Publications, Teachers College, Columbia University, 1927.

TABLE XXXIII

Professional Literature Published as a Cooperative Enterprise between Training School and College Faculty Members*

Cooperative Publications	Faculty Members Who Cooperated	Activity Initiated by: President of College	College Instructor	Critic Teacher	Mutual	Supervisor of Training
English						
"An Exchange of Letters," article in an English periodical	English instructor, fourth and sixth grade critics		1			
Collection of poems by training school children[c]	Supervisor of student teaching,[a] Demonstration teachers, training teachers					1
"English Work Book"[c]	Head of English department, critic teacher	1				
"English Work Books for Elementary Schools"	Head of English department and sixth grade critic		1			
Grammar textbook[c]	English instructor and eighth grade critic		1			
Language bulletin[c]	English instructor and fourth grade supervisor			1		
"Spelling Work Book"[c]	Head of English department; critic teacher	1				
Geography						
Course of Study in Geography for grades 4, 5, and 6 of the Training School (units of work organization)	Director of training, head of geography department[b], fourth, fifth, and sixth grade critic teachers		1			
"Geography Work Book for grades 5 to 8"	Head of geography department; critic teachers	1				
Mathematics						
Standardized Tests in Arithmetic—grades 1 to 8	Director of research, fourth grade critic		1			
Physical Education						
"Physical Education for Elementary Schools" (a textbook)	Head of physical education department and physical education critic in training school	1				
"Teaching Helps for Physical Education Students" (mimeographed)	Head of woman's physical education department and physical education supervisor in training school				1	
School Bulletins						
Articles contributed to quarterly bulletin of the school	Half of the critic teachers	1				
Student Teaching Reports						
Rating scales for student teaching[c]	Director of training[a] and training school faculty		1			
Report of experiment in having Early Elementary Education students teach in training school prior to student teaching period[c]	Early elementary education instructor and primary and lower intermediate grade supervisors		1			

TABLE XXXIII (*Continued*)

Cooperative Publications	Faculty Members Who Cooperated	Activity Initiated by				
		President of College	College Instructor	Critic Teacher	Mutual	Supervisor of Training
Training School Units						
Collection of units of work[c]	Supervisor of student teaching,[a] demonstration teachers, training teachers					1
Report cards for training school[c]	Director of Training[a] and training school faculty		1			
Reports on training school curriculum, college symposiums, classroom situations—*State Journal of Education*[c]	College instructors solicit help from critics		1			
Reports of units of work—college bulletin[c]	Training school critics	1				
Reports of units of work in Training School[c]	Director of Training[a] and training school faculty		1			

* No cooperative publication reported for thirteen schools.
[a] Teaches courses in education department.
[b] See pages 98-99.
[c] One school represented.

tive importance in the judgment of the juries[16] further justifies their inclusion in any study of cooperation between training school and college faculties.

A. Through Faculty Personnel

1. By Having an Administrative Officer Whose Work Is to Direct the Coordination of the Training School and the Other Departments of Teacher Training Institutions

Constructive proposals concerning desirable programs for cooperation stress the importance of making one officer responsible for promoting reciprocal relations between the college departments and the training school. The following officers were listed as fulfilling that function, by a person in authority in each of the 25 schools:

a. A director of training who is administrative head of the department of education. In one of these, the principal of the campus laboratory school offers a course in Reading Methods in the department of education.......................... 3 schools

b. Director of the training school offers college courses in the department of education.......................... 9 schools[17]

c. Director of the training school supervises college instruction to see that it relates to the professional education of teachers..... 2 schools

d. Principal of the campus training school,who directs college courses in Participation and Student Teaching, works closely with the head of the education department.......................... 1 school

e. Dean of women supervises and directs instruction in the college and training school to see that it relates to the professional education of teachers (no director of training employed).......... 1 school

f. Supervisor of the elementary training school teaches Observation and Participation to elementary major students; the director of training teaches High School Observation and History of Education.......................... 1 school

g. Director of training teaches courses in Early Elementary Education and General Education, and closely supervises student teachers in the laboratory school (a city school)............. 1 school

h. Supervisor of training teaches Introduction to Teaching and supervises campus and off-campus schools.................... 1 school

[16] See pages 26–28, Chapter II.

[17] One school uses three schools, all off-campus, demonstration teaching being done in each by teachers who have no student teachers. Critic teachers do no demonstration teaching in these schools. In three others the director of training also has off-campus schools in charge.

TABLE XXXIV

Rank Value Which Three Juries Assigned to Methods for Carrying Out the Cooperative Activities Which Were Given a Weighted Evaluation in Table I

	Jury I More than 1,000			Jury II 500 to 1,000			Jury III Less than 500			Mean of Juries
	P	D	M	P	D	M	P	D	M	
III. *Participation of the Entire Faculty in Activities Which Concern the Teacher Training Institution as a Unit*										
A. By determining the policies of the institution relative to such matters as entrance requirements, attendance regulations, school athletics, graduation requirements, scholarships, loan fund, etc.										
1. As members of standing faculty committees which consider individual policies	2.0	1.7	1.8	2.0	2.2	2.1	2.0	2.3	2.2	2.0
2. As members of temporary committees which are appointed to consider an individual policy	2.3	2.9	2.6	2.6	1.6	2.0	1.9	1.5	1.7	2.1
3. By attending group meetings which include the entire faculty	2.0	2.2	2.1	1.8	2.8	2.3	2.4	2.5	2.5	2.3
4. Through individual conferences with various faculty members	3.7	3.3	3.5	3.6	3.5	3.5	3.6	3.7	3.7	3.6
B. By agreeing upon the methods by which common equipment may be made accessible to faculty members, students, and training school children										
1. By assigning this work to a person who directs the materials bureau where common equipment is kept	2.4	2.5	2.5	2.2	2.6	2.4	2.6	2.4	2.5	2.5
2. As a member of a standing committee which has this work in charge	2.8	2.0	2.4	3.1	3.0	3.0	2.4	2.3	2.4	2.6
3. As a member of a temporary committee which is appointed for this purpose	2.8	3.1	3.0	2.4	2.9	2.6	2.9	3.3	3.1	2.9
4. Through individual conferences with the faculty members most concerned	3.0	3.1	3.0	3.5	3.0	3.3	3.8	3.2	3.5	3.3
5. Through group meetings which include the entire faculty	4.0	4.3	4.2	3.9	3.5	3.7	3.4	3.8	3.5	3.8
C. By participating in planning such college activities as college assembly, social programs, school clubs, school publications, special day programs, commencement, etc.										
1. As members of a general faculty committee which determines all such activities	1.8	1.3	1.5	2.0	1.6	1.8	1.9	1.7	1.8	1.7

TABLE XXXIV (*Continued*)

	Jury I More than 1,000			Jury II 500 to 1,000			Jury III Less than 500			Mean of Juries
	P	D	M	P	D	M	P	D	M	
2. As members of standing committees for specific activities	1.8	1.9	1.9	1.5	1.8	1.6	1.7	1.5	1.6	1.7
3. Casual or irregular participation in such activities as requested by faculty members or students individually....	2.4	2.8	2.6	2.6	2.6	2.6	2.4	2.8	2.7	2.6
D. By cooperating on the placement of graduates										
1. Maintaining a placement bureau to which all faculty members contribute records of students................	1.2	1.1	1.1	1.4	1.0	1.1	1.3		1.2	1.1
2. By individual conferences with faculty members regarding qualifications of individual students for definite positions...	2.5	2.5	2.5	2.4	2.4	2.4	2.3		2.3	2.4
3. By individual conferences with employers regarding students..	2.3	2.4	2.4	2.3	2.6	2.5	2.4		2.5	2.5
E. By follow-up work with graduates										
1. By visiting graduates in the field to supervise their first year of teaching experience and to gain material for revising and improving the training curricula										
a. By visiting these teachers alone....................	1.1	1.2	1.2	1.4	1.4	1.4	1.3	1.4	1.4	1.3
b. By visiting in company with other faculty members..	2.4	1.9	2.1	1.9	1.9	1.9	1.8	1.9	1.9	1.9
c. By visiting in company with college students........	2.6	2.9	2.8	2.7	2.8	2.8	2.9	2.7	2.8	2.8
2. By presenting the findings of visits to students in-service to the other faculty members										
a. To committees of the faculty who are most concerned (e.g., material on teaching technique to a committee of critic teachers)...................................	1.7	1.4	1.6	1.5	1.4	1.4	1.6	1.5	1.6	1.5
b. To individual members of the faculty who are most concerned..	1.8	2.0	1.9	2.0	2.4	2.2	2.4	2.3	2.4	2.2
c. To the entire faculty in a group meeting............	2.5	2.5	2.5	2.6	2.3	2.4	2.0	2.2	2.1	2.3
3. By considering the written appeals for teaching helps from graduates										
a. As a project for individuals who are most competent on the problem concerned.........................	1.4	2.1	1.8	1.4	1.6	1.5	1.7	1.8	1.8	1.7
b. As a subject committee which considers only those problems concerning its own subject................	2.5	2.1	2.3	2.2	2.1	2.1	2.4	2.8	2.6	2.3
c. A committee which is appointed to answer to such appeals..	2.5	2.1	2.3	2.6	2.7	2.6	2.5	2.1	2.3	2.4

TABLE XXXIV (*Continued*)

	Jury I More than 1,000			Jury II 500 to 1,000			Jury III Less than 500			Mean of Juries
	P	D	M	P	D	M	P	D	M	
d. As in a general faculty meeting where all such problems are considered	3.7	3.8	3.8	3.9	3.6	3.8	3.5	3.3	3.4	3.6
4. By holding conferences with graduates who return to the institution to visit										
a. By individual conferences with such students	1.1	1.2	1.2	1.4	1.2	1.3	1.4	1.3	1.4	1.3
b. By departmental conferences with such students	1.9	1.9	2.9	1.8	1.9	1.9	1.8	1.9	1.9	2.2
c. By attending meetings of the entire faculty as a group to which these students are invited	3.0	2.9	3.0	2.8	2.9	2.8	2.8	2.8	2.8	2.9
F. By publishing as a joint enterprise such professional literature as										
1. Courses of study for the training school	4.1	2.7	3.3	3.1	3.6	3.3	3.3	3.6	3.4	3.4
2. Reports of experiments in the training school	2.7	4.4	3.6	3.8	4.3	4.1	3.6	5.4	4.4	4.0
3. Student teaching manuals	4.6	3.1	3.8	5.1	4.5	4.8	3.3	4.3	3.8	4.1
4. Reports of experiments in college departments	5.1	5.7	5.4	4.2	4.3	4.2	4.5	5.6	5.2	4.9
5. Courses of study for the college courses	6.3	5.4	5.8	5.2	4.7	4.9	5.3	4.0	4.7	5.2
6. Reports of cooperative activities within the college	5.6	6.2	5.9	6.6	5.1	5.8	6.0	4.7	5.4	5.7
7. Children's textbooks	5.8	6.5	6.2	5.6	6.2	5.9	6.2	7.3	6.7	6.3
8. Rating scales for student teachers	6.4	5.3	5.8	6.9	7.2	7.1	7.1	6.6	6.9	6.6
9. School news bulletins	6.8	8.4	7.1	8.2	7.6	7.9	7.8	5.7	6.9	7.3
10. College textbooks	7.6	6.5	8.0	6.4	7.5	7.0	8.0	7.7	7.9	7.6

* In this table, the subitems have been rearranged in order of preference according to the combined rating of the three juries. For example, of the three subitems, item II A 1 a, As members of a general curriculum committee composed of representatives of each college department and the training school, is considered most important by the combined juries, and item II A 1 c, Through individual conferences with the college instructors, is considered least important. Therefore the former is listed first in the table, and the latter is listed last.

The numerals at the right of this table represent the relative values assigned subitems by the group of professors of education and directors of training within a jury, the mean ranking of a jury, and the mean of the three juries combined. The numeral 1 would represent a perfect score for any subitem, and the numeral represented by the number of subitems (in this case, 3) would represent the lowest possible rank of a subitem.

When ranking the three subitems under Item II A 1, it is clear that the professors and directors, when considered as juries, give subitem 1 first rank; but it is also clear that the vote was not unanimous by the three juries and that the vote of Jury III was more favorable than that of Juries I and II. A fuller explanation of the technique used in this connection may be found on pages 30–31.

Jury I was composed of eleven professors of education and thirteen directors of training. Jury II was composed of eleven professors of education and fourteen directors of training. Jury III was composed of fourteen professors of education and twelve directors of training.

i. Director of training supervises off-campus and on-campus training schools, but has little relationship with the college departments.. 2 schools

j. Director of training is also superintendent of city schools (one campus, one city, and three rural schools under his supervision).. 1 school

k. Director of training who supervises campus elementary and high school, represents the laboratory department in the curriculum committee and the faculty council.......................... 3 schools

l. Director of training supervises campus and off-campus training schools, and, in addition, offers courses in later elementary education.. 1 school

m. Two schools employ a dean of instruction in addition to the directors of training mentioned in (*b*) and (*i*) above. The former officer supervises instruction in college and training school to see that such courses provide adequate training for the intending teacher.

It is apparent from the above data that each school delegates the work of coordination to one officer in the school, and that in the majority of the schools such work is done in varying degree by the director of training.

As is tabulated in Table XXXV, the juries ranked first the suggestion that the coordinating officer should be both director of training and head of the education department; and, closely second, that he should be a director of training who also supervises college instruction to see that it is related to the professional education of teachers. In light of these data, those officers described in items (*a*), (*c*), (*e*), (*k*), and (*m*) above, most nearly fulfill the requirements set up by the juries.

2. *By Having a Consultant Advisor for Each Student, Who Advises Him Throughout His Pre-service Training and Who Decides When the Student Is Ready to do Student Teaching and When Ready to Graduate* [18]

Three schools report that students majoring in elementary education are aided by the type of consultant advisor described above. In each case these advisors were members of the education department.

[18] *School 1.* One for first two years (lower division) and a second for last two years—all members of education department.

School 2. Dean of instruction is consultant advisor.

TABLE XXXV

Rank Value Which Three Juries Assigned to Methods for Carrying Out the Cooperative Activities Given a Weighted Evaluation in Table I A*

	Jury I More than 1,000			Jury II 500 to 1,000			Jury III Less than 500			All Juries
	P	D	M	P	D	M	P	D	M	
IV. *Administrative Devices Which May Facilitate Cooperation*										
A. Through faculty personnel										
1. By having an administrative officer whose work is to direct the coordination of the training school and the other departments of teacher training institutions										
a. As administrative head of the department of education and principal of the training school	1.7	1.7	1.7	1.7	1.6	1.7	1.6	1.6	1.6	1.7
b. As principal of the training school and as supervisor of college instruction to see that it relates to the professional education of teachers	1.9	1.8	1.8	2.0	2.4	2.0	1.7	2.0	1.9	1.9
c. As a teacher of college courses in the department of education and as principal of the training school	2.4	2.5	2.5	2.3	2.0	2.4	2.6	2.4	2.5	2.5
3. By having supervisors of each grade level in the training school (e.g., primary, intermediate, upper) who										
a. Supervise the critic teachers and student-teachers in their grade level in the training school	1.2	1.2	1.2	1.1	1.1	1.1	1.1	1.2	1.2	1.2
b. Supervise their students in the training school, no critic teachers being employed	1.8	1.8	1.8	1.9	1.9	1.9	1.9	1.8	1.9	1.9
B. Through the status of the training school										
1. By having a training school building which is accessible to the college faculty by being										
a. On the campus near the college buildings	1.4	1.1	1.2	1.2	1.2	1.2	1.4	1.3	1.3	1.3
b. A city school not more than a ten-minute walk from the college buildings	2.1	2.3	2.2	2.2	2.4	2.3	2.1	2.1	2.1	2.2
c. In the main college building	2.6	2.6	2.6	2.6	2.4	2.4	2.6	2.7	2.6	2.5
2. By interlocking the training school and the college departments										
a. By making the training school an integral part of the education department	2.5	2.1	2.3	2.1	2.4	2.3	1.9	1.9	1.9	2.1

TABLE XXXV (*Continued*)

	Jury I More than 1,000			Jury II 500 to 1,000			Jury III Less than 500			All Juries
	P	D	M	P	D	M	P	D	M	
b. By making the training school nearest the college departments an experimental and model demonstration school operated independently as such and open for observation and visitors at all times, student teaching being carried on in other training schools	2.1	2.8	2.4	2.4	2.4	2.4	2.5	2.8	2.6	2.5
c. By making the training school the laboratory of the college, existing primarily to experiment with, and to demonstrate, the theory taught in any college course	2.5	2.6	2.6	2.0	2.4	2.2	2.7	2.8	2.8	2.5
d. By making the training school an independent unit of the college and giving it equal rank with the academic and education departments	3.0	2.5	2.8	3.6	2.9	3.2	3.0	2.4	2.7	2.9

* In this table, the subitems have been rearranged in order of preference according to the combined rating of the three juries. For example, of the three subitems, item II A 1 a, As members of a general curriculum committee composed of representatives of each college department and the training school, is considered most important by the combined juries, and item II A 1 c, Through individual conferences with the college instructors, is considered least important. Therefore the former is listed first in the table, and the latter is listed last.

The numerals at the right of this table represent the relative values assigned subitems by the group of professors of education and directors of training within a jury, the mean ranking of a jury, and the mean of the three juries combined. The numeral 1 would represent a perfect score for any subitem, and the numeral represented by the number of subitems (in this case, 3) would represent the lowest possible rank of a subitem.

When ranking the three subitems under Item II A 1, it is clear that the professors and directors, when considered as juries, give subitem 1 first rank; but it is also clear that the vote was not unanimous by the three juries and that the vote of Jury III was more favorable than that of Juries I and II. A fuller explanation of the technique used in this connection may be found on pages 30–31.

Jury I was composed of eleven professors of education and thirteen directors of training. Jury II was composed of eleven professors of education and fourteen directors of training. Jury III was composed of fourteen professors of education and twelve directors of training.

3. *By Having Supervisors of Each Grade Level in the Training School (e.g., Primary, Intermediate, Upper) Who—*
   a. *Supervise their students in the training school, no critic teachers being employed*
   b. *Supervise the critic teachers and student teachers in their grade level in the training school*

This type of faculty personnel has also been described for the 25 schools in Chapter III, page 58. To summarize here it may be said that of the two schools which reported 3*a* above, in one instance the teachers college used a public school for laboratory purposes, the state bearing no responsibility in the payment of salaries to the city teachers. In the second school these supervisors do the work generally assumed by critic teachers, except that student teachers are given more authority and responsibility in the training school. Of the five schools checking 3*b* above, two use city schools for student teaching. Consequently the critic teachers are not as well trained for the supervision of students as for teaching children and therefore require the aid of supervisors. In the remaining three cases, the work of so-called supervision of critic teachers is coordinate rather than supervisory in nature.

4. *By Requiring That Every Member of the Faculty Shall Have Had Some Experience in Teaching in the Types of Schools for Which He Is Preparing Teachers*

Three of the 25 schools checked this item as descriptive of their faculty. The investigator found by checking through the professional history data requested on the first page of each questionnaire, this to be a 100 per cent true statement in each case.

5. *By Paying Equal Salary for Equal Training and Experience to Every Member of the Faculty, Including the Training School Staff*

Nine of the 25 schools checked this statement as descriptive of their salary schedules. In the remaining schools critic teachers received less remuneration than college instructors, though their training may have been equivalent.

6. *By Adjusting the Service Load of Each Member of the College Faculty to Provide for Regular Contacts with the Training School. Reported by 7 schools* [19]
7. *By Adjusting the Service Load of Each Member of the Training School Staff to Provide for Regular Contacts with the College Departments. Reported by 1 school*

In the judgment of the juries it is equally important for the service load of each group to be adjusted to provide for regular contacts with the other part of the school. That this is not true in practice may account for the fact that many more activities and participants were reported for Part I than for Parts II and III of the study.

B. Through the Status of the Training School

1. *By Having a Training School Building Which Is Accessible*[20] *to the College Faculty by Being—*
   a. *In the main college building—1 school*
   b. *On the campus near the college buildings—21 schools*
   c. *A city school not more than a ten-minute walk from the college buildings—3 schools*

2. *By Interlocking the Training School and the College Departments*
   a. *By making the training school an integral part of the education department—11 schools*
   b. *By making the training school an independent unit of the college and giving it equal rank with the academic and education departments—9 schools*
   c. *By making the training school the laboratory of the college existing primarily to experiment with, and to demonstrate, the theory taught in any college course—4 schools*
   d. *By making the training school nearest the college departments an experimental and model demonstration school operated independently as such and open for observation and visitors at all times. Student teaching being carried on in other training schools—1 school*

[19] Instructors in the education department only.

[20] Only teacher training institutions with an accessible laboratory school were visited for this study.

3. *By Basing Each Professional Course of the College upon Constant Observation in the Training School from the Freshman Year to Graduation—6 schools*[21]
4. *By Requiring Participation Teaching in the Training School in Each Year of the Student's Study, Leading to Responsible Room Teaching in the Last Year—5 schools*[22]

[21] *School 1.* Accompanying each professional course with observation.
School 2. Only Reading and Speech, Technique of Teaching, I and II, Rural Methods and Management, Children's Literature, Child Development and Parent Education, Lower Primary Education, Handwriting.

[22] *School 1.* In two-year course.
School 3. During second year.

CHAPTER VII

SUMMARY AND RECOMMENDATIONS

Summary

CURRENT professional literature is permeated with treatises which emphasize the importance of coordinating the functions of the academic departments and the laboratory schools in institutions which train teachers. The entire 1932 meeting of the American Association of Teachers Colleges was devoted to a consideration of such correlation of theory and practice. Cooperative activities and administrative devices were proposed and descriptions of their functioning in individual schools reported.

In view of the prominence accorded to this problem through published plans suggested for its solution, the present study does not attempt to propose original programs of cooperative endeavor. Instead it is limited to a consideration of reciprocal relations between campus elementary training school and college department faculties in state teachers colleges and normal schools and treated in the following ways:

1. A present practice survey was made to determine the extent to which plans of coordination are in progress. The findings of the survey are based upon visits to a representative selection of 25 teachers colleges and normal schools throughout the United States.[1]

2. Juries of experts were asked to evaluate the list of cooperative activities suggested by frontier thinkers, using the score card technique.[2]

3. A plan is proposed for using the score card in conducting self-surveys of cooperation between theory and practice faculties in individual schools.[3]

[1] The present practice survey is reported in detail in Chaps. III–VI.

[2] The technique is described in Chap. III, pages 14–30; and the findings are presented in Table I.

[3] See Chap. II, pp. 30–48.

4. A constructive program is outlined to follow up the self-survey, based upon the jury evaluation of cooperative activities.[4]

CONCLUSIONS CONCERNING THE SURVEY OF PRESENT PRACTICE

The degree of cooperation between the faculties of the campus elementary training school and the other departments as reported in the 25 schools visited for this study is probably a cross section of what would be found in all state teachers colleges or normal schools throughout the United States since these schools were selected by the representative sampling technique.

The following specific conclusions are presented, using the main topics of the questionnaire as headings, to give a brief picture of present practice in cooperative activities.

Part I. Participation of Members of the College Departments in the Functions of the Training School

A. By Aiding the Training School Staff in Supervising Student Teachers

1. Few college department instructors observe the teaching of student teachers with any degree of regularity, unless they have been designated as training school supervisors or administrators by the administration of the school. Since such supervisors are rarely appointed from departments other than education, art, music, and physical education, we may conclude that these are the only college departments which engage in this cooperative activity with regularity and frequency.[5]

2. Without exception, college instructors who are designated as training school supervisors follow up student observation with a conference; and a majority of the others who observe also follow up.[6]

3. A majority of the college department instructors who help students plan work they are teaching in the training schools are those who offer courses in professionalized subject matter or who are training school supervisors.[7]

4. Except for the training school administrative officers and

[4] See Chap. VII, pp. 227–234.
[5] See Table III. [6] See Table IV. [7] See Table V.

supervisors, few college instructors aid critic teachers in rating or grading student teachers. This would seem to be in agreement with expert opinion since only six out of fifty-eight points (divided among five items) were allotted to this as a desirable cooperative activity.[8] The reason for such judgment is clear, for unless a college faculty member devotes much time to observation, conference, and planning, his rating would have little value as compared to that of a supervisor or critic teacher.

5. No appreciable amount of cooperative endeavor in the construction or revision of student teaching manuals was reported at the time of this survey.[9]

B. By Aiding in Carrying on the Training School Curriculum

1. Most of the cooperative training school curriculum construction and revision is concerned with the elementary school course of study as a whole, rather than with separate subject categories. The majority of the officials who participate in this activity are from the group of training school administrators and supervisors, or are members of the education department.[10]

2. Few college instructors other than training school officials engage in cooperative selection of textbooks and other materials of instruction for the training school. Such aid is usually given in a conference with individual critic teachers.[11]

3. The cooperative testing of training school children is assumed by the instructor in Tests and Measurements or Educational Psychology, and by the training school administrative and supervisory staff in a major portion of the schools.[12] Contrary to rankings by the juries,[13] this college instructor usually administered the tests himself. Seventy per cent of those who engaged in testing training school children cooperatively also engaged in analysis of the findings and in suggesting remedial measures.[14] Those who do not participate in this cooperative analysis report that such tests are administered to training school children to provide material for college class discussion.

[8] See Table VI. [9] See pp. 87–89. [10] See Table VII.
[11] See Table VIII. [12] See Table IX. [13] See p. 112. [14] See Table X.

4. Participation in extracurricular and community activities of the training school cannot be listed as a significant evidence of cooperation in the present practice study, since few academic instructors other than those working closely with the training school as a part of their service load reported such work in the laboratory school. Assembly programs and parent-teacher association meetings are most frequently named by such staff members.[15]

5. Most teacher training institutions report cooperative experiments as an evidence of faculty coordination. Though not a long list for any school or department, the experiments are significant in their attempt to improve instruction and to coordinate the contributing elements in a teacher training program.[16]

C. *By Having College Classes Observe Teaching Done by Critic Teachers in the Training School*

1. Few college classes observe in the training school unless the course has been definitely organized to include training school observation. This can readily be understood since no school has more than one campus training school, and the scheduling of many observations would impede the work of student teaching. The juries weighted training school observation heavily, assigning as much importance to cooperative preparation and follow up as to the actual observation. Contrary to the opinion of these experts, cooperative preparation and follow up was usually done in a conference between the critic teacher and the college instructor rather than in a joint meeting with the college class as a contributing element.[17]

2. The majority of the instructors who take classes to observe teaching done by critic teachers are members of the education department, who do so because it is an administrative policy that the course shall include scheduled observation in the campus training school. In accord with jury judgment, college instructors usually accompany their classes during observation.[18]

[15] See Table XI and Table XII. [16] See Table XIII.

[17] See Tables XIV and XVI.

[18] See Table XV.

D. By Personally Teaching Children in the Training School

Only training school administrative or supervisory officers habitually teach classes of training school children and the majority of these are supervisors from the special departments of music, art, and physical education. Contrary to the mean jury rankings, more of such instructors teach for observers than without.[19] This seems justified, however, since training school supervisors or administrators are usually employed because of their ability to teach children as well as adults.

E. By Assisting in Adjusting Personality Problems in the Training School

1. Cooperative adjustment of the personality problems of training school children is not considered of major importance either in theory or in practice. Few college instructors other than training school officials or members of the education department engage in this type of cooperation.[20]

2. The score card shows that the juries considered it twice as important for college instructors to aid in adjusting personality problems with student teachers as with training school children. The same groups participate in both types of endeavor, usually through individual conferences with critic teachers or student teachers in the former case.[21]

F. By Aiding in Determining Policies of the Training School[22]

1. Though a minority of the schools report progress in cooperative decision as to which students are prepared to be admitted to student teaching on bases additional to the completion of prescribed courses, the plans are both challenging and constructive.

2. Fewer than one-third of the schools report that the determination of student teaching content is being attempted as a faculty group project.

3. In a few schools groups similar to those in (1) and (2) above participate in determining the kind and amount of contacts students

[19] See Table XVII.
[20] See Table XVIII.
[21] See Table XIX.
[22] See pages 170-178.

should have with the training school prior to entering upon student teaching. In addition, a few individual faculty members meet with critic teachers to plan such contacts in connection with their courses in professionalized subject matter. Most of these participants are members of the education department.

Part II. Participation of Members of the Training School Staff in the Functions of the Other College Departments

Comparatively less emphasis is given in present practice, but not on the score card, to ways in which critic teachers may aid in the functions of the college departments. Probably this is due to the fact that, in the past, critic teachers were less well trained than academic instructors, and their ability to aid the college faculty has not yet been fully appreciated in practice, though the experts gave such cooperative endeavor a heavy weighting.

Only eight types of activities are suggested in the score card by which the training school faculty may participate in the work of the college departments, as compared with 21 in which college department instructors may participate in functions of the training school. Very little cooperative endeavor in these eight activities is in progress and in no case do critic teachers participate in the work of college courses other than in professionalized subject matter.

A. By Aiding in Formulating the College Curriculum

1. Critic teachers have little part in determining the content of college courses. They are seldom consulted concerning any courses other than those in Early and Later Elementary Education which are offered in the education department. Special critic teachers in music, art and physical education are usually invited to aid in determining the content of the professionalized subject matter course in their respective fields.[23]

2. Training school critic teachers have little part in the selection of textbooks for the college courses.[24]

3. Cooperative experimentation concerning techniques to be used in the college departments is reported by few schools, most of which

[23] See Table XXI.
[24] See Table XXII.

is described in connection with education department courses.[25]

B. By Participating in the Teaching of College Courses

1. Critic teachers seldom aid the college instructor in teaching college courses, either by offering occasional units when more of an authority than the regular college instructor, or through aiding college students in preparing work for college courses.[26]

2. Critic teachers in the elementary grades offer college courses in the education department throughout the year in approximately one-third of the schools.[27]

C. By Being Cognizant of the Content of College Courses

1. Critic teachers in eight schools report that they visited one college course during the year of the survey, but took no part in the discussion.[28]

2. Critic teachers receive outlines of certain college courses in eleven of the schools, and for all college courses in one school.[29]

Part III. Participation of the Entire Faculty in Activities Which Concern the Teacher Training Institution as a Unit

Cooperative endeavor was infrequently reported but those activities which were listed presented challenging and meritorius achievement.

1. Critic teachers attend all group meetings of the faculty in 14 of the institutions visited, and in 9 of these are also appointed members of temporary and standing faculty policy committees. They aid in planning extracurricular activities of the college in 14 of the schools.[30]

2. Three institutions maintain a materials bureau to which all members of the faculty contribute. Cooperative agreement as to the mutual use of equipment rarely occurs.[31]

3. Cooperative follow up with graduates either by visitation or in group conferences is engaged in infrequently. Four schools report

[25] See Table XXIII.
[26] See Tables XXIV and XXV.
[27] See pp. 187-191.
[28] See pp. 191-192.
[29] See Table XXVI.
[30] See Tables XXVIII and XXX.
[31] See Table XXIX.

yearly conferences with graduates in which critic teachers play an important part.[32]

4. Twelve schools list publications contributed to by college and training school faculties. Though not exhaustive, the list gives evidence of splendid cooperative endeavor.[33]

Part IV. Certain Administrative Devices Which May Facilitate Cooperation

A. Through Faculty Personnel[34]

1. One officer in each school directs the coordination of the training school with the other departments. In a majority of the cases this official is the director of training who also offers college courses in the education department.

2. Equal salary for equal training and experience is paid to every member of the faculty (including the training school staff) in approximately one-third of the schools.

3. Teacher training institutions do not adjust the service load of each member of the college faculty to provide for regular contacts with the training school, though a minority makes such provision for certain members of the education department. Neither is it customary to adjust the service load of each critic teacher to provide for regular contacts with the college departments.

4. Few teacher training institutions require that each member of the faculty shall have had some experience in teaching in the types of schools for which he is preparing teachers.

5. Only a small percentage of the schools assigns each student to a consultant advisor who counsels him throughout his pre-service training and decides when the student is qualified to begin student teaching, and when ready to graduate.

6. It is customary for an institution to maintain supervisors in art, music, and physical education who offer college courses, supervise student teachers, and direct the organization of their respective fields in the training school. Fewer than one-third of the schools maintain supervisors of each grade level in the training school (e.g.,

[32] See Table XXXII. [33] See Table XXXIII.

[34] These summarized items are reported in the order of importance assigned them on the score card. See Table I.

primary, intermediate, upper) who aid critic teachers in the supervision of student teachers. Usually such supervisors are members of the education department.

B. Through the Status of the Training School [35]

1. A majority of the state teachers colleges and normal schools maintain a campus training school which is housed in a separate building, but readily accessible for use by the college faculty.

2. A small percentage of the institutions requires that each professional course of the college be based upon constant observation in the training school from the freshman year to graduation.

3. An interlocking relationship between the training school and each college department has not yet been achieved in the majority of the schools. When such relationship does exist, it is usually with the education department.

4. Participation teaching in the training school under the supervision of a college department instructor, during each year of the student's study, is in force in only a few schools. In cases where the policy is in progress, the college instructor is a member of the education department, who has been designated as a training school supervisor.

General Conclusions Concerning the Present Practice Study as a Whole

1. Few reciprocal relations are reported between training school and college faculty members unless such contacts are fostered by the administration of the institution and provided for through service load adjustment. This is evidenced by comparing the frequencies listed by college instructors who are assigned to training school supervision and those listed by instructors who teach college courses only.

2. College instructors in subject matter courses only make little or no report of cooperative endeavor through individual contacts with the training school faculty in the activities of Parts I and II of the questionnaire. When the schools were visited the investigator was

[35] See footnote 5.

always referred to the instructor in the professionalized subject matter course for such information.

3. The minority of the 25 schools participate in a majority of the activities suggested by the questionnaire, though no school reports participation in all. Institutions with small student enrollments, training elementary school teachers only and not granting degrees, record more cooperation than larger schools training both elementary and secondary teachers and granting degrees.

4. No more cooperation is reported between the academic faculty in the special fields and their training school critic teachers than between the education department and the general critic teachers.

5. The jury evaluations indicate that as much or more emphasis should be placed upon cooperation through large group organizations, such as a general curriculum committee, as upon individual contacts which are usually casual in character.

Conclusions Concerning the Score Card

It is evident that the recommendations in this study of cooperation between the training school and college faculty should grow out of (1) the weighted evaluation of cooperative activities presented in the score card, Table I, Chapter II, and (2) the ranked evaluation of methods for carrying out the activities on the score card, which are included in the discussion of present practice in Chapters III-VI, and in Tables XX, XXXIV, and XXXV.[36]

If the cooperative activities within a given section of the score card are listed in order of their average weighted rank from highest to lowest as assigned by the juries, we shall be able to locate each subdivision in its respective group of importance. The greatest weight assigned to any subdivision was 33 points; and the least weight, four points. Though no item was considered sufficiently undesirable to receive a weight of zero, we may arbitrarily assume that those allotted 17 to 33 points are of greater importance than those allotted 0 to 16. Since the specific recommendations to be summarized in this final section of the study will be cited in terms of each of the large sections of the score card, the above analysis should be applied to each group. For example, the points allotted to the eleven items in

[36] See pp. 178, 209-211, 213-214.

Part IV range from 14 to 32 and we may assume that the activities receiving 16 to 32 points are of greater importance than those receiving 0 to 16. Similarly, the points allotted to the eight items in Part II range from 16 to 31; those receiving 16 to 31 are more important than those allotted 0 to 15. Again, points ranging from 6 to 21 were allotted to the twenty-four items in Part I; those receiving 11 to 21 are more important than those allotted 0 to 10 points. To summarize, in the following recommendations only the more significant cooperative activities are cited within each group.

A plan was proposed in Chapter II for using the score card as a guide in conducting a self-survey of the extent of cooperation between the faculties of the campus elementary training school and the college departments in individual teachers colleges and normal schools. Such a survey should be followed by constructive effort for improving coordination in the activities which failed to meet the standards. In this final section of the study the writer wishes to outline a follow-up program to cover a three-year period following the survey.

I. During the first year the program of improvement may be planned in group meetings attended by the entire faculty, when the more desirable administrative devices for facilitating cooperation as recommended by the juries may be studied and inaugurated. These should include the following devices from Part IV of the score card.

a. The administrative device receiving the greatest number of points (32 out of a possible 237) in Part IV of the score card is the recommendation that *the college should maintain an administrative officer whose work is to direct the coordination of the training school and the other college departments*.[37] He should be administrative head of the education department as well as principal of the training school;[38] or as principal of the training school, he should also supervise instruction to see that it relates to the professional education of teachers. Present practice and expert opinion are not in agreement, for the most frequently reported status of such an officer, namely,

[37] See Table I.
[38] See Table XXXV.

that he should be principal of the training school and a teacher of college courses in the department of education, was ranked third by the juries.

b. The administrative device receiving the second greatest number of points (29 out of 237) in Part IV [39] of the score card is that the training school building should be accessible to the college faculty. Theory and practice are in accord in this instance since the juries recommend that such a laboratory school should be on the campus near the college buildings.

c. The score card assigns 28 points to the subdivision which states that each professional course of the college should be based upon constant observation in the training school from the freshman year to graduation. Jt has been cited in the summary that this is not yet true in practice.

d. The training school and college departments should be interlocked in relationship (26 points). The jury rankings show that there is little difference in value among the four suggested ways for achieving this, slight preference being shown for making the training school an integral part of the education department.[40] The faculty groups should select one or more of these philosophies, and treat all subsequent relationships with the training school in accordance with the philosophy selected.

e. Equal salary for equal training and experience should be paid to every member of the faculty, including the training school staff (21 points).

f. Participation teaching in the training school should be required in each year of the student's study, leading to responsible room teaching in the last year (21 points).

g. The service load of each member of the college faculty should be adjusted to provide for regular contacts with the training school (18 points).

h. The service load of each member of the training school staff should be adjusted to provide for regular contacts with the college departments (18 points).

[39] The subdivisions of Part IV which are recommended in this section are discussed in the order of importance assigned on the score card. See Table I.

[40] See Table XXXV.

i. In employing new faculty members, it should be required that each shall have had some experience in teaching in the types of schools for which he will prepare teachers (16 points).

II. During the same year in which the administrative devices are being considered and put into practice, those items in Part III of the score card may also be given major attention. The lettered divisions A, B, C, and D of the score card[41] have no subdivisions and probably have been treated as Arabic-numbered subdivisions by the juries. However, since divisions E and F have several subdivisions, it would be invalid to arbitrarily include A, B, C, and D with E 1, E 2, E 3, etc. Therefore the six-lettered divisions will be discussed in order of their ranked weights.

a. College instructors and critic teachers should be encouraged to publish professional literature as a joint enterprise (71 points).[42]

Suggested publications weighted as especially important cooperative ventures are:

1. Courses of study for the training school (11 points).
2. Reports of experiments in the training school (10 points).
3. Student teaching manuals (8 points).
4. Courses of study for college courses (7 points).
5. Reports of experiments in college departments (7 points).
6. Reports of cooperative activities within the college (7 points).

b. College instructors and critic teachers should cooperatively follow up graduates of the institution (64 points) [43]:

1. By visiting them in the field to supervise their first year of teaching experience and to gain material for revising and improving the training curricula (22 points).
2. By presenting the findings of visits to students in service to committees of the faculty (15 points).

c. Every member of the faculty, including critic teachers, should participate in determining the policies of the institution in such matters as entrance requirements, attendance regulations, graduation requirements, scholarships, loan funds, etc. (33 points),[44] preferably as members of standing or temporary committees which consider in-

[41] See Table XXXIV.

[42] Table I.

[43] *Ibid.*

dividual policies, or by attending group meetings which include the entire faculty.

d. Every member of the faculty should cooperate on the placement of graduates (33 points),[44] preferably by contributing records to the placement bureaus.

e. College and training school faculty should agree upon the methods by which common equipment may be made accessible to faculty, students, and training school children (27 points).[44] Preferably this should be accomplished by maintaining a materials bureau to which the entire faculty contributes.

f. Every member of the faculty (including critic teachers) should participate in planning such college activities as college assembly, social programs, school publications, etc. (23 points),[44] preferably as members of faculty committees.

III. During the second year the administrative devices for facilitating cooperation should be in progress, but in addition, special emphasis should be given in faculty meetings and in practice to those activities in Part I of the score card,[45] the conduct of which are not so dependent upon the administration as upon personal volition.

a. College instructors should arrange for their classes to observe the teaching of critic teachers in the training schools (21 points), and preferably should accompany them when they observe.

b. The college instructor and college class should cooperatively follow up all training school observation (21 points), preferably in a meeting attended by the critic teacher who was observed.

c. The college instructor and college class should cooperatively prepare for observation in the training school (20 points), preferably in a meeting attended by the critic teacher who is to be observed.

d. College instructors may aid in adjusting personality problems of student teachers (20 points). The jury ranking evidences little preference as to whether this aid may be given in a conference with the critic teacher under whose supervision the student is working, in a conference attended by both student and critic teacher, or in a con-

[44] *Ibid.*

[45] The subdivisions of Part I which are recommended in this section are discussed in the order of importance assigned them on the score card. See Table I.

ference with the student teacher only.[46] We may assume that all three types are desirable.

e. The juries recommend that college instructors help students plan work they are teaching in the training school (15 points), preferably in a conference at which student and critic teacher are present.

f. That college instructors and critic teachers should cooperatively plan and conduct experiments and new techniques in the training school was allotted 15 points by the juries. No preference was shown between conducting the activity as a general curriculum committee, or as a special subject committee.[47]

g. The juries assigned: (1) 15 points to the item which recommended that college instructors teach in the training school without observers to try out experimental units; (2) 13 points to the suggestion that college instructors teach occasional units in the training school in fields in which the instructor is more of an authority than the critic teacher; (3) 12 points to the suggestion that college instructors teach in the training school for college classes to observe.

h. College instructors should cooperate in deciding which students are prepared to begin student teaching (15 points), preferably as members of a committee which includes critic teachers, director of training, and representatives of each college department.[48]

i. College instructors should observe the teaching of student teachers (14 points), preferably in company with the critic teacher;[49] and should confer with the students to evaluate and analyze the teaching observed in a conference conducted by the critic teacher.[50]

j. The juries allotted 13 points to the item which proposed that college instructors should cooperate in determining the kind and amount of contacts students should have with the training school prior to student teaching; and recommended that it be done by a committee composed of critic teachers, director of training, and representatives of each college department.[51]

[46] See ranked list, p. 171.
[47] See ranking table, p. 130.
[48] See Table XX.
[49] See ranking table, p. 51.
[50] See ranking table, p. 73.
[51] See Table XX.

k. College instructors should aid in constructing and revising courses of study for the training school (12 points), either as members of a general curriculum committee or as members of a special subject committee.[52]

IV. During the third year, administrative devices should still be in operation, and, in addition, special attention should be given in faculty meetings and in practice to the activities in Part II of the score card, which are more dependent upon personal volition. Each of the eight ways in which the training school staff may participate in the functions of the academic departments received heavy weighting and are located in the group of the more important items of cooperation.[53]

a. Critic teachers should participate in determining the content of college courses (31 points), as members of a general curriculum committee.[54]

b. Critic teachers should be cognizant of the content of college courses (1) by receiving outlines of each course (31 points); and (2) by visiting college courses as an observer (30 points).

c. Members of the training school staff should be invited to offer occasional units in college courses, when they are better authorities on the unit than the regular college instructor (29 points), preferably by having definite sections assigned when the course is organized for a semester.[55]

d. The training school staff should participate in planning experiments and new techniques for the college departments (27 points), preferably as members of a general curriculum committee.[56]

e. Critic teachers should be invited to aid students who are preparing work for their college classes, e.g., obtaining data for case studies, conferences regarding routine details of classroom management, etc. (24 points), preferably in individual conferences with students at other than scheduled class hours.[57]

f. Qualified critic teachers should be given the opportunity to teach college courses (21 points), either during the academic year or during the summer session.[57]

[52] See ranking table, p. 92.
[53] Technique of selection described on p. 227.
[54] Table XXVII.
[55] *Ibid.*
[56] *Ibid.*
[57] Table XXVII.

g. Members of the training school staff should participate in the selection of such college materials as textbooks, supplementary books, laboratory equipment, etc. (16 points), as members of either a special subject committee or a general curriculum committee.[58]

V. At the end of the three-year period, the standards for judging the activities in the score card should be re-evaluated in the same manner in which it was done for the self-survey.[59] The school should once more engage in a self-survey to measure its growth during the three-year period. Those activities which have been particularly helpful and of real worth in the estimation of the faculty should be retained and others substituted for those of less importance.

Recommendations

This study of cooperation between the faculty of the campus elementary training school and the other departments of teachers colleges and normal schools has been based upon the following assumptions:

1. That coordination of the laboratory phases of teacher education with the academic and professional phases contributes to the efficient pre-service training of the teacher.

2. That the laboratory school is the proving ground of the institution about which all interest should center, for facts, principles, and theories are useless unless applied to situations in which they are relevant.

3. That the most effective way to integrate theory and practice is by making it possible for members of the training school and college faculty to understand and participate in one another's work.

It is evident from the survey of present practice, from the judgment of the juries on the score card, and from the literature of the field that no single philosophy dominates the coordination program in the many institutions which train teachers. If we may look to a future of scientifically planned programs of experimentation, with accurate measures that determine achievement, perhaps it is a hopeful sign that such a variety of patterns is in operation.

Within the various patterns for training elementary school teach-

[58] *Ibid.*

[59] Chap. II, pp. 44–48.

ers are certain types of organization and activity which seem to retard or accelerate, as the case may be, cooperation between the members of the training school and college faculties. Those elements which seem to accelerate such cooperation are embodied in the following recommendations which have grown out of the author's research, observation, reading, and experience in the field.

Personnel of the Faculty

The attitude of the faculty members toward the use of the laboratory school is one of the strongest determinants of the nature and degree of integration within the school. If the majority believe that the only essential equipment for a teacher is a thorough mastery of the subject matter he is to teach, then there is little or no faculty cooperation in that school. It is recommended that any candidate being considered for a position in a teacher training institution be selected with the professional aim dominating; that, in addition to being an expert in an academic field, he shall have had professional education concerning the work of the teachers college and shall have had teaching experience in the types of schools for which he is preparing teachers.

If such a plan is followed there need be no distinction between training school and college staff, for the latter may be assigned as critic teachers from time to time until eventually all have accepted such assignments. In like manner critic teachers may be assigned to teach college courses.

Some of the values resulting from this organization are:

1. A laboratory for experimentation is provided where each college instructor may test various techniques and procedures which he wishes to recommend to his classes.

2. Members of the college faculty are in close contact with children and are more conscious of problems which arise from day to day.

3. The college teacher of educational theory may become just as much an academician as the subject matter specialist if he fails to teach children at frequent intervals to see if his theories are functional.

4. Illustrative material for the professional subject matter courses is obtained at first hand.

5. College faculty members are kept in close touch with contemporary developments in the education of children, for they feel the urge to teach on a high level of proficiency for the observing students.

Each teacher training institution should maintain an administrative officer whose work is to direct the coordination of the training school and the other departments. It should be within his province to reduce the conflict in aims and purposes that exists among various departments and the laboratory school, and to see that proper emphasis is accorded the laboratory, academic, and professional phases of the teacher education program. He may be entitled the director of training, or the dean of instruction but, above all, he must have had wide experience and training in all of the various phases of teacher education.

Activities of the Faculty

In colleges where a rather definite distinction between laboratory and college faculty is maintained, members of each group should be asked to participate in the work of the other in an advisory capacity. In this way opportunities are provided for the teachers of subject matter and of educational theory to become familiar with, and to feel themselves an integral part of, the training school. In like manner, the critic teachers should have a voice in academic and professional preparation of their student teachers. Specific ways in which this organization may function are suggested below. No institution need incorporate all; but the more that are in operation the higher the degree of integration within the school.

Participation of the College Faculty in the Work of the Training School

A. Members of the college staff may, in company with the critic teacher and such other faculty members as wish to be present, aid in the supervision of student teachers by (1) observing their teaching, (2) holding conferences to evaluate and analyze the teaching observed, (3) helping them plan work they are teaching in the training school, (4) assigning a rating or grade, (5) making out and revising manuals or handbooks to be used with laboratory teaching, (6) assisting in adjusting personality problems of training school children or of student teachers.

B. College instructors may aid critic teachers in planning and carrying on the training school curriculum by (1) participating in the construction and revision of training school courses of study, (2) assisting in the application of details and enrichment of state or city prescribed courses which are used in the training school, (3) aiding in the selection of materials of instruction and equipment, such as textbooks, supplementary books, art materials, science equipment, films, slides, maps, etc., (4) participating in the testing of children, the analysis of results, and the planning of remedial measures, (5) participating in planning and conducting the school and community activities of the training school, such as assembly programs, publications, parent-teacher association programs, field trips, community civic and recreational projects, etc., (6) aiding in planning and conducting experiments and new techniques relating to instruction, materials, children, students, etc.

C. All college classes in educational theory, and professional subject matter should observe the teaching done by critic teachers in the laboratory school, for theory should be supplemented by observation of its application. If theories of teaching cannot be demonstrated, it is doubtful if they should be taught. Bulletins, issued weekly by the training school staff, to announce specific units of work in progress and the methods being used are of help to those who make use of the laboratory school. The college instructor should plan for the observation with his class and the critic teacher, he should accompany the class when it observes, and he should follow up the observation by means of discussion with both the critic teacher and the college class.

D. Though he may not be assuming the work of a critic teacher, the college instructor should seek and welcome opportunities to work with children in the training school by (1) teaching for his college classes to observe, (2) teaching without observers to try out experimental units, and (3) teaching occasional units in fields where he is more of an authority than the critic teacher.

Participation of Members of the Training School Staff in the Functions of the Other College Departments

Just as it is important that members of the college faculty should become familiar with and feel themselves an integral part of the training school, so should opportunities be provided for the critic teachers to bear a similar relationship to the academic and education departments of the college. It has been stated earlier in this discussion that in teachers colleges where there is no definite distinction between training school and college staff, college instructors being assigned as critic teachers from time to time, and critic teachers being assigned to teach college courses, the desired integration of theory and practice is more easily achieved. In colleges where a definite distinction between the two faculties is maintained, members of the training school faculty should participate in the work of the college departments in an advisory capacity as follows:

A. Critic teachers should be thoroughly familiar with the content of the various academic and professional courses which are pursued by student teachers. They should, therefore, aid in formulating the college curriculum, visit college classes, and be given recent outlines or syllabi of each college course.

1. Each professional course in the college should be systematically planned and organized in a faculty seminar attended by critic teachers and specialists in the theory and subject matter involved. Other members of the subject matter departments should be invited to present, for discussion, summaries of their courses.

2. Critic teachers should participate in the selection of college materials of instruction, such as textbooks, reference books, laboratory equipment, etc.

3. They should participate in planning experiments and new techniques to be used in the college relative to such matters as size of classes, prerequisites to courses, the advisability of having consultant advisors for students, etc.

B. Critic teachers may participate in the teaching of college courses:

1. Through offering occasional units in courses where more of an

authority than the regular instructor, such as lesson planning, teaching through units of work, etc.

2. By aiding students who request information to be used in college courses, such as providing data for case studies, giving routine details of classroom management, etc.

3. Through teaching an entire course, preferably one course each school year. While the critic teacher is meeting his class, an elementary school teacher of superior quality, employed to relieve the service load of critic teachers, will carry on the work with children.

Participation of the Entire Faculty in Activities Which Concern the Teacher Training Institution as a Unit

I. An important method in bringing training school and college faculty into closer relationship, where mutual respect exists, is to require that all staff members attend the large general faculty meetings where policies of the school are discussed and determined. Members of both training school and college faculty should be appointed to committees which study such matters as entrance requirements, attendance regulations, school athletics, degree requirements, scholarships, loan funds, etc.

II. Effective coordination of effort may be brought about through a council or committee, the personnel of which may include all the representative interests of the college. Its chief function should be to determine the guiding principles that govern integration in the particular institution and to discover ways and means by which these principles may be effectively worked out. This committee, part of the personnel of which should change each year, should be fact-finding rather than administrative. The specific work of the committee may include such activities as the following:

a. College and training school teachers who have visited graduates to observe their teaching should present their findings to this group.

1. Cooperative follow-up visitation should be fostered by institutions which educate teachers because their responsibility does not cease with graduation but continues as an extension of the professional education begun on the campus. Visits to the schools in the area which the college serves should be made jointly by college and training school staff in an effort

to study public school practices in order to learn what is being done in the more progressive schools and to keep in touch with the work of former students.

2. The results should be presented to the faculty, either in large or small groups. It is probable that the content of student teaching and of certain college courses may be modified, enriched, or reorganized to meet deficiencies noted.

b. The committee on integration should determine the extent of use that teachers of professionalized subject matter and educational theory make of the training school, and should hear discussions by them of its value.

c. All conflicts in educational theory and practice should be presented to the committee by the people concerned, and an agreement reached.

d. New techniques being tried out experimentally in training school and college should be presented to this group for evaluation.

e. The committee should study the content of all college courses to discover overlapping and possible ways of making them of greater service to students.

f. It should aid in determining such training school policies as the following:

1. Deciding which students are prepared to begin student teaching by setting up standards of admittance.
2. Determining the length and content of student teaching by analyzing such elements as observation, participation, responsible teaching, conferences, lesson planning, etc.
3. Determining the kind and amount of contacts a student should have with the laboratory school throughout his training course prior to student teaching.

III. It is also important that both training school and college faculty should participate in planning and directing such college activities as social programs, assembly, clubs, publications, special day programs, commencement, etc.

IV. A materials bureau should be maintained where common equipment, units of work, and other teaching aids are made readily accessible to faculty members, students, and training school children. Both critic teachers and college instructors should contribute to this bureau, and should cooperatively evaluate the long units of work, tests, and the like before students have access to them.

V. Members of both staffs should be encouraged to publish professional literature as a joint enterprise, collaborating on such materials as reports of experiments in college or training school, books for children or adults, syllabi for training school or college courses, rating scales for teachers, student teaching manuals, etc.

The core or center around which this suggested program is built lies in the professional aim and organization of the institution. Each member of the faculty should be recognized as a component part of the whole, as an active contributor to the professional aim of the institution, and as a worker who understands the broad implications of public education. If that is true, the staff, the administrative policy, the curriculum, the laboratory phases, and the field relationship of the institution have a common base upon which to build an integrated program of teacher education.

Problems Suggested by the Study

Listed below are the problems which have grown out of the present study and which the author feels to be of immediate importance.

1. To what degree should members of the college departments cooperate with the off-campus elementary training school faculty in state teachers colleges or normal schools?

a. In schools having one campus and one off-campus laboratory school, the latter being a near-by city school.

b. In schools having one campus and several off-campus laboratory schools, the latter being in other cities.

c. In schools having only one laboratory school, it being a city school at some distance from the college buildings.

d. In schools using several city schools for laboratory purposes, but at some distance from the campus.

e. In schools maintaining a campus school and one or more distant rural laboratory schools.

2. Is the type and degree of cooperation influenced by the fact that an institution trains both elementary and secondary teachers?

3. How would each of the above apply to a university school of education?

BIBLIOGRAPHY

ADE, LESTER K. "How May a Closer Correlation Between the Theory Departments of the Institution and the Training School Be Secured in Student Teaching?" *American Association of Teachers Colleges, Yearbook*, 1932, p. 75–80.

ALEXANDER, THOMAS. "Coordination of the Laboratory Schools with the Subject-Matter Departments in the College." *Bulletin 95, North Texas State Teachers College*, May, 1931, p. 138–143.

———. "Plan for a Demonstration Teachers College." *The Virginia Teacher*, October, 1931, p. 192–195.

———. "Significance of New College." *National Education Association, Proceedings*, 1933, p. 730–735.

———. "A Wider Extension of the Content of Student Teaching." *Educational Administration and Supervision*, May, 1930, p. 352–359.

ANTHONY, KATHERINE M. "The Harrisonburg Program." *Educational Administration and Supervision*, May, 1931, p. 351–356.

ARMENTROUT, W. D. "Four Major Problems in the Professional Training of Teachers." *Educational Administration and Supervision*, Vol. 10, 1924, p. 568–573.

———. "Making Observation Effective for Teachers in Training." *Supervisors of Student Teaching, Fourth Yearbook*, 1924, p. 9–15.

———. *The Conduct of Student Teaching in State Teachers Colleges*. Colorado State Teachers College, 1928, p. 35–37; 165–172.

AYER, ADELAIDE M. "Learning Educational Principles Through Experience." *Educational Administration and Supervision*, May, 1931, p. 357–362.

BAGLEY, W. C. "Twenty Years of Progress in the Professionalization of Subject Matter for Normal Schools and Teachers Colleges." *American Association of Teachers Colleges, Seventh Yearbook*, 1928, p. 72–77.

BAGLEY, W. C., ALEXANDER, T., and FOOTE, J. *The Report of the Survey Commission for the State Department of Education*. Baton Rouge, La., 1924.

BAKER, F. E. "Integrated Professional Experiences as the Basis for Learning and as a Substitute for Formal Courses in Education." *American Association of Teachers Colleges, Twelfth Yearbook*, 1933, p. 70–85.

BENSON, C. E. "A Weak Spot in Teacher Training." *Educational Administration and Supervision*, March, 1924.

BROWN, H. A. "An Experiment in Organizing Courses in Education for Elementary School Teachers." *Educational Administration and Supervision*, September, 1933, p. 451–462.

BURGESS, W. R. "Education of Teachers in Fourteen States." *Journal of Educational Research*, Vol. 3, 1921, p. 161–172.

BURRIS, W. P. "Constructive Plan for the Cooperation of a Public School System and a University in School Improvement." *School and Society*, Vol. 13, 1921, p. 271–277.

CAZIN, A. *et al.* *Content and Conduct of Courses in the Introduction to Teaching Including the Place and Function of Observation and Demonstration Problems in Teacher Training.* Contributions to Education, Vol. 2, p. 260–274. Yonkers, N. Y.: World Book Co., 1928.

CHARTERS, W. W. "Basis and Principles of Curriculum Construction For State Teachers Colleges." *National Education Association, Proceedings*, 1926, p. 903–906.

———. "The Technique of Determining Content of Student Teaching Courses." *Supervisors of Student Teaching, Yearbook*, 1929, p. 9.

CHITTENDEN, M. D. "Oswego Normal and Training School Plan of Cooperation." *Educational Administration and Supervision*, Vol. 10, May, 1925, p. 325–332.

CLARK, R. "The Professional Phase of the Teachers College Curriculum in 1950." *American Association of Teachers Colleges, Eighth Yearbook*, 1929, p. 44.

CLEMENT, J. A. "Reciprocal Relation Between Theory and Practice in the Scientific Secondary Education." *Educational Administration and Supervision*, Vol. 8, 1922, p. 198.

CRABB, A. L. "What Professional Preparation Should Faculty Members in Teachers Colleges and Normal Schools Possess?" *American Association of Teachers Colleges, Eleventh Yearbook*, 1932, p. 31–34.

CUMMINS, R. A. "Functions of Supervisors of Student Teaching." *Educational Administration and Supervision*, Vol. 9, May, 1923, p. 272–276.

DAVIS, E. M. and DISTAD, H. W. "A Plan for Vitalizing the Teaching of Two Courses in Education." *Educational Administration and Supervision*, March, 1932, p. 178–184.

DAVIS, S. E. "The College Faculty in 1950: Its Type, Preparation, Background, Relations, and Duties." *American Association of Teachers Colleges, Eighth Yearbook*, 1929, p. 21.

DEARBORN, F. R. "A Tentative Plan for Integrating Theory and Practice." *Teachers College Journal*, Terre Haute, Ind., September, 1930, p. 17–26.

DEARBORN, N. H. "Different Procedures in the Practice Schools of New York State Normal Schools." *Supervisors of Student Teaching, Seventh Yearbook*, 1927, p. 54.

DISTAD, H. W. and CAREY, F. M. "Contrasting Teaching Situations as a Means of Developing Principles of Education." *Educational Administration and Supervision*, September, 1933, p. 468–472.

DUNKLE, J. L. "Plan of Cooperation at Frostburg State Normal School, Maryland." *Educational Administration and Supervision*, May, 1925, p. 320–24.

ECKELBERRY, R. H. "Need for Unity in Teacher Training Courses." *Education*, February, 1929, p. 321–330.

EUBANK, L. A. "Articulation of the Laboratory School with the College." The *Organization and Administration of Laboratory Schools in State Teachers Colleges.* Northeast Missouri State Teachers College, 1931, p. 54–60.

EVENDEN, E. S. "Cooperation of Teachers of Academic Subjects with the Training Schools." *Educational Administration and Supervision*, May, 1925, p. 307–319.

———. "The Critic Teacher and the Professional Treatment of Subject Matter: A Challenge." *Supervisors of Student Teaching, Yearbook*, 1929, p. 39.

———. "Criteria for the Construction of Training School Curricula." *National Education Association, Proceedings*, 1926, p. 285–293.

———. "Findings of the National Survey of the Education of Teachers: Implications for their Improvement of Current Practice." *American Association of Teachers Colleges, Twelfth Yearbook*, 1933.

———. "Proposals for Correcting Professional Myopia of Subject-Matter Teachers in Teachers Colleges." *Educational Administration and Supervision.* May, 1930, p. 372–382.

FITCH, H. N. *An Analysis of the Supervisory Activities* and *Techniques of the Elementary School Teaching Supervisor.* Bureau of Publications, Teachers College, Columbia University, 1931.

FLOWERS, J. G. "How May a Closer Correlation Between the Theory Departments of the Institution and the Training School Be Secured in Observation of Teaching?" *American Association of Teachers Colleges, Eleventh Yearbook*, 1932, p. 65–70.

———. "Organization of a Teacher-Training Program." *Educational Administration and Supervision*, May, 1931, p. 362–367.

FRAZIER, G. W. *Experiments in Teachers College Administration.* Baltimore: Warwick and York, 1929.

FRYKLUND, V. C. "Conduct of Student Teaching Through Individual Instruction: Observation and Participation Methods. A Bibliography." *Industrial Education Magazine*, February, 1929, p. 279–283.

GARRISON, N. L. "A Program for Coordination of College and Training School Work." *Educational Administration and Supervision*, December, 1929, p. 655–659.

———. *Current Practice in Coordination of College and Training School Work.* Michigan State Normal College, 1931.

———. *Status and Work of the Training Supervisor.* Contribution to Education, No. 280, p. 10; 76–98. Bureau of Publications, Teachers College, 1927.

———. "How May a Closer Correlation Between the Theory Departments of the Institution and the Training School be Secured in the Mastery of Subject-Matter so that Theory Courses may be Properly Professionalized?" *American Association of Teachers Colleges Eleventh Yearbook*, 1932, p. 80–83.

GILLAND, T. M. "The Contribution of a Campus Elementary School to a Program of Teacher Education." *Educational Administration and Supervision*, October, 1933, p. 481–495.

GREINER, H. E. "Buffalo Plan of Teacher Training." *American School Board Journal*, June, 1921, p. 45–46.

HAETTER AND SMITH. "An Investigation into the Methods of Student-Teaching in Thirty-two Colleges and Universities." *Educational Administration and Supervision*, December, 1926.

HALL, C. B. "Studies in Student Observation of Teaching." *Educational Administration and Supervision*, January, 1931, p. 43–51.

HALVERSON, L. H. "Geography in Teachers Colleges." *Education*, December, 1928, p. 193–205.

HATCHER, M. L. "How to Secure a Functional Relationship Between the Course in Methods of Teaching Reading and Supervised Student Teaching." *Educational Administration and Supervision*, January, 1934, p. 45–58.

HECKERT, J. W. "Extra-Mural Practice Teaching at Miami University." *Supervisors of Student Teaching, Yearbook*, Fourth Annual Session, 1924, p. 31.

HENDERSON, J. L. "Some Phases of the Uses of City School Systems, by Student Teachers in Colleges and Universities." *Educational Administration and Supervision*, May, 1925, p. 350–352.

HINES, L. N. "Relationship Between the General Administration and the Training School." *Teachers College Journal*, September, 1930.

HOPKINS, L. T. and ARMENTRAUT, W. B. "Principles of Integration." *National Education Association, Ninth Yearbook*, p. 367–78.

HORN, J. L. "Educative Values of Practice Teaching." *Journal of Educational Research*, March, 1925.

HUMBE, H. L. "Cooperative Teacher Training and Evansville College." *School and Society*, August, 1926, p. 206–207.

HUNSICKER, L. "Concerning Overlapping of Professional Courses in Teacher-Training Institutions." *School and Society*, June, 1929, p. 776–778.

IRWIN, F. A. "The Work of the Teachers College in Preparation for Student Teaching Educational Administration and Supervision." *Educational Administration and Supervision*, March, 1932, p. 223–228.

JARMAN, A. M. *The Administration of Laboratory Schools*. Ann Arbor, Mich.: George Wahr, 1932.

JOHNSON, L. "Cooperation Between Training School and Subject-Matter Instructors." *Virginia Teacher*, State Teachers College, Harrisonburg, Va., February, 1931, p. 27–37.

JOHNSON, L. M. "Training School Building—A Factor in Teacher Training." *Educational Administration and Supervision*, March, 1923, p. 139–145.

KENNEDY, K. and SHANNON, J. R. "An Experiment in Directing Observation." *Educational Administration and Supervision*, March, 1931.

KINDER, J. S. "Training Teachers on the Cooperative Plan." *American Educational Digest*, 1924, p. 6–10.

———. "Vital Points in Teacher Training: Observation and Practice Teaching." *Education*, May, 1929, p. 556–560.

LANDSITTEL, F. G. "Cooperation in Teacher Training." *Educational Review*, December, 1922, p. 377–382.

LANGSAM, W. C. "International Cooperation in the Schools of Education of the United States." *School and Society*, August, 1927, p. 342–349.

LATHAM, O. R. "The Training School Faculty in 1950: Its Type, Preparation, Background, Relations, and Duties." *American Association of Teachers Colleges, Eighth Yearbook*, 1929, p. 24.

LEARNED and BAGLEY. *The Professional Preparation of Teachers for American Public Schools.* Bulletin No. 14 of the Carnegie Foundation for the Advancement of Teaching, 1920, p. 199–204.

———. *Curricula Designed for the Professional Preparation of Teachers for American Public Schools.* Section 9, Bulletin of the Carnegie Foundation for the Advancement of Teaching, 1917.

LULL, H. G. "Teacher Training in Curriculum Building." *Supervisors of Student Teaching, Fifth Yearbook*, 1925, p. 46.

MADSEN, J. N. "The Normal School Curriculum through the Eyes of Its Graduates." *Elementary School Journal*, November, 1928.

MCKENNY, C. "Predicted Changes in Faculty Standards by 1950 as Shown by the Experiences of the Committee on Accrediting and Classification." *American Association of Teachers Colleges, Eighth Yearbook*, 1929, p. 27.

MCMULLEN, L. B. "The Service Load of the Critic Teacher in State Teachers Colleges." *Supervisors of Student Teaching, Sixth Yearbook*, 1926, p. 8.

MEAD, A. R. "Advantages and Disadvantages of Campus and Off-Campus Laboratory Schools." *Educational Administration and Supervision*, 1928, p. 196–207.

———. "Cooperation of Academic and Professional Departments in Teacher Preparation at Ohio Wesleyan University." *Educational Administration and Supervision*, May, 1925, p. 333–337.

———. "Example of Cooperation in Teacher Training in a Small City." *School and Society*, October, 1919, p. 393–397.

———. *Staff of the Laboratory School; Supervised Student Teaching.* Johnson Publishing Company, 1930, p. 594–628.

MEADOR, J. L. "The Training School Curriculum." *Supervisors of Student Teaching, Fifth Yearbook*, 1925, p. 13.

———. "What Are the Most Effective Plans for Securing Faculty Cooperation in the Making and in the Progressive Revision of the Curricula of our Normal Schools and Teachers Colleges?" *New York Society for the Experimental Study of Education, Proceedings*, 1927, p. 110–113.

MORRISON, R. H. "The Demonstration School as a Factor in Integrating the Professional Education of Teachers." *Educational Administration and Supervision*, February, 1934, p. 115–122.

MYERS, A. F. "The Fifteen-Hour Load of the Critic Teachers at Ohio University." *Supervisors of Student Teaching, Sixth Yearbook*, 1926, p. 16.

———. "The Course in Observation and Participation in its Relationship to Courses in Principles of Teaching, Methods, School Management, etc." *Educational Administration and Supervision*, September, 1928, p. 404–412.

NEAL, E. "Closer Coordination Between Professionalized Subject-Matter Instructors and the Training School." *Kentucky School Journal*, May, 1933, p. 39–41.

NUTT, H. W. "Essentials in the Supervision of Student Teaching." *Educational Administration and Supervision*, September, 1922, p. 368.

PAYNE, B. R. "Difficulties in the Integration of Subject-Matter and Method in Teachers Colleges." *School and Society*, June, 1930, Vol. 31, p. 821–827.

PEARCE, D. W. and WILLIAMS, O. H. "Trends in the Development of American Teachers Colleges." *Educational Administration and Supervision*, November, 1933, p. 621–629.

PECHSTEIN, L. A. "Cooperative Ideal in Teacher Training—The Cincinnati Plan." *School and Society*, September, 1923, p. 271–277.

PIERCE, M. D. "A Plan for Measuring the Critic Teachers' Load in Terms of College Class Hours." *Supervisors of Student Teaching, Seventh Yearbook*, 1927.

QUIMBY, E. M. and HICKS, H. "Integration of Theory and Practice." *Educational Administration and Supervision*, December, 1933, p. 687–698.

REYNOLDS, H. M. "Demonstration Schools and the Administration Staff." *School Executive's Magazine*, November, 1929, p. 134–135.

ROCHEFORT, A. "How May a Closer Correlation Between the Theory Departments of the Institution and the Training School be Secured in Student Participation?" *American Association of Teachers Colleges, Eleventh Yearbook*, 1932, p. 73–75.

ROCKWELL, H. W. "How May a Closer Correlation Between Theory Departments and the Training School Be Secured in Organization?" *American Association of Teachers Colleges, Eleventh Yearbook*, 1932, p. 62–64.

ROEMER, J. "How a Closer Correlation Between the Theory Departments of Teacher Training Institutions and the Training Schools May Be Secured in Demonstration Teaching." *American Association of Teachers Colleges, Eleventh Yearbook*, 1932, p. 71–73.

ROSE, E. J. "Coordinating the Special Methods Course for Student Teachers with Observation and Student Teaching." *Journal of Home Economics*, May, 1931.

ROSIER, J. "What Should Be the Professional Status of Teachers in the Training Schools?" *American Association of Teachers Colleges, Eleventh Yearbook*, 1932, p. 34–37.

RUSSELL, C. "Laboratory Technique for Observing Practice Teaching." *Teachers College Record*, September, 1923 and November, 1923.

SHARP, L. A. "Uses Made of Demonstration Schools by College Teachers of North Texas State Teachers Colleges." *Peabody Journal of Education*, p. 332–336.

SKARSTEN, M. "Requirements for Admission to Student Teaching." *Educational Administration and Supervision*, October, 1933, p. 529–543.

SMITH, F. W. "How Far Are Normal Schools Professional Institutions?" *School and Society*, September, 1927, p. 355–358.

SMITH, R. N. "Student Teaching in a Two Year Curriculum for Primary Teachers." *Educational Administration and Supervision*, January, 1932, p. 47–63.

SPRAGUE, H. A. "Coordination of Theory and Practice in Normal Schools." *National Education Association, Proceedings*, 1918, p. 212–214.

STALKER, F. M. "Cooperation of Departments and Training School in Supervised Teaching." *Educational Administration and Supervision*, April, 1926, p. 233–237.

STRATEMEYER, F. "Guiding the Student-Teacher in the Development and Use of Principles." *Educational Administration and Supervision*, May 1931, p. 346–351.

———. "A Proposed Experiment in Teacher-Training." *Educational Administration and Supervision*, May, 1932, p. 353–358.

SUHRIE, A. "The Professionalization of the Curriculum in Teacher Training Institutions." *Problems in Teacher Training*, 1930, p. 178–185.

———. "What Are the Most Effective Plans for Securing Faculty Cooperation in the Making and in the Progressive Revision of the Curricula of our Normal Schools and Training Schools?" *Problems in Teacher Training*, 1930, p. 100–110.

TOWSON, MARYLAND (Faculty Study). "A Plan for the Closer Coordination of Professionalized Subject Matter and Student Teaching in a Normal School." *Educational Administration and Supervision*, April, 1930, p. 257–286.

WAGER, R. E. "Trends and Problems in State Supported Teacher-Training Institutions." *Peabody Journal of Education*, July, 1925.

WALK, G. E. "Student Teaching as an Integral Part of Teacher Training." *Supervisors of Student Teaching, Eighth Yearbook*, 1928, p. 3.

WEST, J. H. "The Status and Training of Critic Teachers." *Educational Administration and Supervision*, November, 1927.

WHITNEY, F. L. "Gap Between Lesson Plan and Student Teacher in the State Normal School Practice Teaching." *Educational Administration and Supervision*, October, 1921, p. 361–371.

WILLIAMS, E. I. F. *Demonstration Teaching and Observation in Teacher-Training Institutions in the United States.* Educational Monograph: No. 8. Society of College Teachers of Education, 1922, p. 104.

WITHERS, J. W. "Articulation in the Field of Teacher Training." *The Articulation of Units of American Education.* Seventh Yearbook, Dept. of Superintendence of the National Education Association, 1929, Part 5, p. 393–472.

WOLTRING, C. "Increasing the Productivity of Demonstration Lessons for Student Teachers." *Educational Administration and Supervision*, Vol. 16, 1930, p. 12–18.

APPENDIX

A. TEACHER TRAINING INSTITUTIONS VISITED FOR SURVEY OF PRESENT PRACTICE

B. PROFESSORS OF EDUCATION AND DIRECTORS OF TRAINING WHO COOPERATED IN EVALUATING THE SCORE CARD

APPENDIX A

TEACHERS COLLEGES AND NORMAL SCHOOLS VISITED FOR SURVEY OF PRESENT PRACTICE[1]

Location	Enrollment in Teacher Training Courses Academic Year	Enrollment in Rank[2]	Enrollment in All Courses All Sessions
Florence, Ala.	590	22	1,165
Conway, Ark.	729	17	1,884
San Francisco, Calif.	1,473	7	2,372
New Haven, Conn.	280	25	280
De Kalb, Ill.	760	15	1,310
Cedar Falls, Iowa	2,521	2	5,189
Bowling Green, Ky.	2,739	1	3,944
Towson, Md.	714	18	714
Bridgewater, Mass.	508	23	508
Kalamazoo, Mich.	2,228	3	3,691
St. Cloud, Minn.	1,020	11	1,537
Warrensburg, Mo.	1,100	9	3,160
Paterson, N. J.	416	24	416
New Paltz, N. Y.	703	19	853
Valley City, N. D.	834	14	1,709
Kent, Ohio	837	13	2,555
Edmond, Okla.	1,473	6	3,278
Monmouth, Ore.	1,055	10	1,636
Indiana, Pa.	1,554	5	1,944
Providence, R. I.	609	21	609
Memphis, Tenn.	902	12	1,670
Denton, Tex.	1,749	4	4,351
East Radford, Va.	641	20	1,344
Glenville, W. Va.	736	16	793
Milwaukee, Wis.	1,411	8	1,703

[1] According to *Biennial Survey of Education, 1928–1930*, 1932.

[2] Enrollment rank was derived from the data given in column 3.

APPENDIX B

PROFESSORS OF EDUCATION AND DIRECTORS OF TRAINING WHO COOPERATED IN EVALUATING THE SCORE CARD*

Ackerman, Jennie	State Teachers College	Indiana, Pa.
Ade, Lester, K.**	State Normal School	New Haven, Conn.
Alger, John S.**	Rhode Island College of Education	Providence, R. I.
Almack, John C.	Stanford University	Palo Alto, Cal.
Anthony, Katherine M.	State Teachers College	Harrisonburg, Va.
Bain, Winifred E.	Teachers College, Columbia University	New York, N. Y.
Beal, Alice	State Teachers College	Bridgewater, Mass.
Benjamin, Harold	Stanford University	Palo Alto, Cal.
Bixler, A. L.	State Teachers College	Madison, S. D.
Bowman, Earl	DePauw University	Greencastle, Ind.
Brandenburg, G. C.	Purdue University	Lafayette, Ind.
Brown, Clara M.	University of Minnesota	Minneapolis, Minn.
Bunce, Edgar F.	State Teachers College	Trenton, New Jersey
Butcher, John T.	State Teachers College	Edmond, Okla.
Campbell, E. C.	State Woman's College	Valdosta, Geo.
Canine, Edwin N.	State Teachers College	Terre Haute, Ind.
Carter, Grace A.	State Teachers College	San Francisco, Cal.
Collins, C. A.	State Teachers College	Warrensburg, Missouri
Cook, W. A.	University of Cincinnati	Cincinnati, Ohio
Cordray, E. E.	State Teachers College	Conway, Arkansas
Craig, Clara	Rhode Island College of Education	Providence, R. I.
Davis, Robert A.	University of Colorado	Boulder, Colorado
Dewey, Delmar R.	State Normal School	Monmouth, Oregon
Evenden, Edward S.	Teachers College, Columbia University	New York, N. Y.

Note: Certain of the officers in this list have accepted positions in other teacher training institutions since evaluating the list of cooperative activities. The list was evaluated for the academic year, 1931-32.

* The list includes several teachers college and normal school presidents. See Chapter II for explanation of the selection of the juries.

** President of teacher training institution.

Foster, Frank K.	University of Washington	Seattle, Washington
Gambrill, Bessie Lee	Yale University	New Haven, Conn.
Garlick, Edith	State Normal School	Paterson, New Jersey
Gray, William S.	University of Chicago	Chicago, Ill.
Griffiths, Nellie	State Teachers College	Denton, Texas
Guiler, W. S.	Miami University	Oxford, Ohio
Harlan, Charles L.	State Normal School	Lewiston, Idaho
Hastings, Mary L.	State Normal School	Gorham, Maine
Heer, Amos L.	Kent State College	Kent, Ohio
Hervey, Charles	State Normal School	Dillon, Montana
Hill, Lawrence B.	University of West Virginia	Morgantown, W. Va.
Hounchell, Paul	State Teachers College	Florence, Ala.
Hunt, Charles W.	Western Reserve University	Cleveland, Ohio
Latham, O. R.**	State Teachers College	Cedar Falls, Iowa
Lehman, C. O.	State Normal School	Geneseo, N. Y.
Luce, Eva M.	State Teachers College	Cedar Falls, Iowa
Mead, Arthur R.	Ohio Wesleyan University	Delaware, Ohio
Mead, Cyrus. D.	University of California	Berkeley, Cal.
Moffet, Mary L.	State Teachers College	East Radford, Va.
Moore, Clyde	Cornell University	Ithaca, N. Y.
Morrison, Robert	State Teachers College	Greeley, Colo.
Myers, Alonzo	New York University	New York, N. Y.
Nanninga, S. R.	University of New Mexico	Albuquerque, N. M.
Newson, N. W.	State Teachers College	Gunnison, Colorado
Nutt, H. W.	Ohio Wesleyan University	Delaware, Ohio
Olson, Willard C.	University of Michigan	Ann Arbor, Michigan
O'Rear, M. A.	State Teachers College	Springfield, Missouri
Phelps, Shelton	George Peabody College for Teachers	Nashville, Tenn.
Pittman, M. S.	State Teachers College	Ypsilanti, Michigan
Pryor, Hugh C.	State Teachers College	Pittsburg, Kansas
Rhodes, Earl N.	State Teachers College	Bloomsburg, Pa.
Rich, Mary E.	State Normal School	Bellingham, Wash.
Robinson, Telulah	State Teachers College	Bemidge, Minn.
Russell, E. A.	State Normal School	New Haven, Conn.
Salisbury, Frank	Ohio University	Athens, Ohio
Schorling, Raleigh	University of Michigan	Ann Arbor, Michigan

Scott, Charles	State Teachers College	Minot, N. D.
Sharp, L. A.	State Teachers College	Denton, Texas
Sholtz, T. L.	University of So. Calif.	Los Angeles, Cal.
Showalter, B. R.	Alabama Polytechnic Inst.	Auburn, Ala.
Shryock, Richard	Duke University	Durham, No. Carolina
Simpkins, R. R.	State Teachers College	Macomb, Illinois
Smith, J. M.	State Teachers College	Memphis, Tenn.
Speare, Guy E.	State Normal School	Plymouth, N. H.
Steele, Irene	State Normal School	Towson, Md.
Turner, Egbert	College of the City of N. Y.	New York, N. Y.
Turney, A. H.	University of Kansas	Lawrence, Kansas
Waddell, Charles W.	University of California at Los Angeles	Los Angeles, Cal.
Waller, J. C.	State Teachers College	Murfreesboro, Tenn.
Williams, E. I. F.	Heidelburg, University	Tiffin, Ohio
Wilson, Guy M.	Boston University	Boston, Mass.